Demographic Angst

Demographic Angst

Cultural Narratives and American Films of the 1950s

ALAN NADEL

RUTGERS UNIVERSITY PRESS

NEW BRUNSWICK, NEWARK, AND CAMDEN, NEW JERSEY, AND LONDON

Library of Congress Cataloging-in-Publication Data

Names: Nadel, Alan, 1947– author.
Title: Demographic angst : cultural narratives and American films
of the 1950s / Alan Nadel.
Description: New Brunswick : Rutgers University Press, 2017. | Includes
bibliographical references and index. | Includes filmography.
Identifiers: LCCN 2017015542 (print) | LCCN 2017038999 (ebook) | ISBN 9780813565514
(E-pub) | ISBN 9780813573052 (Web PDF) | ISBN 9780813565507 (cloth : alk. paper) |
ISBN 9780813565491 (pbk. : alk. paper)
Subjects: LCSH: Cold War in motion pictures. | Motion pictures--Social aspects—
United States—History—20th century.
Classification: LCC PN1993.5.U6 (ebook) | LCC PN1993.5.U6 N34 2017 (print) |
DDC 791.43/6581—dc23
LC record available at https://lccn.loc.gov/2017015542

A British Cataloging-in-Publication record for this book
is available from the British Library.

♾ The paper used in this publication meets the requirements of
the American National Standard for Information Sciences—Permanence
of Paper for Printed Library Materials, ANSI Z39.48–1992.

www.rutgersuniversitypress.org

Manufactured in the United States of America

This book is dedicated to:
Maja Nadel, my daughter-in-law,
and
Richard Conway Nadel, my son-in-law

CONTENTS

ACKNOWLEDGMENTS

A shorter version of chapter 2 was delivered as a keynote address at the Conference on Cold War Narratives at the University of Lausanne. A portion of chapter 4 was delivered as a plenary talk at the International Conference on "The American Legacy in Japan: Sixty Years from the End of the Occupation, 1952–2012" in Venice, and subsequently published in *1952–2012: The American Legacy in Japan Sixty Years after the Occupation*, edited by Duccio Basosi. A shorter version of chapter 7 appeared in *The Cambridge Companion to Hitchcock*, edited by Jonathan Freedman. In addition, many versions of many portions of this book have been presented as talks at Northwestern University; Goethe University; the University of Zurich; and several annual meetings of the American Studies Association, the Society for Cinema and Media Studies Association, the Modern Language Association, and the International Society for the Study of Narrative. I am extremely grateful for the feedback of all the audiences and editors involved in these sundry speaking and publication venues.

PREFACE

My childhood was not a happy one. While not scarred by the extremes of deprivation or abuse, it was lonely, full of the rejections and insecurities endemic, we now know, to growing up. My parents, well-intentioned, late to have married, seemed to have come from a different world—my father, in fact, was born in Victorian London—a different world with which I could communicate only through the dense static of mutual frustration, anger, and disappointment. Although the term "dysfunctional" was not part of my vocabulary, I did have the acute sense that my home life differed drastically from that of the functionally contented American family that was—as television relentlessly assured me—the norm.

I remember in that context very specifically wondering as I reached puberty what it felt like to be "well-adjusted." There was at that moment a presidential election taking place, the first presidential election in which I took serious interest. Since being normal was inextricably wed, in the lexicon of Cold War American culture, to success, I accepted as prima facie that the two most successful people in the nation, the nominees of the Democratic and Republican parties, must epitomize normality. And I vividly remember wondering at age thirteen whether I would ever know what it felt like to be as well-adjusted as John Kennedy or Richard Nixon.

These great figures whom I saw on the evening news provided me a reference point. Since I did not recognize myself in the available wherewithals of my existence—not the way my family members spoke to one another other, or the topics that concerned us, or the what and how of our avoidances—I readily, perhaps eagerly, assumed there was an elsewhere in proximity to my life. From the perspective of over fifty years, I understand belief in that approximate elsewhere was the lynchpin of my citizenship. If my neighbors were normal, I lived in America; if I believed they were, I was patriotic.

But the cost of such patriotism was exacting, in the way that living in a dream that teeters always on a nightmare is, for whenever I sought glimpses of that definitive normality, I found only its allusions, pointing me to yet another elsewhere, the "real" site of wisdom, available to me only as blurry shadows and faint echoes. The quest for that elsewhere guided the American Dream of my childhood. Guided it to the movies. The weekly TV series around which I and my parents scheduled our lives, or the weekly double bills at the neighborhood movie theater that consumed so many Saturday afternoons, issued a cornucopia of filmed stories avowing not only that elsewhere's existence, but also its perfect structure.

Could it not be more clear how intertwined were desperate faith and pathetic longing in my construction of America and of my place in it? And has history not shown that that form of angst was the most normal aspect of growing up in the 1950s?

As any deconstructionist knows, the center—that place furthest on average from the margins—depends for its centrality on everything the margins render marginal. Hence the symbiosis between the *there* of Cold War America and the *elsewhere* that enabled it. The traces of the margin and the center intersected crucially at the movies, that happily negotiated space between, in which we tried to live. The historical conditions that made the movies cogent—the Production Code, the studio system, the classical Hollywood style, the modes of mass distribution that engaged the staunchest first-run consumers and the most casually indifferent patrons—created the perfect crucible for Cold War ideology.

But Cold War ideology, like ideology in general, was by definition imperfect. In *Containment Culture* (1995) I argued that American postmodernism reflected the breakdown of the ideological binaries of the Cold War, revealing the dualities no longer containable by the monologic axioms of the 1940s and 1950s. Those axioms were forms of population control, that is, forms controlled by the unprecedented demographics that the anomalous conditions of postwar America produced. At the same time that it obsessed about normality, American culture proliferated historical aberrations that impacted how and where families lived, who worked at what jobs, how the economy and the educational system operated in the context of national and geopolitical mandates, and what kind of future America promised for each of its constituencies.

To better understand this cultural upheaval and, even more important, how it passed for normal, I look at a number of canonical 1950s movies (and one released in 1961) in an attempt to articulate the angst that they engaged, both actively and tacitly. My goal is to highlight the tension that informed the 1950s and demonstrate the artistry with which major American films absorbed the ideological apparatus of the era.

My debts in this project are many. The readings here follow, very humbly, in the footsteps of Roland Barthes's essays in *Mythologies*. In his short preface, Barthes succinctly articulates the inspiration for the bulk of my work: "In the account given of our contemporary circumstances, I resented seeing Nature and History confused at every turn." Also influential has been Donald Pease's work over the last thirty years on the American imaginary, important at every stage of that work to my formulation of the concept of cultural narratives and my understanding of their broad implications. The meticulous film scholarship of

Steven Cohan has been an inspiration to me, and his insights about the films of postwar America have been invaluable. Over the years we have found ourselves discussing the same films from very different perspectives without contradicting one another, demonstrating the rich dynamics of popular film and the inexhaustible array of cultural forces they reflect.

I am also indebted to my graduate students in several courses at the University of Kentucky and in the Masters of Liberal Arts Program, at Dartmouth, where I first offered and later refined my course Cold War Film. I am also very grateful to my fellow faculty at the Futures of American Studies Institute at Dartmouth, especially Eric Lott, who in a casual remark, which I doubt he remembers, highlighted the importance of my focusing on the anxieties surrounding postwar demographics.

The manuscript has also benefited from advice from Brenda Austin-Smith, Kate Baldwin, Virginia Blum, Tom Byers, Tim Corrigan, Tom Doherty, and Ellen Schrecker. Several chapters were developed at Ohio State University, where, supported by a sabbatical leave from the University of Kentucky, I spent a productive year as a Project Narrative visiting scholar. And the invaluable work of my research assistants—Matt Bryant Cheney, Ashleigh Hardin, and Amanda Konkle—during this book's evolution secured countless details in every chapter.

Leslie Mitchner is my favorite editor—smart, savvy, supportive, and insightful; without her urging, I would not have decided to push this project to the top of my "to-do" list. Thank-you, Leslie.

And finally, great affection and gratitude go to my wife, Sharon Kopyc, for whom this book represents a pile of forgone vacations and an even larger pile of books and papers, which for extended periods of time made dining tables unusable, large pockets of our home unsightly, and walking in certain areas a hazardous experience. All this and more she endured with grace and patience and love.

Demographic Angst

1

The Character of
Post–World War II America

In the fall of 1946, the United States was unique. Exceptionally so.

No nation, until then, had ever won a monumental war without incurring significant civilian deaths or major structural damage. The remnants of triumphant London and victorious Stalingrad differed little from the rubble and ash of Berlin and Dresden. England by 1945 had endured six years of relentless bombing that, as the war progressed, included rocket attacks. France was the site of extensive ground fighting—the short period surrounding D-Day produced 20,000 French casualties in the Normandy countryside—and Russia's brutally Pyrrhic victory brought Hitler to his knees through systematic sacrifice and self-destruction: the siege of Leningrad, scorched earth, 20 million Russian deaths. For the losers, the situation was even worse. By the time of the German surrender, Berlin was a pile of scattered bricks, and the prolonged air raids over Tokyo alone killed 100,000 Japanese civilians; two Japanese cities spared by conventional bombing instead became radioactive debris.

But the United States, with much of its war budget financed by taxes, war bonds, and rationing, had a solid and relatively stable economy. The nation also prospered from the destruction World War II had visited on the rest of the industrialized world. Although Franklin Delano Roosevelt was profoundly effective in allowing the Great Depression to bottom out slowly, his policies did more to avert catastrophe than restore prosperity, so that World War II, not the New Deal, proved most instrumental in ending the Depression. Prior to the attack on Pearl Harbor the US market included both Axis and Allied customers, making the war in Europe especially lucrative for Detroit, which at the time was the adrenal gland of the American economy. In 1945 the United States of America produced one-half of the entire world's goods and services (Endy 7).

In addition, the unprecedented generosity of the G.I. Bill kept the postwar economy robust by providing 16 million veterans with short-term support, long-term opportunity, and lifelong health care. These benefits fostered the creation of millions of new families in need of homes and cars and appliances, families fueling the rapidly expanding education and recreation industries,[1] families blessed with a national economy able to underwrite an abundance of low-interest mortgages. Thriving activity in banking, housing, manufacturing, and education produced the highest standard of living in the world.

Despite accolades for the American work ethic, however, and a homiletic faith in the opportunity afforded to a society putatively allowing class mobility, the confluence of good luck and hard work, of effort and fortune, inspired for many people—in much the way US ascent to atomic power did—a sense of ordination.[2] What Tom Englehardt called "Victory culture" seemed to ring forth from every mountainside, in effect proclaiming that the "shining City on the Hill," symbolizing for John Winthrop the New World's potential, had become a reality.

But Not a Happy Reality

Much evidence nevertheless indicates that the citizenry, despite prolific rhetoric to the contrary, experienced the postwar period with significant angst. It would take a very different kind of book to speculate on the array of reasons for the disparity between positive data and negative emotions in the postwar period. Suffice it to say that such disparity has a long precedent in America. Since the nation's inception, conventional wisdom has always intertwined egomania and paranoia into a national discourse reflecting America as beleaguered and threatened. Throughout the nineteenth century, popular culture and public rhetoric iterated such beliefs as: Indians—even those guaranteed sovereignty by signed treaties—attacked the advance of civilization and the rule of law; papists or Freemasons or Jews conspired to subvert the nation in the interest of an international cabal; abolitionists or suffragettes sought to destroy the social order; and the Irish, the Chinese, the Mexicans, or the Southern Europeans, if not monitored or restricted, threatened to dilute the gene pool and thwart the manifest destiny of the Anglo-Saxon race.[3]

"We Americans are unhappy," announced Henry Luce at the beginning of his famous 1941 essay, "The American Century." Looming large for Luce, as war raged in Europe, was the relationship between isolationists and internationalists; his call to abandon isolationism was focused not as much on attacking the Axis powers as on calling US citizens to a spirit of global responsibility, *independent* of immediate decisions or short-term military outcomes. By claiming that, on the one hand, the United States was already "in" the war and, on the other, that it had nothing immediate to fear, regardless of the war's outcome, Luce projected a prototypically Cold War sensibility, uncannily anticipating a union between the ethos of victory culture and the philosophy of containment.

Announcing, with a heft for which Cold War rhetoric would provide resonant echoes, that America was the most prosperous and powerful nation in the world, Luce demanded an invigoration of the American spirit commensurate with its panoply of *a priori* virtues: "The fundamental trouble with America has been, and is, that whereas their nation became in the 20th Century the most powerful and the most vital nation in the world, nevertheless Americans were unable to accommodate themselves spiritually and practically to that fact. . . . And the cure is this: to accept whole-heartedly our duty and our opportunity as the most vital and powerful nation in the world and in consequence to exert upon the world the full impact of our influence, for such purposes as we see fit and such means as we see fit" (63). By claiming that we were already in the war while also making entry into it irrelevant, in other words, Luce was presuming exactly what World War II had yet to prove: that the bridge of American power and influence extended back to the century's incipience and forward to the millennium. Or at least it had the potential to do so, hampered only by the will and focus of the (discontented) population.

The year after Luce's essay appeared, Philip Wylie's *Generation of Vipers* launched a diatribe that shared with Luce the assumption that Americans were troubled, identifying the sources of their discontent as the failure of religion and science to provide the American man with the means for self-scrutiny: "Man must now approach himself, if he still has a chance, with the detached and sincere passion he has applied to the world of things. He must give as much energy to his soul as he does to his job. And the best men with the best brains must research as feverishly into themselves and each other as they have into atoms" (20). Wylie was sure such research would provide the means for the American "man—individual man—[to] enlarge his attitudes toward himself" (19). It is important to underscore that Wylie's "man" was not a grammatical convention to designate human descendants of *Homo erectus*. Rather, his call for "enlargement" was profoundly and foundationally gendered. Wylie saw the psychological, intellectual, and emotional flaccidity of American men as resulting from the privileged situation they had afforded American women, whom they had turned into Cinderellas, that is, women who escape from the world of work by virtue of the support of men: "Our rags-to-riches theme gives scant attention to the virtues rags may conceal; it deals mainly with the lucky escape from rags. The American version of the Cinderella story, retold ad infinitum by the magazines, in the movies, and on the radio, puts all its emphasis on the reward. Each story opens with our heroine having a hell of a time. Along comes the prince. Fade-out." Wylie, in his introduction to the book's twentieth edition (1955), situated his "psychodynamic" argument in distinctively Cold War terms, explaining that 1955 was "a year far more threatening to American freedom, American security, and even to American existence than the year 1942" (xviii). Making explicit Luce's Cold

War agenda, Wylie foregrounded the relationship between maintaining global supremacy and overcoming the malaise that beset the American populace.

Although, contra Wylie, Ferdinand Lundberg and Dr. Marynia F. Farnham extolled motherhood in their 1947 book *Modern Woman: The Lost Sex*, they not only agreed that Americans were unhappy but shared Wylie's belief that misguided women were to blame:

> [Women] are the pivot around which revolves a problem of concern to everybody. . . . The problem concerns the increasing difficulty millions of people experience today in getting along satisfactorily with each other. . . . It also concerns the growing inability of millions of people to get a sense of enjoyment out of life itself, no matter how favorable immediately surrounding material circumstances may be. It really concerns, at its core, mass unhappiness and uneasiness in our time. . . .
>
> *The personal maladjustment of women, reflected by all the questions raised recurrently about them, underlies the spreading unhappiness.* (20; emphasis added)

In this way, Lundberg and Farnham joined Wylie in connecting the psychological problems of women to the unhappiness of all Americans, an unhappiness made more acute by postwar prosperity: "The multiplication in the contemporary world of material means to enjoyment and diversion on an unprecedented scale—movies, radio, phonograph, automobiles, yachts large and small, vacation resorts, television, sports amphitheaters and equipment, colorful magazines and newspapers, comic strips, elaborate toys for children, and an additional variety of appliances and devices for furthering feelings of momentary pleasure—is a rough yardstick of the extent to which people increasingly feel the lack of a capacity for enjoyment within themselves" (21).

A Threat to Containment

The connection of this theme to Cold War survival becomes clearer when we note how much Luce's prewar manifesto and Wylie's wartime diatribe share with George Kennan's postwar plan for Cold War victory. Like Luce, Kennan portrayed the nation as equipped to claim the future only if its citizens achieved the goal Wylie pursued, that of living happy lives, which would demonstrate that the American way of life, from day to day and year to year, was the most attractive in the world. Kennan believed that the image of a happy and prosperous American population would, in effect, deprive the Soviets of partners and thus foment a Communist frustration so profound as to impel the collapse of the Soviet state. Almost as if in response to Luce's prewar secular sermon, Kennan announced that no people were more suited for the challenge; to win the Cold War all Americans had to do was to be normal and act happy:

The issue of Soviet-American relations is in essence a test of the overall worth of the United States as a nation among nations. To avoid destruction the United States need only measure up to its own best traditions and prove itself worthy of preservation as a great nation.

Surely there was never a fairer test of national quality than this. . . . [Providence] by providing the American people with this implacable challenge, has made their entire security as a nation dependent on their pulling themselves together and accepting the responsibilities of moral and political leadership that history plainly intended them to bear. (36–37)

From the perspective of the twenty-first century, making national security contingent on individual attitudes may seem somewhat odd. Certainly the flaws in the Soviet system would have become apparent regardless of how happily Americans cheered at baseball games, how united they seemed in their hyper-vigilant satiation, or—a point crucial to Richard Nixon's 1959 "Kitchen Debate" with Khrushchev—how content they appeared when purchasing their nifty appliances. And certainly American ennui could not have made Stalin's purges or gulags seem prettier. Nevertheless, the demand that Americans behave willfully content must have posed some problems for citizens who, according to broad consensus, were discontent.

A major contributor to that consensus was Arthur Schlesinger's influential *The Vital Center*, the first chapter of which is titled "Politics in the Age of Anxiety." Eight years after the publication of "The American Century," Schlesinger's opening sentence elaborated on Luce's: "Western man at the center of the twentieth century is tense, uncertain, adrift" (1). Like Luce, Schlesinger connected that feeling to American exceptionalism. "Only the United States" he asserted, "still has buffers between itself and the anxieties of our age: buffers of time, of distance, of natural wealth, of national ingenuity, of a stubborn tradition of hope" (1). Although praising that tradition of hope, the title of Schlesinger's book alludes to Yeats's "The Second Coming," written in the midst of the Irish Civil War, which presented a dark millennial vision: the era of Christianity, its 2,000 years of moral dominance about to conclude, faces cyclical replacement by an unfathomable "rough beast" that "slouches toward Bethlehem to be born." Wrestling with the same contradictions about the American character as had Luce, Schlesinger asserted, "Optimism gave the progressives a soft, shallow conception of human nature" (40). From what he saw as a more "realistic" perspective, Schlesinger argued that American success had created a characterlogical bankruptcy: "Industrialism is the benefactor and the villain of our time. . . . In the wake of its incomparable economic achievement it has left the thin, deadly trail of anxiety" (243).

To construct a policy that would replace the fragile center with a more robust (masculine?)[4] form of liberalism, one strong enough to withstand the threats of Fascism and Communism, Schlesinger addressed what he saw as the psychological vulnerability of citizens in a capitalist society. Because "organization impersonalizes all it touches" (26), he explained, "there will be no one ready to go down swinging for institutions so abstract, impersonal and remote" (27). But in the face of the hard, dogmatic systems, that was what was needed, Schlesinger believed, because "Fascism and Communism . . . rise from a genuinely revolutionary dissatisfaction with existing society" (63), for which the soft—what Schlesinger called "Doughfaced"—progressives were no match, as they did not provide the sense of surety that many psychologically and emotionally discontent Americans desired. "America has its quota of lonely and frustrated people, craving social, intellectual and even sexual fulfillment they cannot obtain in existing society. For these people, party discipline is no obstacle; it is an attraction" (104).

Since both Schlesinger and Luce took for granted the superiority of the American system, forging the "American century" depended less on structural adjustments than on a populace able to readjust its image and attitude. Schlesinger thus came to the same conclusion as Kennan had two years earlier: "If the democratic world continues stable and prosperous," Schlesinger stated, "the disintegration of Soviet power will accelerate" (239). However, he cautioned, unless we could soon "make the world safe for democracy, we may commit ourselves too late to the great and final struggle to make it safe for humanity" (242). Thus Americans must commit themselves not only to the worldwide struggle against Communism and Fascism, but also to "the struggle within our country against oppression and stagnation [and] the struggle within ourselves against pride and corruption" (256), for if "democracy cannot produce the large resolute breed of men capable of the climactic effort, it will founder" (256). The foundation for Schlesinger's vital center, therefore, was vigor, a "climactic" vitality he saw as absent in industrialized, organizational America. Schlesinger thus echoed Luce's proclamation that "the world of the 20th Century if it is to come to life in any nobility of health and vigor, must be to a significant degree an American Century" (Luce 64).

Two years after Schlesinger published *The Vital Center*, C. Wright Mills, another major American social thinker, albeit one of a different political stripe, affirmed one of Schlesinger's central perceptions. "[T]he institutions under which we live," Mills wrote, "the framework of our existence, are without enthusiasm. . . . ours is an era of wide moral distress" (350). Mills labeled the new middle class—those white-collar workers who had none of the prerogatives of the bourgeois or petit bourgeois yet identified with the managerial rather than the working class—"little men." They "are worried and distrustful, but . . . they have no targets on which to focus their worry and distrust. They may be politically irritable, but they have no political passion. They are a chorus too afraid to grumble" (353).

Public thinkers across the political spectrum at mid-century noted a passive discontent in the American people. This "observation" provided the central motivation for David Riesman's *The Lonely Crowd*, published in 1950. In the preface to the 1961 edition, Riesman assumed the state of discontent as the fact his study sought to explain:

> We rejected as explanations of American malaise, especially among the more privileged, the usual complaints about the power and greed of the business classes, nor did we think that the shallowness, the lack of conviction of many Americans reflected merely the loss of hegemony by a traditional aristocratic upper class, or the violations of democratic procedures by corrupt politicians. In stressing *the passivity and joylessness of Americans*, their obedience to unsatisfying values, we followed the wake of other observers, notably Erich Fromm, Karen Horney, Harold Lasswell, C. Wright Mills, and John Dollard. In emphasizing cultural and psychological matters, we implicitly made clear our lack of confidence in easy political remedies, although in urging individuals to "feel free," we understand the depth of our political despair. Our understatement reflected not only our lack of moral clarity but genuine doubt about contradictory trends in American life. There is great generosity among Americans; there is also enormous meanness and mindlessness. There has been an immense increase of openness, tolerance and empathy—not only an equality resulting from envy and the fear of eminence but also from a more humane and accommodating responsiveness; this increase must be balanced against the political passivity and personal limpness which *The Lonely Crowd attacks*. (xxxiii; emphasis added)

The fact that the period's most canonical work of social science would join the consensus about American malaise by openly calling itself an "attack" rather than a "study" suggests how much Cold War dogma consolidated around the object of *The Lonely Crowd*'s attack, that "limpness" denounced by Luce and by Schlesinger.

Hence, as K. A. Cuordileone points out: "When postwar American intellectuals and social critics turned their attention toward the self, the nature of intellectual discourse shifted markedly. Disposing of old Marxian categories that failed to explain the complex and irrational dimension of human nature and political behavior, postwar intellectuals placed America—past and present, real or fictional—under psychological scrutiny. Historians and sociologists declared America a consensus society and transmuted class conflict into 'social stress' and 'status anxieties' as sources of historical or social change; conflict now lay deep in the psyche" (101). In this context, as Cuordileone makes clear, the "plight of the American male—trapped, manipulated, struggling against the forces that robbed him of his freedom, his individuality, his will, his sexual potency, and his soul—became a central theme for many postwar cultural critics, novelists, and filmmakers" (134).

Not Being Happy Is Not Being Normal Is Being Un-American

If the premise that America suffered from malaise, ennui, joylessness, and passivity was correct, then perhaps the simplest explanation for the cultural revolution of the late 1960s is that that the generation that grew up during this limp and tepid era thought it was about time to enjoy prosperity. The formative years of the baby boomers manifest great disparity between the ebullient exceptionalism of the Cold War propaganda factory and the alleged joylessness of its producers and consumers. Disneyland at its 1955 opening (broadcast live on television, coast to coast), as the self-proclaimed avatar of America values, called itself "The Happiest Place on Earth." Yet according to the best minds of that postwar generation, Disneyland comprised not the quintessence of passive, repressed, and depressing America life, but rather its utopian alternative.

Disneyland, in other words, concretized the message of the Hollywood Production Code, which since 1934 had required that all films demonstrate that America was a place where corruption always failed and crimes were always punished. To secure wide distribution, American movies had to affirm that religion and government were self-purifying, so that authority figures ultimately merited the power with which Americans had entrusted them. The local movie theater always justified faith in God and country. There, the Movie Production Code reiterated, the success of America's perfect social system depended on broad adherence to narrowly delimited practices. Most significant among these were monogamy, heterosexuality, acceptance of rigid gender roles, appropriate grooming, mild anti-intellectualism, racial segregation, and an ethos of conformity. In exchange, Hollywood-style narratives promised Americans boundless opportunity as well as financial, emotional, and spiritual security.

For the baby boomers, this message was reinforced relentlessly by the new mass medium, television, which underscored the parameters of normality with exponential redundancy and puritanical intensity.[5] The typical baby boomer, by his or her teen years, had watched more than 15,000 hours of television, all of it rigorously censored and thoroughly proscribed by the limits of taste and behavior upon which the rewards of American justice and its instruments of quotidian fairness ostensibly relied. Like the eponymous hero of the 1950s series, *The Adventures of Superman*, Cold War television fought "a never ending battle for truth, justice, and the American Way."[6]

The common message of postwar film and television, therefore, was that America was the happiest place on Earth for those who adhered to strict limitations on what constituted happiness and were also able to believe that institutional injustice, authoritarian clergy, dogmatic teachers, and sadistic police were rare to nonexistent. Ruthless bankers, corrupt industrialists, and brutal law enforcement officers were all atypical in America and always doomed to exposure and punishment. Because that's how things normally worked out, as long as everyone behaved normally and respected social norms, nothing much could go wrong (for the normal, white heterosexual).

There has been extensive discussion of Cold War normativity as it impacted everything from standardized testing to sexual practices. Nevertheless, William Whyte, in *The Organization Man*, a detailed exposure of how corporate America inhibits individualism, made clear that his book was "not a plea for nonconformity. . . . As an abstraction nonconformity is an empty goal, and rebellion against prevailing opinion merely because it is prevailing should no more be praised than acquiescence to it" (11). Whyte, like so many others, found himself uncomfortably championing individuality while advocating conformity. He thus conformed to the impossible rhetorical model that danced around the inherent logic of 1950s conventional wisdom: the solution to the widely noted joylessness was a more willing, happier conformity to the norms that had produced it. As popular culture asserted and public intellectuals confirmed, conforming to normal social and political codes, no matter how unenjoyable, was the path to happiness. At the height of the Cold War, moreover, conformity was also represented as a geopolitical necessity upon which American democracy and, following its model, the entire "free world," depended. How Americans lived their lives, as Luce prophetically predicted, would determine the fate of the American century.

It would take (in fact *did* take) a Joseph Heller to illustrate the absurdity of this logic. Americans were not normally happy; to remedy this problem they had to be more normal. And that remedy would make the United States exceptional, which in some strange construction of causality would make the Soviet Union more fragile. Articulating the apparent flaws in this argument—as the Beats did—was considered dangerous. (My junior high school social studies teacher taught us that the Beatniks provided the "perfect opening" for the Communists.)

And yet no body of intelligent scrutiny arose to confront postwar hysteria; no consensus in the apparatus of mainstream America gave cogency to obvious questions. For example, could one's choice of sexual partners (or positions) promote the construction (or demise) of the Berlin Wall? If Hollywood showed married people sleeping in the same bed, would more Americans join the Communist Party or support the Communists in Italy or Vietnam? If on television a white person were seen touching (not to mention kissing) a black person, would the North Atlantic Treaty Organization (NATO) falter? Would wearing button-down shirts and jackets with lapels of the appropriate width make the newly independent African nations bond with a country that practiced legal and *de facto* racial segregation? Would using the word "pregnant" on broadcast television to describe Lucy Ricardo's "condition" damage public morality so severely as to jeopardize the American character, such that its government of the people, by the people, and for the people would indeed perish from the earth? Apparently the Communist, atheist, totalitarian, state-owned, and state-regulated enemy posed so virulent a threat that showing movies with people kissing for more than three seconds or women who didn't sleep wearing their bras was risky. Clearly rock 'n' roll could encourage such tribal impulses in impressionable adolescents as to make them indifferent to the moral codes that America, as leader of the free world, had volunteered to enforce.[7] If American global leadership demanded that it check music, film, or television programming that might promote deviance, with the world teetering on the brink of nuclear annihilation, no reasonable person ought risk abnormality.

Achieving normality, however, was virtually impossible. Perhaps the biggest absurdity of 1950s normativity was the fact that the "norms" of Cold War America, like its postwar prosperity, were totally anomalous. Most simply, Americans could not become cheerful exemplars of the joys of capitalism by returning to normal life because, from a historical, social, technological, and especially demographic perspective, *nothing* about postwar America was normal. Rather, huge demographic changes had reorganized and redefined the tenets of mid-century American culture such that its obsession with normality functioned as mantra and myth.

Troubling the New Demography

Demographic shifts radically reorganized the size, location, composition, interactions, values, and pastimes of the American population, making any resemblance to America before the stock market crash at best a metaphor and more appropriately a mix of nostalgia and whimsy. The end of World War II; the return of more than half of the male population between the ages of twenty-two and forty-six, two-thirds of those in their twenties and thirties; the rapid creation of large suburban populations; the exodus of women from significant roles in the workplace; the baby boom; court-ordered desegregation; the explosion in college attendance; the rapid expansion of the white-collar class; the vast technologies of domestic life (cars, highways, televisions, home appliances); and the proliferation of mall consumerism created a world in which "normal" American life—for which deviance was a political and social anathema—was an inherent and profound deviation.

Although these changes might have been greeted with joy, even euphoria, they instead fomented an angst reflected clearly in two influential works I mentioned previously, David Riesman's *The Lonely Crowd* and C. Wright Mills's *White Collar*. Published one year apart, these books articulated a common fear about a radically altered American society, a fear of something vaguely related to the middle class and explicitly connected to population.

Although Riesman's preface to the 1961 edition of *The Lonely Crowd* attempted to address the criticism of his immensely successful and influential examination of the changing American "character," Riesman never acknowledged the book's fundamental flaw, as articulated to me by an earnest undergraduate history major a few years ago, after she read an assigned excerpt: "Does he ever supply evidence?"

To respond "never" might be slightly unfair. Riesman did illustrate one point with an extended discussion of the 1944 film *The Cat People*, and another point, perhaps a bit more briefly, with an examination of family relations in a Swedish film. But for the most part, Riesman's analysis, spanning more than 2,000 years and referring to societies around the globe, supplied, for example, no support for the claim that "the type of character I shall describe as other-directed seems to be emerging in very recent years in the upper middle class of our larger cities: more prominently in New York than in Boston, in Los Angeles than in Spokane, in Cincinnati than in Chillicothe" (19). He never indicated how he knew that what differentiated "the metropolitan, American upper middle class, from similar types . . . whether in Imperial Canton, in eighteenth- and nineteenth-century Europe, or in Athens, Alexandria, or Rome, [was that] in *all these groups* fashion not only ruled as a substitute for morals and customs, but it was rapidly changing fashion that held sway" (22; emphasis added). The tradition-directed social character, Riesman claimed, "refers to a common element, not only among people of precapitalist Europe but also among such enormously different types of people as Hindis and Hopis, Zulus and Hawaiians, North African Arabs and Balinese" (12), but he never provided the basis for that claim by listing the qualities that Hopi society shared with Hindi or by articulating the striking commonalities of life among the Zulus and the Balinese. In *The Lonely Crowd*, the only thing they have in common is that they are listed together as antithetical to either Los Angeles or Spokane. Oblivious to Kinsey's first report and prior to his second, to the work of Masters and Johnson, and even to a reality-based dose of what would by the end of the decade be called the "*Playboy* Philosophy," Riesman provided these "facts" about mid-century American sexual attitudes:

The other-directed person, who often suffers from low responsiveness . . . cannot handle his sex life in this way. Though there is tremendous insecurity about *how* the game of sex should be played, there is little doubt as to *whether* it should be played or not. Even when we are consciously bored with sex, we must still obey its drive. Sex, therefore, provides a kind of defense against the threat of *total* [emphasis added] apathy. This is one of the reasons why so much excitement is channeled into sex by the other-directed person. *He looks for reassurance that he is alive* [emphasis added]. The inner-directed person . . . oriented toward the more external problems of production, did not need this evidence. (146)

Making a deductive rather than an inductive argument apparently absolved Riesman of the need to conduct research. Reasoning—incorrectly—from what he called a population "S-curve," he divided the history of the world—all cultures, nations, and ethnicities—into three categories based on the reproduction-to-death ratio, each category distinguished by a concomitant "social character." Until roughly the mid-twentieth century, that is, just about the time that Henry Luce announced the American century, there were, according to Riesman, only two kinds of social character in the history of the world. Eras in which death and reproduction were both high produced societies dominated by "tradition directed" social characters, Riesman deduced, assuming that under such circumstances (much birth, much death) people had inadequate time to think for themselves. More recent societies, in which reproduction outpaced death, produced people, Riesman concluded, who were more productively individualistic, that is, "inner directed."

At the moment of the book's writing, however, Riesman had uncovered the emergence of a new social character, only the third such since the advent of *Homo sapiens*, a character type dominant only in some parts of the United States and some places in Western Europe. The product of a population with both low birth and low death rates, this "other directed" character type is guided by others rather than by his (or her) own judgments and values.

However fuzzy Riesman's knowledge of history and culture, however murky his logic, two things are clear. The first is that the book's argument is counterfactual. Incredibly, Riesman expressed relentless anxiety about low birth rates in the midst of a massive baby boom. Whether or not parts of America were being dominated by an other-directed social character, empirical evidence makes clear that the cause was *not* the birth rate. Riesman's anxiety thus represented something harder to articulate, something transcending the facts, having to do with his perception that present and future generations would not behave as their ancestors had, or at least as he guessed they had. (History and anthropology were not his bailiwick.)

A second, even more startling, fact is that *The Lonely Crowd*'s audience—popular and academic—was impervious to its dubious methodology. It rapidly became both a best seller and the most widely read and universally assigned work of sociology in the postwar period. It would be hard to imagine a college undergraduate in the social sciences from the mid-1950s through at least the 1970s who had not encountered it. During that period, anyone with even vague aspirations to being thought of as an intellectual had to read it or at least pretend to have read it. It spoke powerfully about something in postwar America that troubled Riesman and his readers alike. (And it wasn't that the number of births in the country barely outpaced the number of deaths!) So cogent was the anxiety into which Riesman tapped that few in his audience noticed *The Lonely Crowd* was simplistically Eurocentric, blatantly racist, and often simply ludicrous. (Did the tribes in Borneo, the elders of the Ming dynasty, the builders of the library at Alexandria,

African pygmies, and contemporary Italians *all* have the *same*, "tradition directed" social character?) The transparency with which Riesman's characterizations passed for fact can only suggest how powerfully his articulations evoked the tacit assumptions of his audience. Like him, that audience was consumed by the new demographics and comforted by his giving their angst an etiology.

This is indeed the way that cultural narratives work. In any culture or sub-culture or social unit, some stories are taken for granted, such that they acquire referential cogency; people refer to them without supporting evidence. In contemporary America, for example, we need not cite authorities when mentioning that the North won the Civil War, even though in some subcultures we might not find commensurate agreement that the altercation should not be called "Civil War" but rather "The War Between the States" or, for some, "The War of Northern Aggression." Similarly, for any given cultural unit, specific narratives have no cogency at all; they are relegated to the kingdom of the absurd or, depending on the cultural unit, the machinations of the satanic. Would we take anyone seriously in contemporary America who explained the disappearance of Malaysia flight 370 on the basis that the earth is flat?

Thus we can define a culture, or describe a moment in cultural history, by sorting those narratives tacitly accepted from those universally denied, isolating those that have possible cogency—that is, that exist among the array of plausible explanations for phenomena. This is basically an ideological understanding of culture, one that situates a culture in regard to the ways it tells itself what is true and the elements it treats as axiomatic to such "truth telling."

We can start to comprehend the ideological world of mid-century America, therefore, by noting the assumptions that C. Wright Mills shared with Riesman. Mills, a far more legitimate social scientist, also expressed concern about the changing character of postwar Americans. For him, this concern emanated not from the sense that the categories of social character had been disrupted, but rather that class categories were deviating from the traditional model upon which Marxist critique, dialectics, and evolution depended. The middle class in the United States was no longer small but large (and still growing), and it was no longer bourgeois but proletarian; that is, it sold labor not merchandise. At its core, *White Collar* worries about what happens when working people, en masse, acquire the economic benefits of the bourgeois or petit bourgeois. What kind of class consciousness does this middle class experience, and what kinds of social or political action do they produce?

The New Normal American Character

In light of extreme changes in the American population, actual and immanent, both Mills and Riesman were pondering the implications of what we might call, using contemporary parlance, the "new normal" of postwar America. Peacetime meant not only that marriages would abound, but also that the millions of new families created by these unions would initiate new communities with a lifestyle organized around the booming population of babies, toddlers, children, and adolescents. These new communities, filled with young families, would create a world dispersed geographically but united by the medium of television and a circulatory system of roadways that made each driveway a capillary flowing into a vessel that connected that domestic egress to a major vehicular artery. Surrounded by farmland that had been converted or was slated for conversion into housing developments, these suburbanites, significantly outnumbered by their progeny, would be the new blood pumping through the asphalt veins of a radically reconfigured American heartland.

These progeny would also redefine the face of American education. For the first time in over a generation, thousands of new schools were being constructed; because the production of buildings could not keep pace with the production of students, overcrowded sites initially operated on split sessions. A young generation of teachers was filling these pristine classrooms with new theories of education, fresh from American universities, which also had undergone radical change. Whereas prior to World War II only 9 percent of the population had attended college, because of the G.I. Bill that number tripled almost instantaneously.

But the change was far more than numeric. Returning veterans from sundry regions and classes, men who prior to the war never imagined earning a college degree, demonstrated the egalitarian potential of higher education, a potential open not just to veterans but also to their younger siblings and to their children. Forced to acknowledge that merit could trump privilege, the elite private universities would never be the same. Nor would the network of public institutions, which would expand exponentially to accommodate the booming birthrate with affordable, quality instruction.

Equally expansive was the white-collar world of corporate America, which was no longer regulating labor by means of an almost impermeable wall between clerical workers and their bosses. Instead the divide was gendered. While women were typically offered a stratified array of paperwork occupations—typist, secretary, executive secretary, "gal Friday," bookkeeper, office manager—for men the entry clerical position was the first rung (trainee, executive assistant) on a managerial ladder. Even those men who retained blue-collar jobs were able, thanks to the growth and power of unions, to live in suburbia and afford to save for their children's college tuition.

This describes, for the most part, the roughly 80 percent of the American population that was Caucasian. Black and Hispanic veterans had much more difficulty enjoying G.I. benefits, and black Americans, veterans or not, fared far worse than the general population. While many white veterans, based on their war records, secured—deservedly so—executive positions without a college degree, blacks found few employers willing to credit their military service, no matter how outstanding. In consequence, black Americans had more difficulty qualifying for the mortgages that would allow them to join thriving suburban communities or reserve seats for their children in the spotless new schools those communities supported.

But the process was even more pernicious in that the Veterans Administration tacitly supported discrimination, because it was prohibited from addressing admissions criteria at the institutions for which it provided tuition or exercising control over any state educational agency. Black veterans therefore could only use benefits at colleges that would accept them, which for the most part precluded elite northern schools as well as most southern schools, aside from the small, underfunded, and generally overcrowded historically black colleges.

With regard to housing loans, the VA was more proactively racist. By the summer of 1947, blacks had secured only 2 of the 3,229 guaranteed loans in Mississippi, and "in the New York-New Jersey metropolitan area in 1950, non-whites owned 2.1 of the properties financed with conventional mortgages . . . and 0.1 percent of those purchased with loans backed by the V.A." (Altschuler and Blumin 199). Moreover, "the FHA and the V.A. forbid government backing for any loan that would result in a black family moving into a white neighborhood" (201).

In the postwar period, black Americans and white Americans, as they had for centuries, occupied different worlds, divided most vividly at that moment by access to the benefits of Cold War America's unprecedented prosperity. By the early 1950s, however, these worlds seemed headed for a collision, a dread of which, in fact, had resulted in the fracturing of the Democratic Party, when, in protest against the civil rights plank of the party's 1948 platform, a Dixiecrat splinter supported South Carolina governor Strom Thurmond for the presidency. Harry Truman, shortly after his victory, desegregated the US armed forces, and a number of cases challenging segregation in education were working their way through the courts.

Other collisions were also taking place. After a brutal half century, organized labor, with the passage of the Wagner Act in 1935, secured legal protections that resulted in major gains for the working class and portended even greater success for the growth of organized labor. But only a few years after Hiroshima, the labor movement was mired in conflict. By linking organized labor with Communism, the supporters of big business mobilized to pass, over Truman's veto, the Taft-Hartley Act of 1947, which undermined many of the most potent tools unions used to organize, influence contract negotiations, and enjoy legal protections. In addition to these assaults from the right, many labor leaders faced opposition from their own rank and file, who often felt that their leaders were too soft and, in some cases, had sold them out.

On college campuses, a new, more mature student, often with intense war experiences, provided a vivid contrast to the traditional college student, who entered college directly from high school and usually came from a background at least privileged enough that he or she did not have to help support the family. The new breed of college students also contrasted with many of their far less worldly instructors. Nor was this new generation a brief interruption in the "normal" college demographic. Rather, it impelled a massive expansion in the size and scope of higher education, which would continue unabated for over thirty years and affect every aspect of American colleges and universities, including the cost, the entrance criteria, the curriculum, the composition of the college body, and their social dynamics. The normal college student was no longer normal, and while initially the new students tended to conform to the old paradigm, very quickly the vast expansion of facilities and enrollments made these formerly aberrant college types the numerical norm. What this portended for the college population or the population in general remained in constant doubt, for as soon as the colleges and universities finished adapting to the veterans and the demographic base of which they were the vanguard, those institutions would have to make even larger readjustments to accommodate the booming population of the largely (lower- to upper-) middle-class children born to those veterans and their cohorts.

The specter of violent or criminal adolescents, not unlike the specter of Communist spies and subversives, haunted the country long before the first baby boomers reached puberty. In the 1940s, almost concurrent with the red scare, psychiatrists, social workers, and law enforcement officials warned of growing juvenile delinquency. Regarding both issues, Federal Bureau of Investigation. director J. Edgar Hoover, not surprisingly, was a prime fear monger. To prevent the juvenile crime wave that Hoover had predicted for the postwar period, in 1946 Truman's attorney general, Tom Clark, appointed the Attorney General's Panel on Juvenile Problems. The Justice Department then sponsored the National Conference on the Prevention and Control of Juvenile Delinquency, which, as James Gilbert points out, "assumed the existence of a serious problem, but nonetheless debated about its size, growth, and danger" (37). "The war raised certain public fears about the extent and causes of delinquency," Gilbert explains,

> and it just as surely reinforced a more general worry about the American family . . . in a general context of heightened attention to young people. It was a part—if a confused part—of the public response to the new teen culture that emerged during World War II. As people became more independent and relatively more affluent, as their peer culture grew more influential, and their parents less so, delinquency emerged as a kind of code word for shifts in adolescent behavior that much of adult society disapproved. This was, of course, over and beyond an understandable reaction to real crimes perpetrated by youth. (39–40)

Juvenile crime, like Communist spies, did exist, but not nearly in numbers commensurate with the concern surrounding it. As the collapse of the Soviet Union has subsequently demonstrated, moreover, these groups posed little threat to democracy, capitalism, or "Western values," no more than, despite Hoover's hysteria, the civil rights movement or the labor movement did. In terms of the angst that the fantasy demographic "juvenile delinquent" generated, however, it was as cogent in the public imaginary as were Communists, suburbanites, baby boomers, and white-collar workers.

Nor were delinquents the only imaginary demographic group to assail the consciousness of mid-century American, in that all Americans held *de facto* dual citizenship in that sovereign body, the United States, and that international unit, "the free world," of which the United Nations was, in the 1940s and 1950s, the unofficial capital. As many scholars have noted, the UN was structured by Western powers to stabilize the organization of power and spheres of influence that antedated the war. In other words, it was an international organization grounded in sovereign interests and an egalitarian institution dependent on a rigid hierarchy of powers. Until the 1960s most of the nations empowered by the UN structure served the interests of the free world. And yet to be a citizen of the free world required union with numerous nations whose policies were inimical to the notion of American democracy, linked so pervasively in the United States to the containment of Communism. Great Britain, our closest ally in the Cold War, had adopted a Labour Party government whose philosophy of social welfare typified the programs and policies that America was combating. The American Labor Party, founded in 1936 and modeled on the British Labour Party, achieved some postwar success in New York State but was destroyed in the early 1950s because it was accused of having Communist influence.

Even more interesting, the construction of the free world initiated a process in the United States and Great Britain of befriending the formerly hostile Axis countries. Given the enmity and destruction that had characterized World War II, the political viability of this conversion necessitated a reformation of the cultural imaginary. As parties to the 1949 NATO treaty, for example, Great Britain and Italy pledged mutual defense, despite the recent hostilities that ought to have rendered dubious in each country the political mandate for such a pledge. Similarly, the United States initiated the Berlin Airlift while three of the Nuremberg trials were still under way. Winston Churchill's 1946 "Iron Curtain" speech in Fulton, Missouri, urged a drastic rearrangement of global loyalties that not only divided Europe but also realigned the Allied and Axis forces that had defined global conflict for almost a decade. Replacing inimical sentiments with imaginary affinities, the demographics of the free world mandated an imaginary global community in which Americans stood side by side with the Italians, the Germans, and the Japanese. The notion of this community, moreover, needed to be compelling enough to erase the image of the Japanese kamikaze pilots or knowledge of the Holocaust.

Nor was anxiety surrounding acceptance of former Axis powers unrelated to the fear of juvenile delinquents. "There was a vague, war-induced fear" Gilbert notes, "that totalitarianism would infect youth. The National Delinquency Prevention Society in 1946 accordingly invoked doom for American society and a fate similar to that of 'Germany, Russia, Italy, and Japan' if delinquency was not stopped" (40). Because Communism was combated through a relentless quotidian demonstration of contented normality, Americans sought to make former Nazi and Japanese war veterans allies in Cold War practices, at the same time that Americans also sought vigilantly to prevent American youths from being like these allies.

In many ways, accepting postwar America's radically redefined normal was something like being placed on an alien planet, or perhaps like being invaded by aliens. If this brave new world appeared normal, something was awry, especially in regard to the absence of credible protest. While numerous social critics and public intellectuals seemed certain that Americans were living in an age of anxiety, few treated angst as a perfectly appropriate response to the radical and radically unacknowledged demographic changes that America had undergone. Thus the traditional interpretations of the 1956 film *The Invasion of the Body Snatchers* tend to view it as a critique of either Communist subversion (the final line is "Get me the FBI") or 1950s conformity. Noting how difficult it is to differentiate the former reading from the latter, however, may get us closer to understanding the angst that the film addressed. The site of audience identification, in other words, was not radically different from that of the reader of *The Lonely Crowd*, wrestling with the fear of becoming other directed without realizing it. To use a term that garnered significant cultural currency in the wake of the Korean War, could the reader have been "brainwashed?" And if so, how so? Was he or she duped, perhaps by a friend or neighbor who was also brainwashed? It is true that twenty-one Korean War prisoners of war refused to come home; many Americans no doubt felt these POWs must have been brainwashed; but if that were so, then how many who came home were altered, behind their mask of normality serving the interests of a foreign power? *The Invasion of the Body Snatchers* doesn't resolve this question so much as allow the audience to engage their angst at a fantasy level and thus articulate at a safe remove their concerns about the norms they were simultaneously being urged to celebrate and penetrate.

Demographic Angst at the Movies

At the center of this book, therefore, resides the idea that if the mandate for normality in the midst or anticipation of radically reconfigured demographics produced angst, one important way to understand key films of Cold War American culture is through the way that they negotiate demographic anxieties. Since angst is the friction of a forced intimacy between inimical concepts or desires—hope and fear, self and other, human and God—my discussion attends especially to the nuanced contradictions that popular discourse exposed most powerfully in the process of attempting to suppress them.

Singin' in the Rain (1952), certainly the most written about of all American musicals, consolidates many of these issues by troping the silent era as prewar and the talkie era as postwar. In that context, the film foregrounds the question of who may speak, with what levels of truthfulness, to what ends, because in the age of McCarthyism, as in the world of *Singin' in the Rain*, one's past could be damaging and speech entailed the possibility of incrimination and unemployment. If the film is about work, it valorizes the romantic pairing of Don Lockwood (Gene Kelly) with Kathy Selden (Debbie Reynolds), based on Selden's willingness to subordinate her career to her man's. In this way, the film replaces the screwball comedy, in which female agency trumped the male ego or career goals. In so doing, *Singin'* demonstrates how postwar growth and opportunity, the subordination of women, and McCarthyism were intertwined.[8]

Singin' is thus a more cheerful interpretation of a cultural narrative that informed two slightly earlier films, *Sunset Boulevard* (1950) and *All about Eve* (1950). Both feature women who, like *Singin'*'s Lina Lamont, attempt to maintain the outdated platform for their stardom at the expense of the men whom they profess to love (see figure 1.1).

Using the film industry to the same allegorical ends as does *Singin'*, *Sunset Boulevard* presents a particularly dark version of this narrative, but Norma Desmond's (Gloria Swanson) inversion of Lina—reflecting the genre difference between noir and musical comedy—makes her a tragic figure rather than a comic foil. Similarly, Joe Gillis (William Holden), in the tragic version, cannot be saved by the girl, Betty (Nancy Olsen), who wants to help him find his true voice. If speaking without self-incrimination is a central problem in *Singin'*, it is a problem that Gillis fails to solve, in that he only finds his voice posthumously,

FIGURE 1-1 Lina Lamont, Norma Desmond, and Margo Channing.

in the form of an incriminating confession. Consider how much more he resembles the authors and performers who failed to avoid blacklisting than those, such as Gene Kelly, who left the country to avoid having to testify, or *Singin' in the Rain*'s writers, Betty Comden and Adolph Green, who testified in secret. If the blacklist informs *Sunset* to the same degree that it informs *Singin'*, it also shares with that film another important concern for the postwar American workplace: that during the war women had demonstrated they could rival men professionally. "In spite of the return to prosperity," Elaine Tyler May reminds us, "the proportion of women in the professions remained below 1930 levels" (67). This issue consolidates equally around Lina and Norma, both of whom, looking to the past as evidence that they can take charge of their careers, are in untenable positions. Both figuratively and literally, Lina wants to speak in her own unbearable voice, and Norma, despite her adulation of the silent era, believes in the power of her verbose script to revive her career. Public exposure thus proves disastrous for both women, but Norma, deprived even of Lina's self-awareness, enters a world of pure ridicule.

For the men to preserve their innocence—or maintain their illusion of innocence—in the age of McCarthyism, they have to avoid the seductive powers of aggressive women, a theme that the prelapsarian world of Norma Desmond's estate comes close to literalizing, as does the film title *All about Eve*, although Margo Channing in the end resists following the path of Norma Desmond, who clings desperately to her past stardom even though she is no longer suited to the role. Margo's salvation, in other words, is that just in time she catches up with the ethos of the postwar moment, by converting from Norma Desmond or Lina Lamont into Betty Schaefer and Kathy Selden, leaving her usurper, Eve Harrington (Ann Baxter), to suffer the fate of the careerist woman in the postwar period.

On the Waterfront (1954) is also all about work, innocence, and fear of Communism, as is *Roman Holiday* (1953), despite its title. Reflecting deep angst about the emerging union class—that is, the uniquely American working middle class—*On the Waterfront* demonizes union power and solidarity by constructing a narrative that justifies the triumph of the "right to work" over the evils of organized labor. The film, as has been widely noted, represents the corrupt union as a form of Communist conspiracy in which the organization ostensibly supports workers while, à la *Animal Farm*, it actually centralizes wealth and power at the expense of those workers. Nothing in the film, however, represents the interests of the workers. Terry Molloy's moving, figuratively, through the Stages of the Cross (see figure 1.2) at the end of the film connects redemption to renouncing, in the words of the film's crusading priest, "the love of a lousy buck."

In effect, Terry symbolizes rejecting the material interests of workers, which is the basis of a labor movement, so when the workers defiantly storm into the warehouse at the end of the film, implicitly extolling their right to work, the film

FIGURE 1-2 Terry Molloy's moving, figuratively, through the Stages of the Cross.

suggests that if the union no longer determines who shall work, then everyone can. The film thus converts an indictment of corrupt unions into an indictment of unions in general by replacing the principles of the Wagner Act with those of Taft-Hartley as the foundation for workers' rights and benefits.

Roman Holiday, made when the Central Intelligence Agency (CIA) and the conservative American Federation of Labor (AFL) were both actively concerned about the more radical Italian labor movement, is also about work. Both Princess Ann (Audrey Hepburn) and the journalist, Joe Bradley (Gregory Peck), are identified throughout the film by their respective jobs and their precarious relationship to them. While initially the princess's rejection of her job responsibilities appears to be the means by which Joe will meet his, in the end exactly the opposite occurs. By destroying his story of her Roman adventure, he subordinates his work to the interests of preserving her "holiday" (and monarchy). As in *On the Waterfront*, spiritual values trump material interests: she must go back to work as monarch because she is ordained to do so, and he must temporarily abandon his work for the same reason. Even more important, just as management remains invisible in the central conflicts of *On the Waterfront*, so does the Italian worker as the object of Peck's identification. The film erases identification with Italian labor at exactly the moment that the AFL was urging disidentification with the Italian left. Despite Italy's entrance into NATO, its unstable government and active Communist Party created an array of problems for Americans attempting to reimagine Italy as neither Fascist nor Communist. Thus the focus on work in the film constructs it as something to be escaped from rather than

FIGURE 1-3 Scene from *Roman Holiday*, which highlighted tourist attractions.

engaged, so that *Roman Holiday*, highlighting tourist attractions, portrays Italy as a site of consumption rather than production (see figure 1.3).

Tourism, as an instrument of the Cold War, complemented the Marshall Plan of 1948–1951 with private tourist dollars that made the rebuilding European nations even more dependent on Americans and helped Americans form informal alliances with and affection for the citizens of those European nations. Rome as the site of love and play and empire, therefore, provides the conditions under which the American working man may bond with a postwar European who represents not the aristocracy or the leisure class, but leisure itself, leisure at the expense of work, not as the reward for it. The film also accesses Rome for American moviegoers, as the camera itself voraciously consumes iconic tourist sites. Thus the film valorizes American cultural imperialism by bringing home the pleasures of Rome, ostensibly from the perspective of the American workingman but surreptitiously from that of the aristocrat. In this regard, *Roman Holiday* resembles the Roman epic films of the period, such as *Quo Vadis* (1951), which rejects Fascist Rome by converting it into a Holy City, a conversion effected, as in *On the Waterfront*, through the working class's renunciation of material interests.

Although without organized labor the working middle class as we know it could not have existed, the postwar period also gave rise to the vast white-collar middle class extensively described by C. Wright Mills in *White Collar*. Mills's "Little Man" referred to a member of an exploding portion of the postwar economy. Overwhelmingly male, many World War II veterans constituted another demographic group around whom anxieties proliferated, the largest being that in epitomizing too well the normal American middle class, they were losing their individuality, becoming other-directed "organization men." A musical comedy that loosely parodies earlier Robin Hood films, *The Court Jester* (1955) establishes the little people (literally a troop of midgets) as crucial to the process by which an honest corporate hierarchy replaces a corrupt aristocracy. The corporate model, epitomized by the Black Fox's band of virtuous outlaws, succeeds by importing the modern assembly line, in which the most heroic agent is a small cog, who happily performs his little tasks in the interest of the next generation. In the process, the film engages the social frenzy surrounding marriage, and class, akin to that impelled by the reorganization of the American population effected by the postwar veterans and the rise of the white-collar world that absorbed many of them.

The opening song, reprised at the end, glosses American prosperity in 1956, representing that historical moment as the happy ending to the Depression and World War II, self-reflexively stating about the film, "What started as a scary tale ends like a fairy tale." If the film presents the economic recovery through the ascent of the rightful king, it actually signifies a radical generational change *disguised* as restoration, in that this infant had never previously held the throne. The film's "return" to normality thus turns the unprecedented baby boom into the new normal, in that all of the actions of the Black Fox's band are motivated by ensuring the future of the infant who rules their lives.

The corporate world of postwar America raised anxiety not only about its conditions of labor but also about its commercial practices, especially as they engaged in manipulation of the general public. The concept of "brainwashing" thus united fears about Communism with anxiety about the power of commercial media's subliminal deceptions. What Vance Packard identified as advertising's "hidden persuaders" uncomfortably resembled what had been branded as Communist "brainwashing," a Cold War invention that gained cogency after the Korean War (1950–1953). Unlike torture, brainwashing was thought to draw on the scientific advances of behavioral psychology to create in a person an understanding of reality contrary to that person's "true" beliefs. The power attributed to brainwashing thus evoked fears of the uncanny—that is, the uncomfortable relationship between science and nature. As the technology of the possible, science revealed natural laws, but as the technology of the impossible, it subverted them.

Since America's technological supremacy depended on science, true science could not easily be rebuffed. Brainwashing, therefore, was regarded as a pseudo-science, only effective on Americans with weak character. The concept was thus lodged in the same concern with the American character manifested by *The Lonely Crowd*. And since the only proof that brainwashing existed was its success, the concept entailed believing that postwar America harbored another new demographic group, who behaved normally while (erroneously) believing something contrary to their own thoughts, something implanted without their knowledge. Just like Communist cell members or closeted homosexuals, they could be anywhere. How could one better hide subversion than by acting obsessively normal?

Even more scary was the fact that, if Riesman was correct, a growing number of Americans were vulnerable, like the citizens of Santa Mira in *The Invasion of the Body Snatchers*. That film and *The Manchurian Candidate* (1962) project the power of hidden persuaders and conditioned reflexes in order to caution and chastise an audience in which an unknown number of people might be thinking thoughts that were not really their own, holding beliefs that were fundamentally un-American. These people, as represented on the screen, comprised an odd mixture of the frenetically obsessed and disturbingly withdrawn. It is less interesting that Major Bennett Marko (Frank Sinatra) and Congressional Medal of Honor winner Raymond Shaw (Lawrence Harvey) represent these extremes in *The Manchurian Candidate* than that the passive, withdrawn, repressed, and in many ways apathetic Shaw—the one who most resembles the Luce-Mills-Schlesinger-Riesman-Packard-Whyte image of the normal American—is the foreign agent, while the tormented and haunted Marko, who shows numerous symptoms of what we now call post-traumatic stress disorder, represents the resistance to brainwashing. The same is true in *Body Snatchers*. The more the possessed bodies advocate unemotional passivity, the more crazed and desperate the "normal" Dr. Bennell (Kevin McCarthy) becomes (see figure 1.4).

In both films, sleep deprivation constitutes a painful virtue of Cold War hypervigilance. Because the body snatchers take over when one falls asleep, one must never relax, never succumb to the allure of the apathy (that typifies normal Americans). In this sense, going to sleep resembles what happens, for

FIGURE 1-4 The "normal" Dr. Bennell becomes more crazed and desperate.

Riesman, when one loses internal balance. Perhaps this is why lack of sleep, as represented by chronic nightmares in *The Manchurian Candidate*, is also a form of hysteria. Marko and others in his division, when conscious, seem incapable of deviating from praise or not praising Shaw, yet when then they fall asleep, their rote conformity is shattered by horrifying dreams that reflect the nightmare of the Communist script. This terrifying sleeplessness is relieved only when the frenzied heroes earn the trust of a higher power, the FBI in the case of *Body Snatchers* and Army Intelligence in *The Manchurian Candidate*. In this way, both Bennell and Marko participate in the same dilemma as does Jim Stark (James Dean) in *Rebel without a Cause* (1955), whose impetus for rebellion is his father's passivity, from which he is saved by submission to the stronger authority figure, the police detective Ray Fremick (Edward Platt). The crucial act in *Rebel* that brands Jim a "rebel" is his decision to report the incidents surrounding Buzz's death to the police, the same kind of rebellion that, a year earlier, had distinguished Terry Molloy in *On the Waterfront*.

The issue of divided and realigned loyalties was being staged as well on the international stage. The US ascension to global leadership in the Cold War significantly diminished the nativist strain in American culture and politics and, in so doing, required cultural accommodation of another new demographic group, the former Axis nations, as a cogent aspect of the American policy of "containment." As in *Roman Holiday*, some of the anxiety surrounding this new demographic group was diffused through the notion of tourism. While cultural narratives surrounding tourism also worked to accommodate the image of post-occupation Japan, the anxieties produced by the wartime anti-Japanese propaganda required more complex—and ambivalent—negotiations. The problematic image of Japan and the Japanese in American popular imagination after World War II is exemplified by a 1951 *Life magazine* article that treated Japan's World War II defeat as a form of Japanese victory, in that it provided the opportunity for the Japanese to escape their debilitating customs and traditions. Japanese amorality, the article contended, well equipped the Japanese to abandon their culture and traditions, such that Hiroshima and Nagasaki became, in effect, aspects of a Western rescue mission.

Two popular mid-1950s films, *The Teahouse of the August Moon* (1956) and *Sayonara* (1957), provide clear examples of the template for accepting the new Japan as Cold War ally. In *Teahouse*, a comedy, Marlon Brando plays the "Japanese" interpreter who must facilitate occupation of his home village on Okinawa, which prospers when it builds a teahouse (rather than a school) and the housewives of the village learn the skills of geishas. Supported by selling moonshine to army bases, the teahouse makes the occupation of Japan synonymous with Japanese leisure occupations, thereby defusing anxiety over Japan as an industrial power, despite its startling economic leaps by mid-decade. The cultural work being performed by *Teahouse* coalesces the merger of technology, capitalism, and white, middle-class Western morality around the problematic figure of the geisha, whose craft is transformed from an alternative to marriage into a domestic skill.

Like *Teahouse*, Brando's next film, *Sayonara*, focuses on the Japanese leisure activities and represents the nation as undergoing a rescue plan that celebrates tradition by eliminating it. Hence, it is not surprising that both films attend to lifestyle and sexual freedom and make the same appeal to the tourist sensibility as does *Roman Holiday*, the film aimed at embracing another World War II foe. *Sayonara* uses the panoramic widescreen to set the melodrama against a lush travelogue, highlighting Japanese performance arts as reflected by the seductive power of the Japanese performer. Like *Singin' in the Rain*, therefore, it develops implicit criteria for selecting the female partner appropriate to the postwar moment, here contextualized by the US military's prohibition against marrying Japanese women. Ritual suicide sorts out those Japanese unable to reject their self-destructive traditions from those, such as Hana-Ogi (Miko Taka), who can renounce her role in Japanese theater to become the Western-style bride of Major Gruver (Marlon Brando).

In this way, Hana-Ogi becomes a citizen of that newly formed postwar entity, the free world, implicitly epitomizing American values and exemplified by another new postwar entity, the United Nations. By the end of the 1950s, however, as the UN's role as an instrument of American containment started to unravel, the institution foregrounded the contradictions entailed in being a member of that amorphous demographic group.

Alfred Hitchcock, with his typical prescience and subtlety, wrestles in *North by Northwest* (1959) with the madness, actual and feigned, entailed in the free world and its imaginary citizenry. Relatively early in the film, ad man Roger Thornhill goes to the Plaza Hotel in an attempt to unravel a mass series of complications emanating from the fact that he has been mistaken for a CIA operative, but instead of clearing up the confusion, he multiplies it in ways that replicate the conventions of bedroom farce.

At the UN, however, violence replaces farce (see figure 1.5), graphing the potential of bedroom hysteria to the reality of international espionage, suggesting that the Cold War may be a farce inherent in the UN Charter, which oscillates between asserting the rule of international law and upholding the sovereignty of member states engaged in multilayered competitions. This organization of power and the panoply of actions, large and small, that it comprises are reflected in the film's organization around issues of scale in which intimacy, romance, and nationalism are powerfully pitted against one another, as they were relentlessly for Cold War Americans.

American racial dynamics provided another stage on which Cold War issues were played out, because, as Mary Dudziak has demonstrated, the practice of segregation became an untenable Cold War liability for the United States, which

FIGURE 1-5 At the UN, violence replaces farce.

meant that both the South and North had to anticipate far vaster racial integration than had characterized prewar America. Even the titles of *No Way Out*
(1950) and *The Defiant Ones* (1958), the two most significant 1950s films dealing with impending change in racial demographics, reveal angst and confusion.
Accurately reflecting ambivalence about racism and integration, both titles suggest an injustice in search of a perpetrator.

To assert the possibility of national values *not* grounded in the institution
of the South without demonizing southerners, both films make racism a function of class and gender, as understood within the spectrum of 1950s social
codes. *No Way Out* continuously links overt racism to crime and promiscuity.
When Ray Biddle (Richard Widmark) and his brother are both wounded in a gas
station robbery, Ray believes that Dr. Luther Brooks (Sidney Poitier), the "nigger" doctor who treats them, has intentionally killed his brother (see figure 1.6).

Ray therefore enlists his brother's wife, Edie (Linda Darnell), who is also
his adulterous lover, to help him argue for Poitier's dismissal. Ray's irrational
vehemence, which foments a race riot, emanates from a lower-class upbringing
that fosters anger and immorality.

If *No Way Out*, made four years before the US Supreme Court school desegregation decision in *Brown v. Board of Education of Topeka*, is about those who defy
the changing racial demographics, *The Defiant Ones*, made four years after the
Supreme Court decision, constructs a narrative from which, for several reasons,
there is no way out. When two chain gang members, a white southern racist
(Tony Curtis) and a southern black (Sidney Poitier) who are chained together,
manage to escape, they learn to overcome their mutual hatred. Despite the
injustice of their sentences, the cruelty of chain gangs, and the injustice of
racism, of which they are both victims, the Motion Picture Production Code

FIGURE 1-6 Ray believes that Dr. Luther Brooks has intentionally killed his brother.

prohibited the film showing their successful escape. Thus, at the same time that civil disobedience as a civil rights tactic was starting to reap rewards, a film that valorized its heroes' defiance of racism was also condemned to punish them. Because punishment is inevitable, the politics of the film emerges in the way that it focuses the blame for the injustice of its own inevitable ending. It does so by concentrating its animus on a small number of characters, falling into the same groups as the racists in *No Way Out*: white lower-class men and a sexually active woman.

In the 1950s anxiety about the reconfiguration of racial demographics rapidly graphed onto the anxieties about juvenile delinquency, which continued to grow as the baby boomers approached adolescence. *West Side Story* (1961) provides an incisive perspective on the anxieties around race that the film occludes and on the narrative of mid-twentieth-century American empire that it promotes in the interest of constructing an urban space reconciling the notion of America as leader of the free world with the racial practices and racialized spaces in the United States. The "place for us" denoted by one of *West Side Story*'s songs is consistent with the cultural and hemispheric imperialism that tacitly characterized US relations with Latin countries, the problems of which were made visible in the early 1960s by Castro's rise to power.

Relying on the presence and the invisibility of African Americans, the film, set in a moment of desegregation, forced busing, and "white flight" in New York

City, reconciles racial conflicts by removing black people from the visual field and converting questions of integration into those of immigration, itself a displacement in which American citizens (Puerto Ricans) must occupy the subject position of aliens who "want to be in America." The Puerto Rican/Nyorican thus facilitates a notion of integration that makes invisible both the imported slave labor used to build the American empire and the subjugated spaces and people used to expand that empire.

In this context, the movie also presents Puerto Rico as the redeemable alternative to Cuba as well as the alternative to America. ("I want to be in America," the Puerto Ricans sing; see figure 1.7.) This constructed Puerto Rico elides the actual history of the island's relation to the United States, the actual history of the black people who live New York, and the specific history of the urban renewal projects of the period, which used a narrative of progress to remove African Americans from their historical neighborhoods. The neighborhood in which *West Side Story* was filmed was emptied of blacks and Puerto Ricans to build Lincoln Center, projected as a "cultural utopia."

West Side Story's attempt to negotiate the changing racial demographics of the inner city is further revealed by the casting, which includes no African Americans and almost no Hispanics. Thus while the relationship between Tony and Maria may imply miscegenation, the fact that they are played by Richard Beymer and Natalie Wood makes the film's racial implications cosmetic. Wood's cosmetics also suggest, when compared to her makeup in *Rebel without a Cause*, the gradual conversion of "juvenile delinquency" from a social to a racial problem. Juvenile delinquency in 1954 was treated in much the way that polio was in the early 1950s: no one was immune. With the implementation of desegregation, juvenile delinquency became more a function of the inner city, with a pivotal character being Gregory Miller (Sidney Poitier) in *Blackboard Jungle* (1955), the only prominent African American in the class, whom the teacher, Richard

FIGURE 1-7 The Puerto Ricans sing "I Want to Be in America."

Dadier (Glenn Ford), mistakenly believes to be a juvenile delinquent. If *Black-board Jungle* disabuses both Dadier and Miller of their prejudices, *West Side Story*, made six years later, inextricably connects juvenile delinquency to racial demographics, at the same time that the music, the dance, and the casting move the racialized inner city into an aracial, imaginary elsewhere, very different from the material elsewhere to which the racial minorities were moved to make room for a cultural utopia.

If all artistic production necessarily bears the marks of its moment of production, these films, which have entered the era's canon of classics, reflect in marked ways the concerns, doubts, tensions, and fears with which the Cold War era at its peak was most commonly associated. Of course numerous films, such as *I Married a Communist* (1949), engaged Cold War themes directly, whereas others, such as *I Married a Monster from Outer Space* (1958), did so in a thinly veiled fashion. But just as the perceived unhappiness of Americans, which Luce attacked in 1941, was not grounded merely in the fear of war or subversion, the angst of the postwar period—a broadly construed era marked at one end by Nagasaki and at the other by Lee Harvey Oswald—was not limited to those films that attacked or allegorized the explicit themes of the Cold War. Rather, it reflected the dense foliage in an American forest of demographic angst, barely visible through the new normal of its trees.

2

Singin' in the (HUAC) *Rain*

Job Security, Stardom, and the Abjection of Lena Lamont

Singin' in the Rain (1952), a musical set at Monumental Pictures, a fictitious 1920s movie studio parodying MGM, traces the film industry's transition from silent films to talkies by following the on-screen and offscreen effects of that transition on a pair of film stars, Don Lockwood (Gene Kelly) and Lina Lamont (Jean Hagen), whom the studio had paired in an array of silent romances. The film starts just before the premiere screening of what will turn out to be the couple's last silent film, *The Royal Rascal*, and ends just after the premiere screening of their first talkie. Between these two moments, Lockwood and Lamont will make *The Dueling Cavalier*, an early talkie so comically disastrous in its negotiation of the new sound technology that it is converted into a musical, retitled *The Dancing Cavalier*. This conversion will require that Lina's voice be dubbed by Lockwood's new girlfriend, Kathy Selden (Debbie Reynolds), and *Singin' in the Rain* culminates with Selden's replacing Lamont as Lockwood's costar in the talkie film era.

Although ostensibly celebrating the moment when the stars of the silver screen acquired voices, *Singin' in the Rain* more accurately reflects the moment of production—the height of McCarthyism and the Hollywood blacklist—when speaking out in public could put one out of work.[1] The Hollywood blacklist, in other words, frames the film's relentless contemplation of stardom, spanning from the opening scene, the radio broadcast of stars at a 1927 premiere of *The Royal Rascal*, to the film's concluding lines, when *The Dancing Cavalier* star Don Lockwood announces at the film's premiere: "Stop her! She's the girl whose voice you heard tonight. She's the real *star* of the film: Kathy Selden." Lockwood's statement immediately segues into the song that ends the film, "You Are My Lucky Star."

Because this moment completes the trajectory by which Don exchanges his silent costar, Lina, for a talkie costar, Kathy, the film is about matching the appropriate female star to the appropriate historical moment. The idea of fashioning identity to keep working thus unites everything in film, from the manipulation of cinematic images and sounds to the management of public personae and private lives. Particularly in the way the film examines how stardom adapts to history, moreover, *Singin' in the Rain* uses the beginning of the sound era as an extended metaphor for the post–World War II period that replaced depression and war with an almost ebullient return to peace and prosperity. That postwar euphoria, however, was married to a commensurate angst most cogently consolidated around a fear of Communists, who in theory might reduce American prosperity to nuclear ash or, through subversion, make it the engine of a totalitarian state. Thus, stardom in the film links—as did the US policy of containment during the Cold War—social behavior, private inclinations, and personal attributes to public success, that is, to survival.

The final exchange of Kathy for Lina culminates a series of substitutions: sound for silence, singing for speaking, and dancing for acting. And all of these consolidate around the abjection of Lina Lamont, which grotesquely represents the conditions of speech in the age of McCarthyism, the stakes and terms of postwar prosperity, the diminishment of female agency after World War II, and the fate of the screwball comedy, the film genre most directly energized by female vitality.

Happy Again

Like the film's title dance number, "Singin' in the Rain," Kelly's description of his intentions for it evokes the postwar euphoria that has been described as "triumphalism."[2] Kelly was adamant that the dance number emphatically illustrate the song's lyrics. "I'm going to have a glorious feeling," he said, "I'm going to be happy again."[3] And indeed, compared to the other participants in World War II, Americans had many reasons to feel triumphantly happy. In Europe and Asia, winners and losers alike were ravaged. In the period between 1946 and 1951, European and Asian nations, in the process of rebuilding their infrastructure, their economies and, in many cases, their political systems, were besieged by issues of survival, while the United States, its physical and social structures virtually undamaged, its economy stable, and its government sound, experienced unprecedented prosperity.

In that context, the glorious feeling Kelly wants to enact clearly reflects an important aspect of the American postwar sensibility. If the war had produced an absence of eligible men, and the Depression before it an absence of employment opportunities for those men, starting in 1946, both of these obstacles to marriage vanished with unimaginable speed; between 1946 and 1950, weddings and births abounded. So too did opportunities for travel and education, opportunities that a decade earlier the majority of American men never contemplated. There were, indeed, many reasons for Kelly to celebrate a glorious feeling.

The lyrics to "Singin' in the Rain," however, place the joyous feeling in a retrospective context: "I'm happy *again*." Kelly is not singing about a moment that produces euphoria, but one that restores it. Like the lyrics and the song itself (written before the stock market crash), the film is steeped in the past. As Peter Chums notes, the project of the film is "the attempt to make the old new again, to recuperate the past for the present" (40). Don, he points out, can be innovative by turning back to the past (44). By drawing on his earlier life as a song-and-dance man, Don energizes the dying medium of the silent film. And that energy is enacted to a score of songs from that earlier period.

Intended by Arthur Freed, who headed the MGM musicals unit, to be a showcase of the songs he had written with Nacio Herb Brown in the 1920s and 1930s, the film is also an homage to the history of the movie musical, in which their work played a crucial part. Their songs were featured in the first two "all talking, all singing" MGM musicals, as well as *Hollywood Revue of 1929*, and many of the songs, including several used in *Singin'*, had been previously revived in subsequent MGM musicals. As Steven Cohan notes: "What's distinctive about the Freed-Brown songs chosen for *Singin' in the Rain* is that so many of these compositions had already been recycled in other MGM musicals" (221).

Repackaging the Past

The recycling of the songs, however, is also muddling. Cohan accurately points out that obscuring through mainstreaming of the film's camp qualities—of the camp qualities of MGM musicals in general, of which *Singin' in the Rain* is the apotheosis—is part of a generic process of political palatability, of repackaging the past so as to make it safe, both for the makers and the viewers. It is not surprising that the rehistoricizing engine works on several registers in the film. It repackages the Freed-Brown songs to give contemporary currency to the nostalgia implicit in the referents. It also puts the imprint of the MGM musical style on its antecedents both in and outside of the MGM system.[4] "Through this prior recycling," Cohan points out: "The Freed-Brown catalogue brings to *Singin' in the Rain* long-standing associations with the MGM musical, a surplus value which gives added texture to the film's retrospective view so that the history of the genre's production at the studio seems to occur logically, inevitably, and immediately after the arrival of sound in 1927. Which is also to say that, by following the lineage supplied by the recycled songs, as far as *Singin' in the Rain* recreates the past, 1927 cannot be conceived of without thinking ahead to what had become MGM's signature genre by 1952" (222).

The recycling thus confers a progressive inevitability on the MGM brand, making it stand for, visually epitomize, postwar American affluence and technology. As General Motors was doing for the American auto industry, MGM was representing the other mode of American cultural domination in the twentieth century, the movie industry, as the culmination of a historical trajectory initiated at the beginning of the century. Nor is it inappropriate in the immediate postwar period to see the millennialism of this trajectory as structurally analogous to the self-glorification attached to America's ascent to nuclear supremacy.[5]

This conflicted relationship with the history informs the film. If Peter Wollen is correct that "as well as a surface of retro pastiche and affectionate parody, it also has a thematic core which raises questions about the relation of sound and image, authenticity and inauthenticity" (30), then the film's self-conscious engagement with the past at that core requires an equally conscious duplicity. While singing that we are going to be happy again, the film returns us to the yesteryear of silent films, reviving that earlier period not to celebrate it but, at least ostensibly, to celebrate its demise. The conundrum of the film, therefore, is that it recounts the death of the same era that it revives. In order to be happy again, to be reenergized, the film invokes a period in which, for the principals, the successful mode of happiness had failed.

The film's self-conscious engagement with the past as the return to normality therefore requires a set of norms identified with a past that never existed. While allegedly returning to normality, the song and the film make normality a substitute for a much more troubled and troubling past. Rather than a piece of nostalgia, the "Singin' in the Rain" dance number is a baptismal moment celebrating the fact that *The Dueling Cavalier* will be given a new name and genre, and Lockwood will be given a new voice and a new career.

These are all good things, for as Lockwood's first words in the film—his speech at the premiere of *The Royal Rascal*—indicate, he wants to cover up the past. While telling the audience about his dignified youth as a conservatory-trained performer, we see the incriminating history that his speech misrepresents. While he underscores the importance in his life of "dignity"—from childhood through his work as a stuntman in silent films, which turns him into a leading man in the days when actors did their own stunts—we see Don's life presented in a series of vignettes in undignified settings, including pool halls and third-rate vaudeville houses (see figure 2.1).

The film's opening event thus establishes Don's need, his professional obligation, to dignify his past, a point that will have several ramifications, especially given that his interviewer is a fictional gossip columnist based on the red-baiting Luella Parsons. Since during the opening credits we have already seen Kelly (along with O'Connor and Reynolds) sing the title song, the obvious question at this point is how Lockwood's desire to be happy *again* can be reconciled with a past he must renounce. To the extent that the film will solve this problem, the rain in which Lockwood will so joyously sing will literalize the process by which the past that Lockwood had been hiding can be washed away.

FIGURE 2-1 Don Lockwood's history in pool halls and third-rate vaudeville houses.

It's About Work

Although the "Singin' in the Rain" dance number starts with Lockwood's kissing Kathy good night, the romantic energy of their clinch is channeled into a routine in which Lockwood replaces her with two phallic props, a large umbrella and a much larger lamppost. At the end of the number, moreover, Lockwood strolls away from Kathy toward his revitalized workplace. His joyous feelings, it turns out, emanate from the prospect of saving his job.

Singin' in the Rain's relentless self-reflexivity, moreover, foregrounds the fact that it is a movie *about the work of making movies*. Almost every scene invokes some stage of film production or distribution. The opening red carpet radio interview with Lockwood engages at the audio level issues of audience, fandom, and publicity, while the visuals review aspects of silent filmmaking: the music played on the set, the privileging of action over nuance, the conversion of stuntmen into stars, and the marketing of star "couples."

The premiere is followed by Don's jumping into Kathy's car to escape crazed fans and, consistent with the work motif, attending a cast party celebrating the successful product of the studio's labor. Kathy too is working; she is part of the entertainment at that party. Next we see Don and Lina at work on the set of their next silent feature, *The Dueling Cavalier*. In the midst of this work, Lina reveals that she was responsible for having Kathy fired, so that the scene merges a personal issue with a personnel issue, and it does so during the act of filming, underscoring how extensively everything personal in *Singin' in the Rain* is framed by professional activity. Because their personal life is a publicity fiction, Don's personal interactions with Lina only occur at work; their relationship *is* their job. Thus, thanks to the silent medium, Lena gloats over Kathy's firing and Don tells Lena how much he loathes her while they are actually filming a scene. This work session, however, is interrupted by the announcement that *The Dueling Cavalier* is going to be turned into a talkie, and the scenes in *Singin' in the Rain* that immediately follow deal with the work of making talkies, such as voice coaching, the development of scripts, the placement of microphones, and the reduction of ambient noise. The segue to these scenes is achieved through a montage that spans the development of the MGM musical, featuring snippets of songs from those first musicals and headlines naming them. The headlines, moreover, coming from both the popular press and the trade journal *Variety*, are not transmitting entertainment news but rather conveying professional information.

The advent of sound production also allows Don to find Kathy, because she has obtained work in one of the newly assembled choruses necessitated by the production of musicals. Don cannot express his true feelings to Kathy, however, unless he does so in a work setting, a vacant set, where his true feelings, it turns out, are best reflected by a recycled song, "You Were Meant for Me," originally used in the 1929 musical *Broadway Melody (see figure 2.2)*. The scene, however, complicates in several ways the generic triteness of the MGM musical tradition that *Singin' in the Rain* also celebrates. The fact that Don can only be sincere on a movie set diverges from the traditional pastoral convention that the lovers escape the world of work and posturing to be themselves. Only within his workplace surroundings can Lockwood express his true feelings, so wedded is his identity to his job. He achieves intimacy not by discarding his star persona but, because his job forms the foundation of his identity, by contextualizing it. The scene distinguishes therefore between two identities that are both grounded in the workplace, one on an active set and the other on a vacant set. In the former, regardless of his actual feelings, Lockwood is Lina's lover. On the vacant set, however, he is just a Monumental employee, identified with his profession, but not with a specific role.

Thus, while the vacancy of the set establishes his sincerity, the set itself maintains his authenticity. This is a distinction that Kathy implicitly understands and that Lina explicitly inverts. For Lina, Lockwood has no existence outside of his role, and thus he *must* be in love with her offscreen just as he is on-screen. Since she sees him only as identified by his role, moreover, she ignores any connection between him and his profession, career, work, or craft.

The preview of the film on which they are working, *The Dueling Cavalier*, exposes unsuccessful labor and portends a questionable future for Lockwood. The incipit script, the foibles of inept sound recording, and most horrifically,

FIGURE 2-2 On the vacant set, Don is just another Monumental employee.

Lina's lower-class accent and screechy voice, render the film unsalvageable. Lockwood's equally poor work in the film jeopardizes his employability. After the preview, Kathy and Cosmo's plan to convert the film into a musical is therefore devised as a way of keeping Don employed. Not just the film *The Dueling Cavalier*, in other words, but Lockwood himself undergoes a conversion to dancing in order to continue working.

As the earlier scenes in *Singin' in the Rain* focused on the work of making silent films, the later scenes attend to the work entailed in using sound technology to make musicals. This work is much more productive, so much so that after the success of the remodeled film, Lina invokes clauses in her contract that will require Kathy to continue to dub Lina's films, uncredited, a demand so outrageous that at the end of *The Dancing Cavalier*'s premiere, Lockwood, Cosmo, and studio head R. F. Simpson destroy Lamont's career by publicly exposing her actual voice.

The Working Man's Dancer

In *That's Entertainment* (1974), a documentary about the MGM musical, when Fred Astaire, the premier dancer of prewar film, acknowledged Kelly as the premier dancer of the postwar period, this passing of the baton was not simply generational but also thematic.[6] For Astaire, in his heyday, song-and-dance numbers were about love: "I know that music leads the way to romance," Astaire sings with Ginger Rogers in *Roberta* (1935), "So if I hold you in my arms. . . . I won't dance." For Kelly, on the other hand, dance was always about work, and thus his dance partners were more often his male work partners. Unlike Astaire, Wollen notes, Kelly never had a regular female partner and preferred male partners, "his buddies" (quoted in Mast 249).[7] In the "Singin' in the Rain" number, however, when Lockwood's longtime partner, Cosmo (Donald O'Connor), is not available, a lamppost will suffice.

The contrast between Kelly's dance style and Astaire's underscores the difference between the Depression and the postwar period. When Astaire in *Follow the Fleet* (1936) sings "Let's Face the Music and Dance," he performs in sync with a world where love will substitute for rather than complement prosperity, his formal wear celebrating a lifestyle of leisure rather than of production. He may look as though he doesn't need to work, but as his empty wallet makes clear, he needs work but doesn't have a job (see figure 2.3). In that number, Ginger

FIGURE 2-3 Formal evening wear serves as Astaire's disguise.

Rogers too has lost her options, but still retains her formal evening gown. They encounter one another on a bridge, both contemplating suicide, but by becoming partners in one another's embrace, by dancing, they save each other's lives. In his dance routines during the RKO years, formal evening wear thus serves as Astaire's disguise, that is, as a sign of his bravura, his assertion that the value in life could be found, had to be found, in love rather than work.

To that end, Astaire's form and gesture hide his knees and elbows even more effectively than the folds of his formal attire. The lines of Astaire's arms, whether cradling his partner or whirling across the stage, were always curved, and he seemed, however impossibly, to tap dance without bending his knees.

Exactly the opposite is true of Kelly. Rarely in formal attire, with his sleeves often short or rolled up, he displays distinctively the sharp angles at which his elbows bend, angles that mirror the acute bend of his knees and of his waist (see figure 2.4).

If bent elbows, bent knees, and a bent waist are signs of work, no dancer has ever looked more as though he were putting his shoulder to the wheel. Not surprisingly, therefore, almost all of Kelly's dance numbers in *Singin'* have to do with work, as does Donald O'Connor's only solo dance, "Make 'em Laugh." The scene begins with Lockwood walking through the studio, past several sets on some of which there is active filming. We see not only the performers but also the director, cameramen, lights, and equipment. From *Variety*, the trade

FIGURE 2-4 Kelly's bent elbows, bent knees, and bent waist are signs of work.

journal, Cosmo reads a story on talkies. Then Cosmo correctly guesses the plot of *The Dueling Cavalier*, about to go into production, implying its heavily formulaic quality, to which Lockwood responds, "Well, it's a living." When they arrive at a set under construction, Cosmo begins his number by reminding Lockwood of his responsibilities as an actor, that is, as a worker. Before and during the number, moreover, we see almost two dozen anonymous workers building sets, hauling materials, sweeping floors, washing walls, and moving props and costumes. While Cosmo's lyrics relate to the job of entertaining, the scene as a whole relentlessly iterates the multifarious aspects of labor involved in film production. Although the number foregrounds the work of the star, we are unable to ignore the fact that a studio is a factory. Everything in the scene reminds us that Cosmo is singing and dancing in the workplace.

And Cosmo works very hard, the number concluding with such abundant energy that he literally climbs the walls of the set (see figure 2.5). "The number led to such a crescendo," O'Connor said, "that I thought I'd have to commit suicide as a finale" (quoted in Silverman 160).

Stanley Donnen, the co-choreographer and codirector of the *Singin' in the Rain*, even more radically experimented with the gimmick of dancing on the walls in the film he made immediately before it, *Royal Wedding* (1951), starring Fred Astaire. The most famous dance number in *Royal Wedding* takes place in the gym of a transatlantic liner, where Astaire dances not with a partner but

FIGURE 2-5 Cosmo literally climbs the walls of the set.

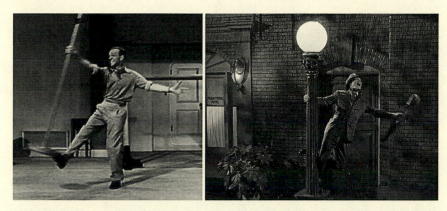

FIGURE 2-6 Astaire assumes a pose very similar to Kelly's with the lamppost.

with inanimate objects, the most prominent being a coat rack. Jane Feuer is correct that this number has a bricolage quality, but not in the sense that Astaire's "tinkering" is a form of play; quite the contrary. In the film he says he is going to the gym *to work out*, and like the "Singin' in the Rain" number, this number is a solo about work, not love. Astaire's sleeves are rolled up and, embracing the coat rack, he assumes a pose very similar to the one Kelly would later with the lamppost (see figure 2.6).

This number may be uncharacteristic for Astaire, but in conjunction with "Singin' in the Rain," it seems to typify, I think, the focus on men returning to work in the early 1950s. Like *Singin' in the Rain*, moreover, *Royal Wedding* evokes an earlier period, in that Astaire's female dance partner in this film, Jane Powell, plays Astaire's sister, alluding to Astaire's early dancing career. At that point—chiefly in the 1920s—he partnered not with a love interest but with his sister, Adele. *Royal Wedding*'s other highly celebrated dance number features Astaire dancing on the floor, walls, and ceiling of his apartment, a trick briefly suggested by O'Connor at the end of "Make 'em Laugh." While celebrating his new love, Astaire nevertheless dances solo.

Singin' in the Rain's dance numbers also foreground work through their relentlessly escalating tempos, especially in the numbers that feature Lockwood and Cosmo. During the shooting of "Good Morning," Kelly was constantly shouting, "Dance harder! More energy!" (Head and Dabholkar 95); the "Fit as a Fiddle" number, shown as part of Lockwood's unnarrated history, features Don and Cosmo singing and dancing in vaudeville. Although the cheap, garish outfits—broadly checked brown and white suits—the hokey routine, and ultimately the hooks that remove them from the stage suggest failure, the perfectly coordinated tap-dancing, maintained through several intensifications of the tempo, demonstrates skill and great energy, devoted to getting and keeping a job, to dodging the hook.

If "Fit as a Fiddle" illustrates men working with all of their effort to secure a career, the "Moses Supposes" number illustrates the fruits of that labor. While the occasion for the number is a diction-coaching session to prepare Lockwood for talkies, the setting, inexplicably, resembles a college classroom that looks as though it were left over from the 1947 MGM musical *Good News* (also produced by Freed and authored by—among others—Comden and Green). Cosmo accompanies Lockwood, and both of them are dressed as though they were undergraduate classmates of the 1920s. The voice coach complements their appearance, looking like the caricature of a professor excavated from the preceding century. If, as Ruth Johnston aptly states, "Don and Cosmo . . . dance like schoolboys taking over the schoolroom" (123), they nevertheless seem far more authoritative than the "professor," whose stuffy, pretentious demeanor seems to invite rebellion, especially in light of the fact that Lockwood's speech sounds more correct for the age of talkies—that is, more appropriately modern—than that of his coach.

While the supposition of the scene is that Lockwood should learn to speak as his coach does, within a few seconds we can see that what the teacher supposes is erroneous, that Lockwood has learned more from life about how to speak than the "professor" has from books, and thus the roles need to be reversed, which they are in stunning fashion. Donnen said this was the best tap number ever done in pictures, better than the closest rival "for its sheer energy" (quoted in Head and Dabholkar 89). By my count, the tempo accelerates a dozen times during the number. In other words, it does exactly what the assembly lines were doing in Detroit, what the housing starts were doing, and what the birthrate was doing: demonstrating a capacity for limitless production. The number clearly establishes, in this regard, the Cosmo-Lockwood partnership as the male dynamo empowering the physical and psychic industry of the postwar boom.

Given that the setting for the "Moses Supposes" number is a 1920s college classroom, and the voice coach who is humiliated by the dance looks like an old-fashioned professor, the connection between the number and the new population of more mature college students taking advantage of the G.I. Bill seems particularly strong. In this setting certainly, and more generally as avatars of postwar production, Don and Cosmo stand for the 16 million men who returned from World War II, were greeted as heroes, as stars, and were privileged with job opportunities. They were also showered with benefits, which included low-interest loans to buy homes, farms, or businesses; a year of unemployment pay at $20 a week (ca. $185 in 2017 dollars); and extremely generous benefits for school tuition, books, and living expenses (more than $45,000 a year in 2015 dollars). This education benefit profoundly changed the composition of American higher education[8] and in the immediate postwar period created a radical change in campus demographics. Able men, older than the average college student and in many ways mature beyond their age, encountered a professorial generation on average already too old to serve at the outbreak of the war, and in many cases far less worldly than the unique generation of their students. These professors were used to teaching students (about 60 percent of them male) heavily drawn from the upper class. Now they were confronted with classes in which the enrollment was over two-thirds male, and a significant portion of that group were men who had commanded planes in bombing raids over Berlin or led platoons through the jungles of Guadalcanal, who had risked their own lives and been accountable for the lives of others. If those professors supposed that they were in the traditional position of handing down wisdom from on high, then many of them no doubt were in effect told that "Moses supposes erroneously."

If the "Moses Supposes" number serves as a paean to the energy of what would much later be called the greatest generation, it is not limited to the campus but endemic to the film. And it is moreover linked inextricably to erroneous suppositions as the means to careerist ends. Lena supposes erroneously that Lockwood loves her, which is also what their fans erroneously suppose. And Lockwood erroneously supposes that he can disabuse Lena while continuing to delude their fans. The energy that overflows from the "Good Morning" number, when Cosmo and Kathy figure out how Lockwood can continue to work as a star, and the "Singin' in the Rain" number, when Lockwood celebrates the effect of their plan on the rebirth of his manhood, funnels for the rest of the film into the work of getting Lina to suppose erroneously—that is, to assume she is speaking while she is actually being dubbed—and the work of getting the audience to suppose the same erroneous thing. It turns out, however, as Head and Dabholkar point out, "to be an almost bizarre exercise. The production company of *Singin' in the Rain* focused on a deceptive, widely known 'secret' in the industry while coolly practicing the deception themselves in the very sequence that makes fun of it. It adds quite another layer of irony to the lyrics [of Lina's dubbed song, 'Would You?']: 'And would you dare to say? Let's do the same as they'" (147).

Avoiding the Blacklist

Lina's dubbed song "Would You?" is also ominous in the way that it echoes the dreaded House Committee on Un-American Activities (HUAC) question, "Are you now, or have you ever been, a member of the Communist Party?" And the levels of deception evoked to deal with it become particularly evident in the dubbing of Lina's speaking voice. Jean Hagen, who plays Lina with shrill, squeaky nasality, uses her normal voice to dub Debbie Reynolds when Reynolds appears to be dubbing Lina. The elaborate measures necessary for us to hear Hagen's real voice reflect the tortuous steps necessary to speak in one's own voice, steps that allow the speaker adequate layers of disguise and the producers plausible deniability. Hagen knew she was speaking for Selden only at that moment when Lina did not know that Selden was speaking for Hagen's character. Such was the kind of machination—actual or imagined—that any potential HUAC witness had to conjure. These machinations were manifest in the don't ask, don't tell relationship between screenwriters and producers that "fronts" facilitated. They characterized the array of rhetorical strategies devised by professional writers as they attempted to script their testimony so as to incriminate the process rather than themselves. The rhetorical contrivances were at the heart of the deals in which HUAC accepted dubious excuses from major celebrities[9] or provided names to "friendly" witnesses with no one to name, for HUAC's primary mission clearly was not to investigate but to intimidate through investigation. To that end, as Tom Englehardt points out, between 1789 and 1925 Congress had only authorized 285 investigations, but "51 anti-Communist investigations were held during the 83rd Congress alone (1953–54)" (126).

HUAC, as Milly S. Barranger explains, "remained in the limelight for a decade by means of its extensive show business hearings of 1951 and 1952. . . . Those writers and artists showcased by the investigative committees usually had star status to generate the headlines so dear to the congressional committeemen and to their constituencies" (2). As a result, no one was exempt from suspicion. "The political and the apolitical, actors and composers, screenwriters and playwrights, film and television artists, were targets of the Cold War crusade to eradicate Communists from American culture and society" (3).

If, as I noted at the outset, the film is about stardom, and these dance numbers make clear that stardom is a form of work, then Lockwood's job, being a star, as the movie constantly reminds us, is in every way circumscribed by work. But the word "work" means not only "effort" but also "employment"; as a nation recovering from more than a decade of devastating depression well knew, working meant *having* a job. In Hollywood, however, especially after 1948, having a job involved more than talent or effort or economic conditions or even luck; it involved politics.

And saving one's job, therefore, often involved the art of successful collaborative deception, because McCarthyism acquired much of its power from the specter of the Depression. My mother, who started her working life a few years before the stock market crash, bragged so frequently that it became a motif in my household, "I was never out of work one day during the Depression." This was her equivalent to being a star; it made her a statistical anomaly on a unique honor roll. For the generation of people who had endured unemployment, often for long periods, and for the children who had grown up in a household where employment was intermittent and/or infrequent, keeping one's job was paramount. Hence, the postwar abundance of jobs did not produce a cavalier attitude toward work, but instead evoked an attitude that regarded employment as a valuable natural resource not to be squandered. And of the many things that could jeopardize one's job, the easiest to avoid was associating with anyone whose politics was deemed suspect; who might have engaged in protests considered questionable by J. Edgar Hoover; or who might have belonged to groups he classified, ex post facto, as subversive. The desire to keep one's job also impelled conformity to specific lifestyles, such that any significant deviation from the norm required closeting. Although it is impossible to produce conclusive data to support this notion, I think it is difficult not to imagine that a cornerstone of Cold War conformity was the trauma of unemployment that the Depression had produced.

At a time when personal history could be particularly incriminating, Lina's voice therefore represents a political danger, as all undoctored speech did in the age of McCarthyism, especially in Hollywood. The word "singing," we should remember, also connotes ratting people out, naming names; indeed, as numerous Hollywood figures—most notably Elia Kazan[10]—proved, singing was a way to save one's career.

Another way to look at the central problem of *Singin' in the Rain*, therefore, is how to speak without incriminating oneself or others at a moment when remaining silent was no longer tenable. Lockwood's speech at the premiere of *The Royal Rascal* has two goals: to misrepresent his own history and to prevent Lina from speaking at all. The antiquation of Lockwood's method, signified by the old-fashioned microphone and the superannuated medium of radio into which it feeds, suggests from the film's outset that a new way must be devised to hide old indignities. In a similar fashion, after the failure of the Hollywood Ten, who were ultimately blacklisted, to assert their First Amendment rights or to use their Fifth Amendment right against self-incrimination (in that doing so became a form of self-incrimination), many in the Hollywood community sought alternatives to naming names.

With a HUAC subpoena always possible, many of the principals involved with *Singin'* no doubt spent much time pondering the relationship between speech and incrimination. Comden and Green, as well as Judy Holiday and Al Hammer, the other members of a theater group they had founded in the 1930s, were called to testify before HUAC. Hammer refused to testify and was blacklisted; Holiday did testify and, in order to avoid incriminating her friends, may have committed perjury. Comden and Green, according to Gerda Lerner, saved their careers by testifying in secret as friendly witnesses.

Ostensibly to take advantage of a new tax loophole that allowed Americans who spent eighteen months abroad to avoid paying US taxes, Kelly left the country immediately after shooting *Singin'*. However, as Kelly biographer Alvin Yudkoff, notes, "There was yet another factor underlying [Kelly's and his wife, Betsy Blair's] decision to live abroad, perhaps the most important" (222). Kelly, as a member of the Committee for the First Amendment (which included Billy Wilder, Danny Kaye, Lauren Bacall, Humphrey Bogart, Fredric March, and songwriter Ira Gershwin), had spoken in a radio ad in 1947 denouncing the HUAC assault on Hollywood: "Did you happen to see *The Best Years of Our Lives*, the picture that won seven Academy Awards? Did *you* enjoy it? Did you like it? Were you subverted by it? Did it make you Un-American? Did you come out of the movie with a desire to overthrow the government?" (quoted in Falk 109).

In California, moreover, Yudkoff points out, "the notorious Tenney Committee, a clone of HUAC . . . had already put out two successive reports criticizing Kelly for membership in 'Communisty Party fronts'. . . . Gene feared being blacklisted—not so much because of his prominence in the liberal-left political movement within the film industry, but because of Betsy's history as a Party member" (222).

In this context, it is striking how successfully the film repackages not only Lockwood's biography, but also Kelly's, such that the copious allusions to Kelly's prior screen roles, as Cohan points out, start to stand in for his life. "Some twenty years after its release, and without appearing to do the film any injustice, a BBC interview with Kelly could simply treat *Singin' in the Rain* as if it *were* telling his life story" (197). The film creates a pastiche of earlier Kelly roles and numbers and then reformulates the allusions into a long dance number appropriately merging "gotta dance" with "Broadway Melody." Thus dance not only saves *The Dueling Cavalier* but also saves the principals from the threatening potentials of sound. (As Cohan notes, the numbers move more progressively away from the human voice.) The long dance number thus refashions the events of Don's life in the same way that the film disguises those of Kelly's.[11]

This is important cultural work, because Kelly, like Lockwood, is an industrial product. Organized as it was on the principles of Fordism, the studio system made "stars" assembly-line material, as definitive an aspect of brand as was, for example, the grill design of a Buick (or of an Edsel). The star's image, therefore, was just as important as the studio's, a point made most explicitly by Lina when she asserts that she is bigger than the studio.

And while the film is about the Hollywood musical in particular, it is about industrial production in general and the boon to productivity provided by technological innovation. This is why technology and stardom must be reconciled; in other words, why the dangers of speech must be evaded. If the film makes apparent—so apparent that even Lina finds it obvious—that industrial profits depend on stars, then it posits dance as the way to evade speech and evading speech as the way to preserve stardom.

The "Broadway Melody" makes this emphatically clear. It starts with Kelly in a cheap, garish, undignified outfit, similar to the one he wore in the "Fit as a Fiddle" sequence (see figure 2.7), approaching Broadway with the iterated imperative, "gotta dance!," an imperative sung sixteen times during the course of the thirteen-minute number that connects the success of the young dancer, who represents both Lockwood's and Kelly's alter ego, to success as a performer, although he is disappointed in his pursuit of an underworld gun moll.

Returning to his Broadway roots, Kelly unites dance with work and with stardom on Broadway, underscored by the number's frame song, "Broadway Melody," sung at the outset and again at the conclusion. These themes consolidate in the remarkable closing shot of the number. Spectacularly, while

FIGURE 2-7 Kelly in an outfit similar to the one he wore in the "Fit as a Fiddle" sequence.

Lockwood is belting out the phrase "Broadway melody," the camera lifts him out of a large ensemble dance number, such that his whole body seems to rise to the heavens—that is, toward the camera—leaving the chorus line behind; then, with the diminished chorus still in the background, the camera closes in on Lockwood just as dramatically as he seemed to have risen toward the camera. The concluding close-up of his head, in full color, is brightly lit so that one can virtually see the stars in his eyes (see figure 2.8).

He almost literally becomes "a star in the firmament," to use the words with which Lina's self-promotional material describes her. In visually fulfilling Lena's prophesy, Don has used dance to avoid the pitfalls of the sound era, which ensnared her.

Silencing Lina

While Lina's voice constantly foregrounds the threat of undignified speech, the fact that Lina's voice is undignified makes her a representative of Lockwood and Cosmo, whose undignified origins Don made a great effort to cover up. Because, as the opening segment makes clear, speech can disguise one's past by giving the appearance of dignity to behavior that lacked it, Lina's raw speech threatens to expose the fragile artifice upon which everyone's job depends. By revealing

FIGURE 2-8 We can virtually see the stars in Kelly's eyes.

cinema's capacity to hide indignity in general, she threatens to blow everyone's cover, to fracture the veneer of stardom, the magic of the magic lantern itself.

Singin' very clearly thematizes the relationship between disguising speech and preserving stardom in a sequence that intertwines the images and voices of several women, momentarily unified in the black-and-white composite of a scene from *The Dancing Cavalier*, a film that is itself a composite of several disparate elements: footage from the scrapped film *The Dueling Cavalier*; new footage including (unseen) dance numbers, the words spoken by Gene Kelly playing Don Lockwood, that Lockwood dubbed onto the silent film; the song sung by Betty Noyes dubbing Debbie Reynolds playing Kathy Selden dubbing Lina Lamont, played by Jean Hagen; and the voice of Jean Hagen dubbing Debbie Reynolds when she plays Kathy Selden dubbing Lina Lamont's speaking (as opposed to singing) voice.[12]

In other words, the viewers of *Singin' in the Rain,* along with the spectators of *The Dancing Cavalier,* simultaneously experience, by virtue of cinema's symbolic order, an imaginary coherence, the illusion of mastery not consistent with the experience of the subjects whose actions contribute to that illusion. That illusion is informed by exactly what the dubbed composite excludes: the voice of Lina Lamont. The first dubbing sequence starts with a shot of Selden singing "Would You" that pans to Lockwood and lingers on him looking lovingly at Kathy, who is outside the frame, while he listens to Betty Noyes's voice. He then moves back into the frame so that we see him looking at Kathy singing into a mike and also see part of the orchestra accompanying her. As the camera moves in on Kathy, the round mike in front of her dissolves into the spinning of an old-fashioned record player, and Betty Noyes's voice is joined by Jean Hagen's singing the same song, using the grating, nasal, lower-class voice Hagen created for Lina.[13] As the camera pans from the record player to the megaphone into which Lina is singing, Noyes's voice fades away, only to return and replace Hagen's as the camera closes in on Lina struggling with the lyrics.

With Noyes's voice as a sound bridge, the close-up of Lina dissolves into a shot of the director and cinematographer of *The Dancing Cavalier* filming the scene in which the song will be used. Following the director from his chair toward the action, we cut to a shot in full color of Lockwood and Lamont in costume, acting the scene into which this song will be dubbed. Although Lockwood and Lamont appear to be singing the duet, the visual, taking place in the studio, and the audio, taking place in the sound stage, merge only from the perspective of the viewer engaged in the conflation of time and space made possible by the cinematic imaginary. Brilliantly, the camera moves in for a rich, color close-up of Lamont in full makeup, looking absolutely beautiful and singing beautifully, in every way and every bit a star, however briefly, for the audience of *Singin' in the Rain,* as she will be, the transition of the shot to black-and-white makes clear, for the audience of *The Dancing Cavalier (see figure 2.9).*

FIGURE 2-9 Lina Lamont looking absolutely, in every way, a star.

An interesting, perhaps poignant, and certainly political fact is that *Singin'*
in the Rain never matches this glamorous (albeit fleeting) color close-up of Lina
with a comparable close-up of Kathy. The substitution of Kathy for Lina, in other
words, indicates the new version: the woman for the new era will never command the same authority or have the same luster as the star she replaced.

Nor does any other shot in the film so totally represent stardom, except
for the shot of Lockwood at the end of "Broadway Melody." Although this shot
echoes the close-up of Lamont at the end of the "Would You" number in the
way that it asserts star power, there are important differences, all portending the end of Lamont's stardom. The shot of Lockwood, held much longer
than Lamont's, is part of the "modern" portion of *The Dancing Cavalier*, and it
remains in color instead of morphing into black-and-white. Moreover, just as
the black-and-white shot associates Lamont with an earlier era in film history,
her eighteenth-century costume and makeup signify an even more distant past,
while Lockwood's black tuxedo appears timelessly contemporary. In juxtapo-
sition, these star close-ups project Lockwood into the future while relegating
Lamont to the past.

This distinction is underscored by the next, briefer sequence, in which
Kathy and Don dub not singing but dialogue. In that scene, they stand in a
sound stage, before a mike, their backs to the camera as they look at a projection of *The Dancing Cavalier* in which Lina is speaking in her own voice, that is,
the abject voice Hagen created. When Kathy is cued, they replay the scene with
Kathy dubbing Lina's speaking voice. The voice we hear in the dubbed version,
however, as I noted, belongs to Hagen. Like the morphing of Lina from color to
black-and-white in the earlier dubbing montage, the dialogue in this sequence
indicates the demise of Lina, the cooling off of her stardom. "Our love," she says,
speaking in Hagen's rich, full-toned, non-Lina Lamont voice, "will last 'til the
stars turn cold."

The power of this manipulation of Lina's voice and image derives from stardom's functioning as abjection's Other. If for Julia Kristeva abjection is linked
to bodily expulsion, which blurs the boundary between that which is a product of the self and that which the self must reject in order to be a "self," then
stardom, in contradistinction, is not expulsionary but absorptive. The abject
object is repelled, and the self that is the object of abjection is repulsive; stars,
on the other hand, are attractive, stardom being defined by the magnetism it
generates. Instead of expelling products of the self, the star accumulates under
the auspices of its identity meanings beyond its own production. Memorabilia,
photos, and autographs, even in their separation from the star and more so in
their circulation apart from the star's knowledge and control, support, bolster,
endorse, and *belong to* the star's identity. If the abject object calls attention to
the fragility of self, stardom masks it. I am not saying that a star's persona is

less fragile than that of the abject, only that it is less apparently so, and thus the disparity between appearance and reality, which informs every aspect of *Singin'*, consolidates around the crisis fomented by the advent of sound and the sound of Lina Lamont.

To put it another way, the myth of stardom is the myth of presence, the belief in a centered subject—Cary Grant, Marilyn Monroe, John Wayne—always present to himself or herself, regardless of the fictions he or she performs. *Singin'*, however, is about the moment when voice would become inextricably connected to star identity through a process that historically has functioned to disavow cinema's lack. As Kaja Silverman has noted, "with each new testimonial in the history of recorded sound, cinema seems once again capable of restoring all phenomenal losses" (42). The advent of sound, in other words, can be viewed as the mirror stage in the life of the contemporary movie star. As in the Lacanian mirror stage, the subject is split, manifesting a coherence in the imaginary elsewhere upon which cinema depends, while being an incomplete conjunction of disparate elements.

Because the fragile psychic elements conjoined by the imaginary to produce the imagined—the star—thus always verge on turning cold, when Lina says, "Our love will last until the stars turn cold," she is addressing the movie audience as much as her character is addressing Lockwood's cavalier. This becomes apparent in the final scene, which immediately follows, when the film's climactic public introduction of the real Lina's voice indeed turns her stardom cold, and the real Lena Lamont is rent from the imaginary Lina Lamont.

Thus one could view the plot of *Singin' in the Rain* as the story of the abjection of Lena Lamont more than of Don and Kathy's love, for in fact Lina provides no serious obstacle to the offscreen relationship between Don and Kathy, her rivalry with Kathy existing only in her own imagination. And Lina's stardom never threatened Don's; he actually benefited from her success. Nor can the plot allow her simply to be rejected. If the beginning required that she not speak in public, the end requires that she disappear completely.

Carol Clover notes how the film's pervasive exposure of artifice masks the larger suppression of its origins in African American culture: *Singin'* "not only footnotes plagiarism but hitches the whole to a morality tale exactly *about* plagiarism. . . . In the world of the film musical . . . it is not enough merely to mention and silence, remember and forget, the source. An entire plot must be accomplished to mobilize the forgetting" (743). "Poor Lina," Clover points out, "carries a heavy burden. She is the scapegoat not only for all the actors, male and female alike, whose voices flunked the shift to sound, but for all the white performers who danced the art of unseen others—which is to say for the film musical itself. No wonder her exposure must be so brutal and her humiliation so complete; she is the repository of a guilt so much greater than her own" (744).

While Clover, from a cultural perspective, erases Lamont's gender, Silverman, from a psychoanalytic perspective, sees Lamont as standing for women in general. "The bewildering array of female voices," Silverman argues, "marshaled at both the diegetic and extradiegetic levels for the purpose of creating direct sound suggests, even more forcefully that the difficulties Lina encounters in attempting to articulate and record her lines, that the rule of synchronization simultaneously holds more fully and necessitates more coercion with the female that with the male voice—suggests, in other words, that very high stakes are involved in the alignment of the female voice with the female image" (46).

Thus, although Clover is very astute, her argument cannot exclude Lina's gender, especially in light of the way that the female voice, as Silverman convincingly argues, has been employed in a compensatory relationship to the threat of castration implicit in cinematic lack. Indeed, Lina's inability to hide the fact that her sound is derivative requires that she be expelled, lest the source of the derivation be acknowledged, but for Lamont's humiliation to be, as Clover puts it, "so complete," Lina has to be expelled not just as an improper black but also as an improper woman, which in the moment of the film's production, she is. As Cohan succinctly points out, "More than just sending up her ability to adjust to the talkies, *Singin' in the Rain* vilifies Lina because she crosses the line of power at the studio as determined by gender" (241).

The film's narrative, as Cohan explains, "views women as disruptive, the source of all of Don's problems because of their voices" (194), despite the fact that what Don's voice has been disguising, disavowing, is his lower-class background, which identifies him with the poor and the working class. This is what his costume dramas have done and what his ballet number does. This process of disavowal is what the "Broadway Melody" number thematizes, resurrecting Don's lower-class background so that it may demonstrate how he rises above it, thematically, and thanks to the magic of moviemaking, physically, ascending at the end of the number into the cinematic firmament that Lina's publicity had reserved for her.

Like the returning GIs, Don replaces a successful woman, assisted in doing so by a compliant woman. Unlike Lina, but like Kathy, the proper woman in 1952 must not acknowledge her professional or personal desires; like Kathy, she must pretend to say no when she means yes; must be pursued rather than give chase; must subordinate her career to that of her (heterosexual) partner; and must cover for his deficiencies rather than expose or exacerbate them in the way that, for example, Katherine Hepburn relentlessly pursues and embarrasses Cary Grant in *Bringing up Baby* (1938). Since, like Hepburn (or Carole Lombard in *My Man Godfrey, 1936*), Lina is a zany character who chases the man she "knows" loves her, despite his insistence to the contrary, we can see that she resides in the great tradition of screwball comedy heroines, such that her expulsion represents a rejection, as well, of the screwball genre and the level of female agency it implied.

This becomes especially clear when *Singin'* is read in the light of *You Gotta Stay Happy* (1948), starring Jimmy Stewart and Joan Fontaine, a film that begins, unmistakably, as a screwball comedy. Dee Dee Dillwood (Fontaine), a multimillionaire (à la Claudette Colbert in *It Happened One Night, 1934*) who has run away from her wedding (the film indicates that she has been "engaged" several times), hides in the suite of a prestigious New York hotel. Marvin Payne (Stewart), a former World War II pilot trying to start up a commercial airline company by hauling cargo coast to coast with two two-prop planes, is staying in the suite because a war buddy, who manages the hotel, allows him to use vacant suites for a nominal fee. When Stewart hides Fontaine and helps her escape from New York as a passenger on his cargo plane (which is illegal), he has no idea that she is an heiress, but comes to believe she is the blonde secretary wanted by the police for helping to embezzle $50,000. Because Stewart's business is in financial straits, his copilot, Bullets (Eddie Albert), has also sold passage to newlyweds—from their accents, rural southerners—and a businessman, Mr. Caslon (Porter Hall). Marv, who is falling in love with Dee Dee despite his suspicions that she is the wanted woman—suspicions exacerbated by her buying an expensive ring for the new bride—decides not to stop for fuel in Kansas City, where the police may be waiting, but instead to fly on to Tulsa. This takes him into a storm that forces him, halfway through the film, to land on a farm field north of Tulsa.

Taken in by a farmer named Racknell (Percy Killbride), Marv, Dee Dee, Bullets, the young newlyweds, and Caslon share a warm family evening in the Racknell farmhouse, dining and socializing with the Racknell family, which includes nearly a dozen children, ranging from teenaged to infancy. Killbride, best known for the Ma and Pa Kettle movies, was at the time sixty years old, and Edith Evanson, the matronly actress who plays his wife, Bella, was fifty-two. Thus, when Marv tells Racknell that he has a fine family and Racknell retorts, "It's going to be a fine family when we're done. We're just getting started," the line is delivered in a way that makes it comic, but not ironic. Racknell clearly believes that fewer than a dozen children do not constitute a full family and seems certain that he and his wife have several fertile years ahead of them. Located in the heart of America and speaking for American values—generosity, warmth, "mom and apple pie"—the Racknells derive humor from the authority with which they define American life, not because they are wrong, but because they are implicitly right. While their family size does not represent the norm in postwar America, the family values it reflects are normative, so much so that they become the means for sustaining the happiness called for in the film's title.

The Racknell farmhouse thus becomes the site of the antidote to the problem, noted by Luce, Wylie, Schlesinger, Riesman, and Mills, that Americans were not happy. This point is made explicit when Dee Dee and the young bride help Mrs. Racknell with the dishes. Dee Dee is distressed because her $800 million

FIGURE 2-10 Mrs. Racknell and the young bride impart wisdom to Dee Dee.

(at least $8 billion in contemporary value) and the agency it provides has, in keeping with Lundberg and Farnham's prognostication, made her neurotic rather than happy. Despite her numerous "engagements," she has never been in love. In this regard, Mrs. Racknell and the young bride, for whom Mrs. Racknell is the implicit role model, impart more wisdom than Dee Dee's psychiatrist, seen advising her at the outset of the film (see figure 2.10).

When Mrs. Racknell casually extols the simple pleasures of farm life and of raising a family of ten or more children—"Don't know what else there is in life for a woman 'side helpin' her man and raisin' some kids"—Dee Dee says, with joy and revelation, "You must be really happy, aren't you?" To this Mrs. Racknell responds, "Why . . . why yes, I suppose I am." Then she asks Dee Dee, "Ain't you happy?" But Dee Dee confesses that she doesn't think she really knows. This leads to what the film treats as the obvious next question: "Did you ever thinks of getting married?" Dee Dee explains that it is a hard decision to make and asks Mrs. Racknell, "How do you make up your mind about a thing like that?" "If you have to make up your mind," Mrs. Racknell explains, "then you have the wrong man." Dee Dee has discovered, at last, from the matronly mother of ten, *what* will make her happy. She then learns immediately from the young—probably teenaged—bride how to discover *who* will make her happy. The young newlywed knew, she explains to Dee Dee, that Billy was for her from the first time she kissed him. Although Dee Dee has "kissed" a man or two, she confesses that she "never got any message." The young bride with great confidence reassures Dee Dee: "Oh, you will . . . when you kiss the right one." Armed with a new knowledge of life and of love, acquired accidentally from the homespun expertise generated over the sink of an Oklahoma farmhouse, Dee Dee seeks out Marv, who is inspecting the plane, so that she can give him the "kiss test" she has learned of from the rural teenager who knows how to recognize true love.

That crash of Marv's plane not only alters the plot—perhaps as much as Janet Leigh's murder in *Psycho*—but also marks a realignment of goals, energy, and power that in effect indicates the end of the screwball plot not only in the film but, for the most part, in American cinema. It is as if the emergency landing of Stewart's two-prop freight plane in mid-America were reenacting the impact on the screwball genre of the plane crash that killed Carole Lombard. For at least the next two decades, the guile, deception, determination, and agency epitomized by screwball heroines such as Lombard were replaced by a compliance, self-subordination, and dependency consistent with the postwar cult of domesticity.

The scene in which Dee Dee, Mrs. Racknell, and the young bride do the dishes thus provides a pastoral moment around which the plot of *You Gotta Stay Happy* pivots. Escaping the complex (and implicitly corrupt) world of wealth, society, psychiatry, and urban life—the world of the city and the court—the confused sophisticate achieves insight grounded in the simplicity of the pastoral world of the Oklahoma countryside. But pastoral is the antithesis of screwball, which thrives on the zaniness facilitated by the complexity and unpredictability of the social world. The zaniness, by providing an antidote to the stolid, gives society a renewed vitality grounded in the vitalism of female agency.

Bearing with her the last vestiges of the vitality and self-determination that connected Fontaine's character to the roles of Lombard, Hepburn, Rosalind Russell, and Colbert, Fontaine marches out into the field that designates the figurative site of Lombard's death, not to resurrect her figure but to mark its grave. First kissing Marv to confirm the validity of the rural teenager's love test, she then reveals that her true identity is not the embezzler's accomplice but the world's wealthiest heiress. Dee Dee's recognition and avowal of love—that is, her reciprocating the affection that led Marv to protect her when he thought she was a fleeing criminal—causes him to reject her as a fleeing millionaire. Although she possesses the teenaged bride's wisdom about marriage, the fact that she has been involved with other men indicates that she lacks the requisite inexperience that must complement it.

The crash landing means that Marv's business will collapse, making Dee Dee, in either identity—criminal or heiress—the untenable alternative to his career. That career, moreover, is connected in Marv's imagination and the film's thematics to the postwar boom and national prosperity. Marv wants to build up his cargo fleet by adding a four-engine plane, so that by 1954 he can be affluent enough to start a family. Although when he thinks Dee Dee is poor he says that "there's nothing wrong with me that a million dollars won't cure," when he learns of her exorbitant wealth, he finds it an even more egregious assault on his masculinity than her numerous "engagements." He would rather lose his business and go broke than have his children think that he was not the family's breadwinner. When Dee Dee saves his business by investing in it, he says, "I'm not working for any woman. . . . You can get somebody else to run your airline for you." Although he clearly loves her, he explains his dilemma: "Now that you own Payne Airline, if I stay around . . . it's just the same as your giving me the money, and I'm not going to have any woman supporting me. If my kids want ice cream cones, they're going to have to come to me for the money and not their mother. . . . So the best thing for you and me to do is just forget about the whole thing. I'm sorry, but that's the way it's got to be. Is that clear?" In the face of the euphoria of discovering how to stay happy and the inverse effect of acting on that knowledge, Dee Dee is confirmed in what she always knew: that money cannot produce happiness. What she discovers, however, is that happiness does come from the particular form of domesticity she has found somewhere north of Tulsa: twenty plus years of pregnancy, cooking, cleaning, and child raising. By convincing Marv that despite her enormous wealth she will be so occupied with domestic activities that he will naturally head the household, Dee Dee makes the screwball heroine antithetical to the tenets of postwar happiness. The film concludes happily when Dee Dee presents Payne Airlines with a new four-engine plane, so that Marv may have a successful business and thereby unburden Dee Dee of distractions from the joy of making dinner and changing diapers. "I know, you don't want to work for a woman. Well, you won't have to. You'll be in complete control. Besides, I'll be busy at home, I hope, like Mrs. Racknell." Whether they are going to be happy again, like Don Lockwood, or gotta stay happy, like Marvin Payne, these postwar narratives reinscribe veterans in narratives of compensatory masculinity, the relentless bolstering of which underscores its fragility.

Dee Dee represents a world in which a woman with Lina Lamont's drive can be funny in humiliation but never in triumph. For that reason, the psychoanalytical and the cultural understandings of Lina's voice are not alternative but interdependent. Her failure to hide the derivation of her art in the moment of the film's production is also her failure as a woman (according to the dicta of 1952 American culture). She aggressively shuns the demands upon women to restore the nation to normality and thereby allow the men to sing that they are "happy again." Lockwood sings his refrain of postwar triumphalism after he has spent the night with Kathy and she has proven herself a proper postwar woman—that is, one who will put her man's career first.

Thus Lina's voice threatens not only the cinematic apparatus and the male ego ideal that grounded classical Hollywood cinema, but also the political economies of gender intended to stabilize the demographics of post–World War II demobilization and reassimilation. Lina's voice does, therefore, echo the acoustics of figurative castration and actual emasculation. This was a political threat perhaps more pervasive in the 1950s than Communism and certainly more long-lasting.

3

It's *All* about Eve

If *Singin' in the Rain* (1952) is a musical comedy that enables us to laugh at the abjection of a female star, it provides a joyful way of dealing with anxiety about the role of women in Cold War America's new normal. That anxiety, connected in popular postwar discourse to the story of Eve, proliferated in cautionary tales about women who resist the project of supporting masculinity in all facets of postwar domestic life. Margo Channing (Bette Davis), observing the machinations of her evil alter ego, appropriately named Eve (Ann Baxter), manages just in time to avoid the fate of *Sunset Boulevard*'s (1950) Norma Desmond (Gloria Swanson), the silent star of whom Lina is a comic interpolation.

For good reason, many overviews of the films of the 1950s discuss in conjunction with each other two of 1950s most heavily Oscar-nominated films, *All about Eve* and *Sunset Boulevard*. Noting that both films are about "the contradiction between stardom and aging," Peter Lev describes *Sunset Boulevard* "as far more bitter" (59).[1] Others have regarded the films as dark comedies. Ed Sikov argues that *Sunset Boulevard* is "one of the great comedies of its time" (89), an extreme position bolstered, at least in part, by the fact that Mae West was director Billy Wilder's first choice for the Gloria Swanson role,[2] and even more so when we view Norma Desmond through the lens of her comic successor, Lina Lamont.

If Nora Sayre finds *All about Eve* (and even more *Sunset Boulevard*) "rather unsettling today because it so sternly rebukes women for being ambitious" (141), Lina mutes the discomfort by allowing a comedic spin on the story of Eve as the conduit of evil splayed across the template of female stardom; she allows us to dismiss with laughter women who privileged their own ambitions and satisfactions over those of men, women who were, in effect, perceived as vipers, capable of destroying the normal relationships—romantic and economic—upon which American prosperity and Cold War victory depended.

These Eves—Norma Desmond, Lina Lamont, Eve Harrington, and for the first two-thirds of *All about Eve*, Margo Channing—conform to the model of evil articulated by Philip Wylie in *Generation of Vipers*, using the same satanic imagery: "Never before has a great nation of brave and dreaming men absentmindedly created a huge class of idle, middle-aged women. Satan himself has been taxed to dig up enterprises enough for them." Wylie's "historical" argument was that in earlier (that is, pre–World War I) periods, the demands of being a mother were consuming and (thankfully?) terminal: "Hitherto, mom has been busy raising a large family, keeping house, doing chores, and fabricating everything in every home . . . and she was rarely a problem to her family or to her equally busy friends, and never to herself. Usually, until very recently, mom folded up and died of hard work somewhere in the middle of her life" (199). But in the modern age, they live long past their usefulness, to form a social burden and a pervasive threat to masculinity:

> Nowadays, with nothing to do, and all the tens of thousands of men I wrote about in a preceding chapter to maintain her, every clattering prickamette in the republic survives for an incredible number of years, to stamp and jibber in the midst of man, a noisy neuter by natural default or a scientific gelding sustained by science, all tongue and teat, and razzmatazz. The machine has deprived her of social usefulness; time has stripped away her biological possibilities and poured her hide full of liquid soap; and man has sealed his own soul beneath the clamorous cordillera by handing her the checkbook and going to work in the service of her caprices. (199)

These evil moms, "an American creation" (197) "launched as Cinderella" (197), evoke "megaloid momworship [that] has gotten completely out of hand" (199), despite the fact that, Wylie pointed out, "one indubitably most-needed American verity [is]: 'Gentlemen, mom is a jerk'" (198). She is a jerk, Wylie contends, because she is the American Cinderella in fullest bloom, and Cinderellas or would-be Cinderellas have created a society in which "we have enshrined, not the honest search of a Prince, which is the positive force in the story, but the girl's reward. And we have turned over most of our fixed wealth to women. Woman spends it. The absurd posturings of chivalry . . . serve to bloat the nonsensical notion of honoring and rewarding women for nothing more than being female. Cash is heaped at the feet of the sweetheart, the bride, the wife and especially 'mom.' Since money does represent a crystallization of human energy, this gave females an inordinate power" (50). Interestingly, these powerful (and powerfully lazy) creatures emerged from Wylie's imagination—*Nation of Vipers* contains no real evidence to support his economic or social claims—in 1942, when women were assuming positions vacated by men at war. The threat Wylie saw in their economic power loomed largest, in other words, at the moment when they verged on receiving a modest portion of it. For Wylie, however, wartime had created the rare modern occasion when women were obliged to work for the wealth they had already acquired, an obligation from which they would flee, he was convinced, as soon as the war ended. And indeed, as Wylie announced in the preface to the 1955 edition, he considered himself prophetic: "The footnotes [in the new edition] often point to a 'prophesy' now proven accurate" (xvii), in the sense that the purging of women from the workplace and the diminishing of their authority and responsibility in Cold War America became the cornerstone of a circular argument about women's true nature.

Although Lundberg and Farnham extolled rather than condemned mothers, their influential book, *Modern Woman: The Lost Sex* (1947), shared Wylie's basic sentiment that American women behaving inappropriately had caused malaise, anxiety, and possible doom for American society. Lundberg and Farnham argued that women trying to escape their natural role as mothers had caused a social crisis so extreme and extensive that, they pointed out, "The woman needs to have in her unconscious mind the knowledge that for her the sex act, to yield maximum satisfaction, terminates only with childbirth or the end of the nursing period" (264–265). This unconscious knowledge allows women to act in accord with, rather than in opposition to, their nature, for the biological differences between men and women, they noted, "have deep consequences for both sexes" (170):

> This is clearly seen in the matter of their orientation. To the male the externals of every situation are decisive, as it is the essence of maleness to realize self externally, objectively. Maleness . . . always manifests itself to man as something outside himself. His sex organs are, so far as he knows them, outside himself. The sexual act for him is something outgoing, and culminates for him in a spurting out and away of sexual fluid. . . .
>
> Conversely, self-realization for the female, is always, in any final analysis, deeply internal. . . . Wom[an] may attempt to realize the self as does the male, but she can never attain more than partial success, offset by deep losses. The partial success in certain cases, may, true enough, greatly exceed the measured performances of many men. But, generally, the female is at an inherent disadvantage when trying to function as men do. . . .
>
> Whereas for the male the sex act involves doing something to someone else, for the female it comes down to something done to her. Fertilization and conception take place outside the male, as a consequence of his outgoing activity; they take place inside the female. The male can be objective about reproduction, as about everything else. Women cannot. (170–171)

Rather than categorize people as "active" and "passive," Lundberg and Farnham preferred to say that men are "external" and women "internal," from which follows numerous mandates that the two groups, for their own happiness and the good of society, comply with nature. Thus, in order to avoid the extensive harm effected by women who try to achieve success by male standards, *Modern Woman: The Lost Sex* recommended that the government provide free psychotherapy, "both long term and short term, to stem the tide of psychic illness. It should be arranged on both an individual and community basis" (356). "The vast amount of neurosis among defense workers," Lundberg and Farnham reminded us, "was highlighted by its prevalence among women. . . . So many women were highly neurotic that many employers came to the conclusion, finally, that they would always rather employ men than women if given a choice" (357). They further recommended that *"all spinsters be barred by law from having anything to do with the teaching of children on the ground of theoretical* (usually real) *emotional incompetence. All public teaching posts now filled by women would be reserved . . . for married women . . . with at least one child"* (365; emphasis in original).

A most damnable example of women adapting male criteria was articulated by Dr. Helene Deutsch, whom they cited: "In her *Psychology of Women* [she] describes what she felicitously terms the 'malicious orgasm' in a woman" (Lundberg and Farnham 264). In the case of the malicious orgasm, Dr. Deutsch pointed out: "The rhythmic contractions follow their own course in complete disregard of the man's rhythm. They have the character of reception and rapid expulsion and give the impression that a kind of duel is taking place. In such cases, the sexual act often becomes a competition: who will be through first (or inversely, who can keep it up longest) and who has achieved the most? As must be expected, this type of orgasm will be found in masculine-aggressive women, who thus fight for the equality of the sexes even in the most intimate part of their lives" (264).

Since for a woman to be fully satisfied by the sexual act, "she must, in the depths of her mind, desire, deeply and utterly, to be a mother" (265), Lundberg and Farnham were particularly condemnatory of the clitoris, a genital organ that has no role in reproduction: "There is something significant in this widespread preoccupation with, and infantile fixation on, an organ essentially similar to that of the male and *completely external* to the *real* genital apparatus of the female that contains a strong suggestion of the denial of femininity. It is not from receiving the male organ with its pleasure-giving and impregnating capacities that such women experience pleasure, but only from stimulation of their *external* genitalia. This leaves them with a lack of inner involvement, bespeaking a very definite lack of acceptance of femininity" (266–267; emphasis added).

Lundberg and Farnham were concerned with women's "infantile fixation" on the clitoris because it is so vastly prevalent a problem: "Of all the conditions met with in marital sexual difficulties of women this one would certainly rate highest. We have no way of determining accurately how widespread the condition is, but the percentage of women so oriented must be enormously high"

(267). Clearly Lundberg and Farnham were faced with an epidemic as prolific as—and perhaps not unrelated to—the production of Cinderellas and their blossoming into Moms, which so troubled Wylie. Given their monomaniacal obsession with self-gratification, Wylie's Cinderellas and Moms, one may presume, are the most likely to indulge that infantile fixation with an organ "external" to their "real" genitalia.

But even more serious than the prevalence of the fixation with the clitoris is the nature of the problem:

> Its general significance is that it is symptomatic of the effort of women in an intimate part of their lives to deny their femininity. Certainly it is at times disturbing to the marital relation because it contributes to a feeling of insufficiency in the man and is derogatory of his organ. His sexual function is penetration and gratification thereby, and the feelings of a man incapable of providing gratification are those of distress or frustration. Furthermore, the woman suffers from similar feelings, along with the deep conviction that there is "something wrong with her" and that she is an odd person because of her inability to function as she believes she should. (Lundberg and Farnham 267)

For a woman, self-gratification is no gratification at all. Rather, it makes women derogate the male organ and (naturally) feel odd about doing so. In combination, the oddity of her actions and the oddity of her feelings render "modern woman" not only a "lost sex" but also a threat to masculinity and thus to the possibility of Americans' achieving the level of happiness necessary to win the Cold War. Women, in other words, must "find" their sex in order to tip the fragile balance between nuclear family and nuclear holocaust.

The Viper's Honeymoon

The film *Niagara* (1953) provides a somewhat discomforting morality tale about the threat to masculinity posed by self-gratifying women. It contrasts two couples who alternately—and both inappropriately, in that neither couple is newlywed—occupy the same honeymoon cabin at Niagara Falls. The first couple, Polly (Jean Peters) and Ray (Max Showalter) Cutler, are visiting the Falls because Ray has won a contest for the employees of a company that produces shredded wheat, a product associated with keeping people "regular." And Ray is a regular guy, that is, a husband, in the 1950s sitcom tradition, far more interested in the external activity of impressing his boss than in making love to his wife, an activity that, according to Lundberg and Farnham's data, risks the derogation of his organ. (See figure 3.1.)

The Cutlers' counterparts, Rose (Marilyn Monroe) and George (Joseph Cotton) Loomis, reflect a dysfunctional marriage in which George cannot please

FIGURE 3-1 Polly and Ray Cutler: a regular couple, in the sitcom tradition.

Rose sexually; in attempting to satisfy her, he abandons his (admittedly modest) career as a farmer. (See figure 3.2.)

Unable to subordinate her own desires to those of her husband, the tantalizingly and overtly sexual Rose conspires with an unnamed lover to kill George in a plot that backfires, ultimately resulting in the death of all three. The cause of all the problems is Rose's ambition. Although her ambition is sexual rather than material, it nevertheless tropes all the dangers of female desire in the postwar moment. Her husband, a psychologically fragile veteran, needs her support, which requires that she suppress her own desires, exactly as Polly does to support Ray. Although Polly wants the Niagara vacation to be a more successful version of her original honeymoon, she instead complies with Ray's interest in socializing with his fatuous boss, Mr. Kettering (Don Wilson).

Rose's desire for sexual satisfaction manifests an infectiousness that not only destroys the men with whom she has relationships, but also threatens the "normal" union between Ray and Polly because Rose undermines Ray's satisfaction with Polly's modest demeanor and appearance and creates, directly and indirectly, a series of circumstances that interfere with Ray's attending to Mr. Kettering. *Niagara* thus reflects a collision between the Loomis's world of *film noir* and the Cutler's world of TV sitcom, the genre associated in the 1950s with domestic situations and nuclear families.[3] The casting of the Cutler story underscores this. Ray is played by Max Showalter, who four years later would appear as Ward Beaver in the pilot episode of *Leave It to Beaver*. Don Wilson,

FIGURE 3-2 Rose and George Loomis: a dysfunctional marriage.

who plays his boss, Mr. Kettering, would have been immediately recognizable to audiences as a longstanding cast member of Jack Benny's extremely popular radio and television sitcom, spanning the period 1934 to 1958.

In *Niagara*, the collision of genres does not invest the noir world with comic absurdity, à la *Abbott and Costello Meet Dr. Jekyll and Mr. Hyde* (made the same year), but rather turns the comedic situation of going to a honeymoon resort in order to impress one's boss into a cautionary tale about how the intrusion of lust and psychological depth into the world of domestic frivolity can terrifyingly corrupt the norms of postwar domesticity.

In *Singin'*, because Lina's seductive powers are burlesqued rather than affirmed, the film need only destroy her stardom—that is, her industrial power— and banish her from the workplace of the talkie (i.e., postwar) era. In this regard, the figurative evocation of an earlier Hollywood era is particularly apt, for the Hollywood of the 1930s, as May explains: "Saw itself as promoting the equality of the sexes. But it did not provide a new model of marriage that incorporated equality. Individual men and women were simply urged to be flexible and some- how find a way to avoid competition and jealousy in marriage—a message that was relevant not only to stars but to couples of modest means trying to survive the depression and the tensions inherent in the two-earner household" (37).

But in *Niagara*, made just a year after *Singin' in the Rain*, even Rose's fatal outcome does not fully remove concern about women who undermine their partners' careers and threaten their masculinity, because, as May underscores, "the independence of wartime women gave rise to fears of female sexuality as a dangerous force on the loose" (59). Rose's death, therefore, is not enough to contain her threat, as even posthumously her actions impinge on the Cutlers' marriage. In the climactic scene, Polly has become an unwitting surrogate part- ner for George, as the two of them, in Kettering's out-of-control cabin cruiser, head for the Falls, while Ray and the authorities look on helplessly. When the boat abuts some rocks, George is able to help Polly escape before he and the boat plummet down the Falls. Out of gas, out of control, on the rocks, sinking, and doomed, the boat provides an elaborate metaphor for the Loomis marriage and a potentially chilling warning for the Cutlers.

If Monroe here is the figure of Eve, whose temptations contaminate all those with whom she has contact, she also invokes a broader concern over ambitious, self-gratifying women such as Lina, Norma, and *All about Eve*'s eponymous ingé- nue turned star, Eve. When Lundberg and Farnham contextualized "the ideal of womanhood and femininity throughout the long career of humanity" (12), they explain that "with the rise of Christianity in the West, ancient ideals yielded slowly to the demonically compelling and mysterious symbol of the virginal mother and child. . . . Eve, also an integral wraith of the same unconsciousness, was retained as a contrasting symbol of the temptation of the male from high purpose; ulti- mately she was transformed into a symbol of temptation to evil" (12). If we follow Lundberg and Farnham's argument, the evils of the postwar era are all about Eve: "The conclusion is inescapable, therefore, that unhappiness not directly traceable to poverty, disease, physical malformation, or bereavement is increasing in our time. This subtly caused unhappiness is merely reinforced and intensified by such factors. The most precise expression of that unhappiness is neurosis. The bases for most of that unhappiness, as we have shown, are laid in the childhood home.

The principal instrument of their creation are women" (71). Here we have the creation story adapted for the needs of postwar America, booming with babies and haunted by the angst entailed in converting 20 or 30 million women from producers into breeders: God created Adam, and women created neurosis.

Not Abject Enough

Exactly how complete did the abjection of Lina Lamont detailed in chapter 2 have to be to perform the requisite cultural work implicit in the promotion of Lundberg and Farnham's creation story? The answer I suggested is extensively, given the pervasive and multifarious modes of cultural discipline the reassignment of women underwent at the end of World War II. And yet it is worth considering that Lina is less severely punished, because she is less a terror and less a star, than her 1950 cinematic predecessor, Norma Desmond. Made two years before *Singin'*, *Sunset Boulevard* represents the menace of female ambition, epitomized as Norma's obsession with stardom, about which Lina, as a comic interpolation, becomes equally grotesque but easier to discount. Norma, whose egomaniacal ambition results in one death and several damaged lives, does not allow us the cheerful safety that enables the viewer to substitute Kathy, as Don's "lucky star," for the potential industrial power of preserving Lina's silent stardom.

In both films, the villainous woman is attempting to deny the limitations that social (i.e., technological and historical) change have placed on her career. In the fictionalized silent era, Norma Desmond was an even greater star than Lina Lamont, in that Norma made the epic dramas of her day, while Lina's genre was the escapist romance/adventure film. Twenty-two years after the moment when Don Lockwood adapts to the age of talkies by reverting to song and dance, Norma lives in seclusion in her splendid but run-down estate, exemplary of the palatial homes of silent stars such as Lockwood and Lamont. Norma's huge living room, rid of its clutter, would in fact resemble Lockwood's mansion, where the "Good Morning" number is set. Inhabited only by Norma and her faithful servant and chauffer, Max (Erich von Stroheim), and accentuated by the neglected grounds and eerie overgrowth, this lonely place exhibits the gothic aura of early 1930s horror films. When Max first greets Joe at the door, his accent and eerily authoritative speech seem reminiscent of Bela Lugosi's *Dracula* (1931), an allusion made resonant by Max's instruction: "If you need any help with the coffin, call me." (See figure 3.3.)

In her seclusion, Norma is writing a massive screenplay, *Salome*, her intended platform for stardom in the talkie era to be commensurate with her silent film fame. Although extremely wealthy, she wants attention and adulation of the kind that she cannot buy and at that moment is unable to earn. She is neither a writer nor a woman young enough to play the role she is scripting. When a broke screenwriter, Joe Gillis (William Holden), pursued by men who

FIGURE 3-3 Max: "If you need any help with the coffin, call me."

are trying to repossess his car, takes refuge on her estate—which he initially presumes to be abandoned—Norma offers him a job editing her screenplay. At first Joe believes that he is conning Norma, but employing his (bogus) editing services, it becomes clear, is the lure Norma uses to make Joe, susceptible to her wealth and assertiveness, her lover.

His comfortable prostitution, however, is disrupted by a reader at Paramount, Betty Schaefer (Nancy Olson), who believes that one of his unproduced scripts contains original material, which she offers to help him turn into a full screenplay. When this collaboration blossoms into a romance, Norma attempts to sabotage it by contacting Betty. In an act of nobility disguised as caddish rejection, Joe convinces Betty that he prefers the luxury of being kept by Norma to his love for her or his career as a writer. But as soon as the heartbroken Betty leaves Norma's estate, Joe attempts to walk out on Norma and return to his job on a Dayton newspaper. As he is leaving, the rejected Norma shoots him several times, and he collapses into her swimming pool. The shock of Joe's rejection, along with her own homicidal action, destroys the vestiges of Norma's sanity, and *Sunset Boulevard* concludes with the police taking Norma away, while she has deluded herself into believing the newspaper photographers gathered at her door are actually cameramen filming a scene from *Salome*.

This tragedy results from Norma's desire to sing in the rain, that is, to be happy *again*, a desire perhaps tolerable in the dormancy of her gothic seclusion, but at the point when she pursues that desire on her own terms, instead of conforming to postwar norms, she is destroyed. To the extent that, as I have argued, being "happy again" represents participating in euphoric postwar prosperity, Norma demonstrates that she does not understand the role she must play to merit participation. The form her lack of understanding takes, moreover, threatens the gender economies of the postwar accommodation. Her desiring more prestige and power than the new generation of adult men demands punishment, for nothing could upset the reassimilation of veterans more than women evoking their prior accomplishments to claim a direct and equal share in postwar prosperity.

It's Still All about Work

In much the same way as does *Singin'*, *Sunset Boulevard* engages the issues of work and female agency. As Norma states emphatically to DeMille, "I just want to work again." In both films, the postwar shift in gender roles and social norms is signified by a rupture associated with the advent of the sound era, an era in which success is measured and distributed according to new criteria, affecting not just box office income but the culturally valorized standards for successful coupling. All of this is suggested visually by the boom mike that harasses Norma when she visits the Paramount soundstage (see figure 3.4) and is encompassed verbally in DeMille's response, "You know pictures have changed quite a bit."

This message is underscored by its extra-diegetic resonance, not likely missed by audiences in 1950: Gloria Swanson was a Paramount star in six DeMille silent films, but, as Mary Beth Haralovich reminds us, his "career [had] continued to grow from the silent to the sound era" while Swanson's, like Norma's, had been lost (32).To the extent, moreover, that movie production stands in *Sunset*, as I have argued it does in *Singin'*, for American productivity and the production of American values, the rupture informing the production of both films is actually the end of World War II. The return of 16 million veterans, as I have noted, rapidly redefined and rigorously enforced a new normal, impacting almost every aspect of American culture. *Singin'* foregrounds the brutality of that rupture between the past and the present by condensing and intensifying the replacement of silent films with talkies, a process that, as Steven Cohan points out, actually took place over several years. (The first "talkie," *The Jazz Singer*, we should remember, had little dialogue and was released in a silent version as well as one with a sound track.) *Sunset Boulevard*, on the other hand, treats the past as already buried, a point made when Joe first hides his car in Norma's garage. Seeing an enormous Isotta Fraschini (in the late 1920s the most elite luxury car in America), Joe tells us, "It had a 1932 license. I figured that's when the owners moved out." For all intents and purposes, 1932 marked the end

FIGURE 3-4 The boom mike harasses Norma when she visits the Paramount soundstage.

of silent films, the production of which had been gradually declining since 1928. Thus the license plate serves as a tombstone marking the moment when silent films officially died.[4]

Instead of portraying, as *Singin'* does, a rapid adjustment to the present, *Sunset* presents a ghoulish unearthing of the past. Appropriately, therefore, when Joe first enters Norma's grounds, the reason he is mistaken for an undertaker is that the real undertaker is long overdue. "Why are you so late?" Norma asks him in light of the fact that the subject should already have been buried. "Why have you kept me waiting so long?" Like much of Norma's dialogue, her opening lines allude to the suspended animation in which she resides, attempting, in relative silence, to write herself into the present.

The estate, moreover, is the cemetery where the deceased, Norma's pet monkey, will be interred that night and, as it turns out, the place where Joe has come to die, something already inscribed diegetically by the fact that the film begins with his corpse floating face down in Norma's swimming pool; his narration explicitly explains how coming to this forgotten place led to his death. "The poor dope—he always wanted a pool. Well in the end he got himself a pool, only the price turned out to be a little high. Let's go back about six months and find the day when it all started."

The gothic style in which the monkey's candlelit funeral is shot, along with the chimp's evocation of the Tarzan films of the early 1930s, in which the plot centers on the search for the elephant's burial ground, all evoke a bygone Hollywood era, as does Joe's commentary, "He must have been a very important chimp—the great grandson of King Kong, maybe." In a literal sense, more-over, this is a ghost story—that is, a story told by a ghost whose ghostliness is a consequence of the world of death into which he wandered or, symbolically, where he belonged, given that his career had dead-ended.[5] In this way, Norma's domain, stagnant, traumatized, obsessed with the past, was everything that vibrant, fertile, forward-looking postwar America was not, and the semiotics make clear from the outset that, despite Joe's belief to the contrary, living in and off of Norma Desmond's world cannot make his career viable in the post-war period any more than sustaining a connection to Lina Lamont could pre-serve Don Lockwood's.

Both Lina and Norma are in completely untenable positions. Lina, despite her exploitation of dubbing, wants to speak in her own voice, as demonstrated by her speech to the audience at the premier of *The Dancing Cavalier*, by her taking charge of her own publicity, and by her numerous comments: "Of course [I] talk. Don't everybody?" or "Tonight I'm gonna do my own talkin'. I'm gonna make the speech." In this way, she is a replica of Norma, who wants to write her own script, control her own publicity, and speak to DeMille in person. Norma is more pathetic than Lina, however, in that Norma thinks that say-ing her own words on screen will revive her career at the same time that she openly denounces the cinematic effectiveness of spoken words. "There was a time when [films] had the eyes of the whole wide world. But that wasn't good enough for them, oh no, they had to have the ears of the whole world too, so they opened their big mouths and out came talk, talk, talk!" Learning that Joe is a screenwriter, she says, "You are . . . writing words, words, more words—but you've made a rope of words and strangled this business—Ha! Ha!"

Underscoring the pathetic nature of Norma's ambitions, the plot of *Sun-set* focuses relentlessly on the verbal, on writing and the production of speech, while the visual qualities of cinema that Norma extols function as a sepulcher, with almost every shot of Norma involving some form of vegetative, historical, psychological, or cinematic death.

Moreover, Joe fills his narration with meta-commentary about writing. His initial meeting with Betty in the Paramount producer's office, for example, involves arguing about whether his most recent story is clichéd. Joe's narra-tion comments on Norma's writing, on editing it, on selling his own scripts, on working as a hack reporter, and on the script he is developing with Betty. His writing is also foundational to his relationship with Betty, initiated by her finding the seed of an original script in one of his earlier projects and convinc-ing him to develop it with her assistance. Their personal chemistry, moreover, is established when they find refuge in the bathroom at a crowded New Year's Eve party (see figure 3.5), where, using stilted British accents and exaggeratedly melodramatic phrasing, they speak to one another exclusively in clichés drawn from the Hollywood toilet bowl:

BETTY: Are you hungry?

JOE: Hungry? After 12 years in the Burmese jungle, I'm starving, Lady Agatha, starving . . .

BETTY: Philip, you're mad! . . .

JOE: Thirsting for the coolness of your lips . . .

BETTY: No, Philip, no—we must be strong. You're still wearing the uniform of the Coldstream Guards! Furthermore . . . you can have the phone now.

JOE: Suddenly, I find myself terribly afraid of losing you.

BETTY: You won't—I'll get us a refill of this horrible liquid.

JOE: You'll be waiting for me?

BETTY: With a wildly beating heart.

JOE: Life . . . can be beautiful.

If the delivery makes clear both of them are speaking ironically, their ability to embrace quotation with self-conscious authority nevertheless demonstrates a mutually seductive mastery of craft and industry. The scene, Daniel Brown argues, establishes "the principles of narrative and generic convention over originality" (1224). Like the interchanges between Don Lockwood and Kathy Selden, the "amusing concatenation of film clichés provides the medium for

FIGURE 3-5 Joe and Betty find refuge in the bathroom at a New Year's Eve party.

their flirtation, playfully establishing the love story as the genre in which they renegotiate their incipient relationship" (Brown 1224). Although Hollywood's illusions may be a joke—"the joke of *Sunset Boulevard*," Sikov argues, "is Hollywood itself" (98)—they are in on it, which distinguishes them from the crowd at Schwab's Drugstore, waiting to be "discovered," as though studios were in the business of finding talent rather than manufacturing it.

Not the Real Stars

The relationship between Joe and Betty is strikingly replicated in *Singin'*. Initially Kathy has the same judgment of Don's films that Betty has of Joe's scripts—that they are hackneyed. "If you've seen one," Kathy says to Don, "you've seen them all." Yet in a revelation resembling Betty's confession to Joe, we later discover Kathy admires Don. Both couples communicate their most intimate feelings, moreover, on vacant movie sets. The dynamic I noted about *Singin'*—that it does not distinguish between the "artificial" movie world and the "real" outside world but rather between scripted and unscripted options, active and vacant sets, within the world of film production—replicates exactly the conditions of interpersonal exchange for Joe and Betty, with the most significant difference being that in *Sunset* prophylactic irony provides inadequate protection, while in *Singin'* it becomes the mechanism successfully diverting criticism away from the fact that the musical version, *The Dancing Cavalier*, is as much an insubstantial formula picture as its "dramatic" processor, *The Dueling Cavalier*. *Singin'* is about Hollywood's adaptation, in a Darwinian sense, to ensure that Kathy's critique—if you've seen one, you've seen them all—will continue to apply. Standardization, as Bordwell, Staiger, and Thompson have made clear, was one of the foundational industrial principles of the studio system, just as it was for the array of manufacturing industries that Monumental Pictures metonymically represents. And predictability was essential to an industry that had to resell the same product each week.

Joe's awareness of genre, therefore, is crucial. When he pitches his script to the Paramount producer, he talks more about the script's generic qualities than about its actual content, and in his first discussion with Norma, he tells her, "Last thing I wrote was about Okies in the Dust Bowl. You'd never know it, because by the time it reached the screen the whole thing played on a torpedo boat."

Instead of rejecting the genre factory, *Singin'* merely rejects a woman who wants too large a share of its profits and prestige. In *Sunset Boulevard,* however, self-awareness is condemnatory. If Joe fails to extricate himself from Norma or to write a successful screenplay with Betty, it is not because he doesn't know better. Nor is it because he doesn't have talent, as is demonstrated by the screenplay he "authors" posthumously: the stunning, insightful, and arch narration of *Sunset Boulevard*. Joe's failure is one of character, exactly the kind of failure that troubled Schlesinger and Riesman, as such a failure threatened the masculinity seen as crucial for the survival of democracy and the fate of the free world. As K. A. Cuordileone points out, "In Schlesinger's case, beyond the defensive, manly, heterosexual pose of the anti-Communist liberal, we see how a fascination with the psychology of sexual will and transgression crept into his imagination of Communism, and especially of his vision of its extraordinary power to seduce and then transform the individual's psyche" (29).

Joe's succumbing to the wrong kind of woman, in other words, demonstrates a character flaw. He should have had the strength to shun Norma, a woman who, like Lina, would put her own career ahead of a man's, would subordinate his wishes to her desires, and would refuse to acknowledge what he says. Nor can Norma see that their alleged romance is just a job, any more than Lina can disabuse herself of the studio publicity's telling fans that she and Don are engaged. Norma too actually believes that Joe loves her, even though, as the film progresses, it becomes more difficult to tell whether Joe's prostitutional relationship with Norma tropes his professional life, or vice versa.

As in *Singin'*, however, the centrality of work remains constant. Initially Joe's work, as did Don's, unites him with a partner linked to the silent era, one who becomes irrationally vengeful when she discovers Joe's real love interest, Betty, who, like Kathy, has a minor role at the studio. Betty shares many traits with Kathy, the most notable being her lack of star power. Since stardom is the matrix of meanings produced by the role and the person who plays that role, the careers of Nancy Olson and Debbie Reynolds are important. Like Betty, actress Olson, who continues to work even today at age eighty-six, has had a modest presence. The bulk of her career has consisted of guest appearances on 1950s and 1960s television series, along with secondary film and television roles. In *Sunset* she plays a woman somewhat like herself. Neither a writer nor an actress, she constitutes no professional rival for either Norma or Joe. When Joe offers to let her use his ideas to write the screenplay under her own name, she says she can't do it.

Like Kathy Selden, whose career opportunities rely completely on her connection with Don, Betty is most distinguished by her desire and ability to help promote a man whose talents are far greater than hers. Despite the projection of Kathy as the "real star" at the end of *Singin'*, therefore, the plot makes clear that she earns her place by helping Don succeed. And Debbie Reynolds, at the time she was cast in *Singin'*, had little star power, a fact that made her selection for the part controversial. According to Kelly, when he met Reynolds in Louis B. Mayer's office and was told by Mayer that she would be his leading lady in *Singin'*, the statement hit Kelly "like a ton of bricks. . . . What the hell was I going to do with her? She couldn't sing, she couldn't dance, she couldn't act" (cited in Silverman 152).

In her subsequent career, more noteworthy for its longevity than its highlights, Reynolds never consolidated the glamor and aura equal to that of an actress like Lina Lamont or her heirs in adventure films of the talkie era such as postwar stars Rita Hayworth, Maureen O'Hara, Susan Haywood, or Deborah Kerr, to name a few. Kathy Selden and, a decade later (the unsinkable) Molly Brown would be Reynolds's most prominent roles, demonstrating that as a movie performer she would never fulfill the promise bestowed on Kathy Selden at the end of *Singin'*. It seems clear she could never be called a "shimmering, glowing star in the cinema firmament," the words describing Lina in her publicity prior to the premier of *The Dancing Cavalier*. Kathy Selden could never deflect any of the starlight, thematic or visual, lavished on Don Lockwood at the end of the "Broadway Melody" number. It is virtually impossible to imagine Kathy played by Reynolds providing the presence of silent star Lina Lamont in something like *Return of the Dancing Cavalier* and, as the use of Jean Hagen to dub Kathy's speech suggests, Reynolds's voice not does have the gravitas for a costume drama. In other words, Reynolds's sound and her appearance reassure the postwar audience that she would not share Don's spotlight.

In the same way, Betty points the man she loves toward the future by evoking what is original in his work rather than derivative:

JOE: Now if I got you correctly, there's a short stretch of my fiction that you found worthy of note.

BETTY: The flashback scene in the courtroom when she tells about being a schoolteacher.

JOE: I had a teacher like that once.

BETTY: Maybe that's why it's good. It's true; it's moving. Now why don't you . . .

JOE: Who wants true? Who wants moving?

BETTY: Stop that attitude. Here's something really worthwhile . . .

Because Betty is helping her man find a voice that will succeed in the new era, Joe's final actions become heroic; he dies saving Betty from him and his lies and the illusions of Hollywood past. The reward for this heroism is that he gets to tell his own story. In effect, the flashback that comprises the film is the filming of his screenplay, an honest screenplay of the sort Betty had been urging him to create. Death thus valorizes Joe, with his humiliation before Betty a work unquestionably of his own orchestration, a way of realizing visually and dramatically the truth he had been withholding not only from Betty but also from himself.

Norma's authorship, in contrast, is never validated, and her fall is pathetic, an act of abjection even more complete than Lina's. Deprived of Lina's self-awareness, facing the photographers at the end of the film, Norma enters a world of pure ridicule (see figure 3.6).

The cinematic apparatus that anchored her identity is replaced by the medium of tabloid headlines, with the flashbulbs portending the next day's

FIGURE 3-6 Norma enters a world of pure ridicule.

journalistic grotesquery. This form of publicity, which she cannot control as she did her star publicity, will permanently replace her stardom with her image as a deranged has-been. Against her will and counter to her every desire, her actions have cast her in a role plucked from the most tawdry of B pictures. This role, the final close-up makes clear, will forever erase her earlier fame. To put it another way, *Singin'* ends with Lina becoming something like Norma at the *outset* of *Sunset*, a has-been who was unable to transition to talkies, one with a humiliating anecdote attached to the moment when this became clear. In short, Lina's complete humiliation at the end of *Singin'* will fade into trivia, while Norma's acquires sensationally grotesque prominence. The horrible deformation, both psychic and visual, with which Norma in the end absorbs the screen makes Lina's banishment from the frame seem merciful.

Humbert Humbert Goes to the Movies

Another way that Norma transgresses more egregiously than Lina is by choosing a much younger man at a time when "normal" American courtship paired returning veterans with younger women. This theme was reflected in increasingly problematic ways throughout the 1950s, during which time a parade of American male stars over age fifty were cast opposite women who were playing teenagers. In 1954, two years after nineteen-year old Reynolds played Kathy

FIGURE 3-7 Reynolds opposite fifty-year-old Dick Powell.

Selden, she played seventeen-year-old Susan Landis in *Susan Slept Here* (1954), opposite fifty-year-old Dick Powell as Mark Christopher, a struggling Hollywood writer who becomes inspired, as did Joe Gillis, by a younger woman.

Mark allows Susan to spend the night at his apartment so that she will not be arrested for vagrancy and have to spend Christmas Eve in jail, in exchange for her facilitating his research on a screenplay about juvenile delinquency. But what starts as a story of convenience turns into a reluctant love story. At first, Susan's sleeping in Mark's apartment gives the wrong impression, especially to Mark's disgruntled fiancée, Isabella (Anne Francis). Susan's innocence and Mark's lack of interest, although apparent to the viewer, become increasingly perplexing to the other characters, all the more so when Susan develops an adolescent crush on Mark. Because Mark is an Academy Award–winning writer, he is a public figure, which requires his friends and associates to do damage control, thwarted when Mark takes Susan to Las Vegas and marries the seventeen-year-old so that she won't be sent to a juvenile detention center.

Although Mark avoids consummating the marriage, the plot conventions—his shrill "longtime" fiancée, his navy buddy Virgil (Alvy Moore), Susan's role as his literary inspiration—make clear that what seems like convenience is really serendipity: Susan, a teenaged virgin, is the appropriate match for the writer twice her age, played by the fifty-year-old Powell, who is *well more* than twice the age of twenty-two-year-old Reynolds. (Gene Kelly was only slightly more than twice Reynolds's age when they filmed *Singin'*.)

Although this is not the first movie romance between an older man and a younger woman, read through the lens of *Sunset Boulevard*, it is notable as a 1950s film because in both cases, struggling Hollywood writers in their thirties (Gillis's age is not specified, but Holden was thirty-two) are inspired by younger women who idolize them. Reflecting the same good-bad template, Gillis is destroyed by becoming the paramour of an older, aggressive woman, who is indifferent to his career, while Mark finds inspiration by marrying an adolescent girl. In this context, Norma Desmond's emasculating qualities consolidate all the threats aggressive women posed in the popular imaginary of the 1950s. The popularity of *Modern Woman: The Lost Sex* and *Generation of Vipers*, as well as all the derivative popular magazines that formed their echo chamber, testified to Cuordileone's persuasive argument that the failure of the American character bemoaned by Luce, Schlesinger, and others was grounded in a crisis over masculinity.

This theme is underscored in *Susan Slept Here* by the fact that Susan's chief rival, it turns out, is not Mark's fiancée but rather his navy buddy, Virgil. If the purging of homosexuals from government positions under McCarthyism, what David Johnson has called the "Lavender Scare," was far more extensive than the purging of suspected Communists, one explanation is that, as Elaine Tyler May, among others, has noted, Cold War homophobia treated homosexuality as the antithesis of masculinity. Although the ostensible reason for purging homosexuals was that they were security risks (because they were deemed "unstable" and because they could be blackmailed), the period's homophobia was anchored to the more deep-seated belief that the American character was masculine—or needed to be in order to prevail—so that any behavior questioning a man's masculinity threatened national security at the characterological level. And as we have seen, the Cold War binaries were pervasively grounded in questions of character.

Lest we miss the power of homosexuality as a threat to both Mark's masculinity and his creativity, Susan has a dream that features Virgil, wearing a bright blue and pink one-piece outfit, dangling a very large, phallic key while he dances around the cage in which she is locked (see figure 3.8). The dream's unmistakably queer semiotics represents Virgil as the chief obstacle to Susan's romance with Mark. When Susan wins Mark, therefore, it seems apt that Virgil decides to return to the homosocial world of the US Navy. Most significantly, Susan's triumph over Mark's male friend posits a seventeen-year-old girl as the appropriate remedy for the postwar masculinity crisis, epitomized, but by not limited to, the fear of homosexual orientation—latent or closeted—concretized by the intense bonding effected over years in combat conditions.

This implicitly contrasts Susan with women at an adult stage in their lives, whose proven success could make it difficult for men to act like men. Although women had handled important responsibilities during the war, for them, as for the successful women in *Singin'* and *Sunset*, past success does not predict future success but instead indicates that the women are no longer appropriate for mating. Cold War survival thus becomes a Darwinian process, such that the gravitation of men ages thirty-five and older to women under the age of consent

FIGURE 3-8 Virgil dangles a bright pink, phallic key while dancing around Susan's cage.

becomes an act of natural selection, one in which the heroine of the screwball comedies has "evolved" into what Humbert Humbert, in Vladmir Nabokov's huge best seller, *Lolita*, would call a nymphet or child bride.

Completed in 1953 and first published anonymously in France in 1955, Nabokov's novel became an enormous (and scandalous) success after its 1958 American publication. Starting in 1958, *Lolita* spent thirty-nine weeks on the *Times* Best Seller list, sixteen at the top of the list and nine more in second place. Its salacious content and transgressive perspective—that of a sophisticated and witty pederast—created a sensation that for much of the public obscured its savage satire of mid-century American culture. Focused through the eyes of a minimally well-educated European who is so delusional a romantic as to have made Poe's "Annabel Lee" his paradigm for true love, the novel is the confession of a pervert who has found his métier in postwar America. In a nation pretentiously devoted to kitsch, Humbert's facility with languages and his rudimentary background in literary classics enable him, to his great amusement, to pass for an intellectual. Surrounded by films with fairytale endings (more or less mandated by the Hollywood Production Code) and a landscape in which every resort or motel bears an enchanted name comically incommensurate with its facilities and parodied by its own fantastic décor, Humbert passes for normal, his detachment from reality understandably undetectable.

Particularly in its excessive adulation of children, postwar America makes Humbert appear typical and feel completely at home. The fashions for preadolescent girls and the names bestowed on those fashions put him in a state of euphoria. (He particularly adores stores that sell "training bras" and have a clothing size called "junior miss.") When the language of postwar "progressive education" proclaims all young girls "exceptional," who is Humbert to disagree? Indeed, he is just singing and dancing in the rain. For Humbert, like Don Lockwood, is happy "again" because in discovering postwar America, he returns to a normal that never existed and that he had never imagined. In that land of delusion, Lolita is his apotheosis of American exceptionalism, despite the fact that she reads little aside from comic books, likes simplistic escapist movies, has bad hygiene, speaks in slang, cannot carry on a prolonged conversation, and has no intellectual curiosity.

Humbert's child love, as Nabokov represents it, is thus his most naive and hence his most American trait. In an assimilation of American values, as he perceives them, Humbert not only believes in the idea of an Annabel Lee, but also in Lolita as her incarnation. This faith in the ideals of his adoptive nation makes him impervious to Lolita's actual sexual experimentation as well as her other very nonideal traits, characteristic of the average American teenager. American culture's refusal to notice the disparity between the behavior of postwar adolescents and the glorification they receive does more than mask Humbert's pederasty; it unwittingly validates it. That validation provides the framework for Nabokov's satirical dismemberment of the mid-century American male, infantile in his romantic delusions, obsessed with younger girls (whom he insists on regarding, despite all evidence to the contrary, as innocent), and irritably uncomfortable in the presence of mature women. Thus the "scandalous" success of *Lolita*, as best seller, could be viewed as reflecting the secret pleasure with which Humbert publicly fulfilled the male fantasy implicit in postwar American culture, to which Nabokov was the bemused witness.

What Miracle Has Made You the Way You Are?

Nothing supports this hypothesis more than the film *Gigi* (1958), the spectacular success released the same year that *Lolita* dominated the best-seller lists. The film, which broke records by winning nine Oscars (every Oscar for which it was nominated), is set in turn-of-twentieth-century Paris. This lavish, beautifully costumed, and sumptuously photographed musical recounts the story of Gigi (Leslie Caron), a fifteen-year-old girl, who descends from a long line of successful courtesans; no woman in her family has ever been married. Although still a schoolgirl, Gigi is being groomed by her grandaunt—a wealthy and revered retired courtesan—to enter the family trade. Gigi lives with her grandmama, also a retired courtesan, in a modest apartment where they welcome and are befriended by Gaston (Louis Jordan), a super-rich member of French society. A celebrity and playboy, he confesses to his uncle, Honere (Maurice Chevalier),

FIGURE 3-9 Gaston, bored with his thirty-year-old mistress.

ostensibly a senior version of Gaston, that he is bored with his beautiful, thirty-year-old mistress, Liane (Eva Gabor) (see figure 3.9).

Using Liane's dalliance with her skating instructor as an excuse, Gaston dumps her in very public fashion, and she "attempts" suicide in an equally public fashion. To counter the bad publicity created by her latest in a series of suicide attempts, Gaston hosts an unending run of extremely lavish galas, which he finds as boring as he had his mistress.

The only thing that does entertain Gaston is sharing simple meals and games with the unpretentious schoolgirl, Gigi, and her grandmama (see figure 3.10). He is attracted to Gigi, in other words, because her grandaunt's lessons ostensibly have not taken, so that he does not perceive Gigi's incipient worldliness and thus can maintain a Humbert-like belief in the incomparable desirability of the eternal child bride. (Gaston and Mark Christopher in *Susan Slept Here*, it should be noted, are exactly the same age as Humbert.)

This idolizing of eternal nymphets is endemic to the first decade of Leslie Caron's career, which was characterized by her being the object of a Humbert-like lyrical gaze. From 1953 to 1958, moving from age twenty-two to age twenty-seven (and having two children in the process), Caron ends up stalled in midadolescence. At age twenty-two she starred in the title role of *Lili*, a musical about a sixteen-year-old orphan employed by a carnival puppeteer because of the crowd-pleasing rapport she has with his puppets. Bitter and off-putting, the puppeteer, Paul Berthalet, played by Mel Ferrer (who in 1953 was the same age as Humbert, Gaston, and Mark) uses the puppets to express his love for Lili (see figure 3.11), a love she comes to recognize in a fantasy dance sequence in which each of the puppets turns into Paul.

Because Paul is an injured (World War I) veteran, haunted and hence emasculated by his lame leg, the sixteen-year-old Lili provides an appropriate cure in

FIGURE 3-10 Gaston sharing meals and games with schoolgirl Gigi and her grandmama.

FIGURE 3-11 Paul uses the puppets to express his love for Lili.

the same way that seventeen-year old Susan remedies Mark's writer's block (and attachment to his navy buddy). Two years later, twenty-four-year-old Caron, in *Daddy Long-Legs*, plays an eighteen-year-old orphan who falls in love with the fifty-six-year-old Fred Astaire, playing the anonymous benefactor who put her through college. Three years after that, at twenty-seven, Caron returns to adolescence as Gigi, a character twelve years her junior.

In each of these films, Caron evokes the aura of an eternal child prematurely navigating the bewildering experiences of teen love. Instead of disillusioning her, however, the plots validate her desire for a father figure. She beguiles these older men by virtue of an endearing resistance to adulthood, rather than through precocious maturity. Importantly, Lili's rapport with the puppets derives from her *pre*adolescent sensibility, from the fact that despite having reached puberty, she retains childlike qualities. Through his puppet creations, Paul relates to these traits just as Humbert admires them in his imaginary nymphets. American audiences found *Lili* charming, in other words, in much the same way that Humbert adored Lolita.

Part of *Gigi*'s "charm" is that, like Lolita, she understands a great deal more than she is given credit for. Whereas Lolita uses her understanding to construct an escape from her molester, Gigi uses hers to preserve her virginity and exact a marriage proposal. And in *Gigi*, Caron's veneer of innocence is even more incredible than Lolita's, not just because at twenty-seven she is nearly twice the age of the character she is playing, but also because that character comes from a long line of courtesans. Thus, when she plays with Gaston in childish ways, Gigi is affirming his innocence as much as hers. Although the film was intended to be a version of the play *My Fair Lady*,[6] its plot is actually much closer to *Lili's*— even the title echoes the earlier Caron film—in that Gaston is not Gigi's instructor, and she is not his Galatea. In direct contrast to *My Fair Lady*, moreover, their union depends on his getting her to *forget* the crash training she has been given, training to which he has only reluctantly agreed. Gaston was not seduced by Gigi's sophistication, actual or latent, but by her cheerful silliness.

But Gigi is not as silly as she appears. Rather, she shrewdly understands that Gaston's "boredom" masks insecurity about his masculinity, which is even deeper than Paul Berthalet's, in that Paul is inhibited by a crippling war wound, whereas Gaston's insecurity has no traumatic cause. There is nothing to account for Liane's cheating on him with her skating instructor, who, although very handsome, is no better looking than Jordan, and not as interesting as Gaston (otherwise why would he be a skating instructor?), and he is far too poor to "keep" any woman, much less a high-end courtesan such as Liane.

All that the skating instructor provides is sexual satisfaction. Gaston's song expressing his boredom with Liane (and with life in general) is more aptly read, in other words, as a projection of Liane's boredom, the depth of which is clear to Gaston. In the song, "She's Not Thinking of Me," Gaston repeatedly notes that Liane is too happy: "She's so gracious, so vivacious—she is not thinking of me." The fact that "she is shimmering with love, oh she's simmering with love" means "someone has set her on fire. Is it Jacques or Paul or Leon? Who's turning her furnace up higher?" Gaston is certain someone else is stimulating her: "Oh she's hot, but it's *not* for Gaston!" These lyrics reflect less Gaston's astute understanding of his mistress than his acute knowledge that he does not satisfy her; the embarrassment that Gaston, with his uncle's advice, seeks to spin through the orchestration of a public breakup, is not Liane's infidelity but his own inadequacy.

Severed from Liane and loath to initiate another relationship with a sophisticated courtesan, Gaston finds his only enjoyment in the company of the unthreatening teenager and her grandmama, which leads to his negotiating for the young girl. In this context, Gaston's negotiations with Gigi's grandaunt and grandmama become a template of 1950s norms. The film attends elaborately to the contract, detailing the material rewards—a nice house in a good neighborhood, a car, a chauffeur, money, jewelry—that Gigi will receive in exchange for becoming Gaston's mistress. ("He said she would be spoiled as no other woman had been before.")

This commodification of Gigi's adolescence is a fantasy version of the contractual terms of the normal, single breadwinner nuclear family of the 1950s. The man will provide material comforts, including a car, for a stay-at-home wife who will organize domestic arrangements conducive to his pleasure. Only a tiny number of the arrangements for that new demographic, the booming middle class, would entail a bevy of servants, but some might include a "cleaning lady" who visited weekly (but did not do windows). And most of these postwar marriages would involve some jewelry. Gaston's contract does not deviate from the implicit conditions of "normal" 1950s marriages; it just fetishistically exaggerates them. Like all the lavish aspects of *Gigi*, from its fantastical setting—the Paris of 1900, Renoir and Degas and the Eiffel Tower and the Moulin Rouge and Toulouse-Lautrec[7]—to Gaston's wealth, the film reduces the angst of middle-class desire by making the social and financial confinement of the nuclear family its most valuable prize. Gaston offers the material abundance to Gigi, after all, in exchange for access to the pleasures enjoyed by the ordinary, suburban husband.

This perspective makes clear why *Gigi*—a film uncritical of sexual relations between people who were not married—was able to gain Production Code approval, with the rationale that "the story proves that in one way or another, because one girl is greedy and grasping, and another unstable, they really are not satisfactory wives for a man with a great family tradition to continue. But Gigi is everything he would want in a wife" (quoted in McLean 215).

The panoramic commodification of middle-class marriage also provides a backdrop for another negotiation between Gigi and Gaston, in her modest living room, where the topic is sex rather than money. "Do you want to, or don't you?" Gaston asks Gigi, to which she gives the only appropriate response for a teenaged girl in her audience, who is set on marriage: "I don't want to. I really don't know what you want." When Gaston discusses the wealth and comfort he will heap on her, Gigi responds with concern about the effect that the arrangement will have on her reputation. "It's not your fault you're world-famous," she explains to him. "It's just that I haven't got a world-famous sort of nature." This leads Gaston to try another strategy, no doubt practiced prolifically on fifteen-year-old girls in the 1950s, albeit more often by boys their own age: "Gigi are you trying to find a way to tell me that you don't like me, that I don't please you?" Gigi, a model for the "good" girls in her audience, affirms her affection for Gaston by underscoring the innocence of their relationship: "Oh no, Gaston. Oh no, I do like you. I'm so happy when I'm with you. Oh Gaston couldn't we go on just as we are? Maybe seeing each other a little more often. . . . You can go on bringing me liquors and caramels and champagne on my birthday, and Sundays we can have an extra-special game of cards. Oh wouldn't that be a lovely little life?" When Gaston plays his trump card, that he is in love with her, Gigi recoils, calling him "a wicked man." "You're in love with me and you want to drag me into a life that will make me suffer. You're in love with me and you think nothing of exposing me to all sorts of terrible adventures?"

Despite the aura of Gay Paree and the umbra of ultra-affluence, the argument retains transparent tenets of the classic 1950s adolescent libidinal dispute: "If I love you, why shouldn't we do it?" / "If *you* love *me*, why do you want me to do it?" Were *Gigi* set in the 1950s, this discussion would less likely take place in her grandmama's parlor than in a car parked at a secluded spot, referred to locally as "lover's lane." Consider, for example, analogous scenes from *Peyton Place*, made the previous year, or *Some Came Running*, directed by Vincent Minelli the same year that he made *Gigi*. Here Gigi occupies the subject position produced by the angst of living in a period that oversexualized adolescent girls while making female virginity the cornerstone of a successful marriage and the most privileged commodity to exchange for one. As I pointed out in *Containment Culture*, *Lady and the Tramp*, the 1955 animated film, while ostensibly naming the film's two principals, a well-bred female cocker spaniel and a male mutt, actually designates the two roles available to young women according to the binary norms of 1950s culture. In consequence, the task of the woman in domesticating the playboy was to convince him that she would gratify him for the rest of his life, without doing so before marriage.

Gigi's success, therefore, comes from her figuring out that the way to prevent Gaston from consummating her relationship as his mistress is by demonstrating how perfectly she has absorbed her grandaunt's instructions. Although she is fifteen, in her public debut with Gaston she epitomizes his former mistress, Liane, rather than offering Gaston an easy-to-satisfy alternative. Nor is Gigi's success accidental. The night of this "first date" with Gaston—in a film set in the 1950s, it would be the night before the prom—she prays for the success of her strategy: "Pray I'll be Wellington, not Bonaparte." Her plan, correctly relying on the belief that her true appeal is her lack of sexual experience, requires that Gaston (like Humbert) find it distasteful (or at least boring) to sleep with a sophisticated woman.

While articulating faith in Gigi's innocence, however, the film never addresses the possibility that she plays the innocent girl as strategically as she does the polished courtesan. Instead of allowing a glimpse at that side of Gigi, Gaston's proposal forever silences her. He addresses the proposal to her grandmama, who gives consent with a sigh that dissolves immediately to a shot of Honere walking among prepubescent girls in a Parisian park, singing what would have been Humbert's theme song, "Thank Heaven for Little Girls." The lavish artistic direction, the intense color palate, and the celebratory orchestration distract us from what is being celebrated: that a never-ending supply of "little girls" will prevent adult men from having to be with adult women, who might find them sexually boring (or have careers that rival or surpass theirs). By marrying Gigi, Gaston prevents her from becoming the sexually experienced woman she accurately imitates on their "prom" date. According to postwar American norms, their gender negotiation portends a happy future: the young girl upholds the man's (fragile) sense of masculinity, in exchange for which he respects her "honor." (Is there unacknowledged irony in assigning the film's pederast anthem to "Honere"?) As McLean accurately points out, the film provides "quite a nice summation of both the era's complacency and its ambivalence about marriage" (216).

Gigi's negotiations are also another way in which *Gigi* echoes *Lolita*. Humbert relentlessly makes trade-offs in exchange for little bits of time with Lolita and little favors from her. The first deal he makes is to rent a room from Lolita's mother after he sees the twelve-year-old girl in the backyard, so that he may steal glimpses of his "nymphet" or have incidental contact with her, despite his revulsion for her mother, Delores, and her house adorned according to decorating hints found in popular women's magazines. His marrying Delores was a similar trade-off in order to be around Lolita, as are all the little bribes that he uses to extort favors from Lolita after her mother's death and the initiation of their sexual relationship.

When Humbert sees one of Lolita's friends interacting with her father, he confesses apologetically that it made him realize that the best he was able to offer Lolita was a *parody* of incest, the unstated implication being that normal families could offer the real thing. In this arch manner, Nabokov ridicules what he perceives as the premise of the normal 1950s American family, which defines the happy return to postwar normality in terms that confine the mother and fetishize the daughter.

To the extent that in the musical genre—by definition a form of idealization—the songs represent an expression of principles, no song more aptly captures the qualities that Humbert so admired in American culture as "Thank Heaven for Little Girls," stating as it does the generic understanding for which the song "Gigi" provides one specific example. Thus when Gaston first sings about Gigi, "What miracle has made you the way you are?," he is extolling the *pre*-transformed Gigi, miraculous because, although she is fifteen, she denies the arrival of puberty.

The same themes proliferate in the career of Audrey Hepburn, who created the role of Gigi on the stage. Two years older than Caron, Hepburn, at twenty-five, played the eighteen-year-old Sabrina in 1954. This love story's success consists of her discarding her crush on playboy David Larrabee (played by William Holden, at the time thirty-seven), opting instead for his more serious older brother, Linus Larrabee, played by Humphrey Bogart, then fifty-five. In 1957 she starred in films opposite Astaire, fifty-eight, and Gary Cooper, fifty-six. In the latter, *Love in the Afternoon*, Hepburn plays Ariane, an innocent Parisian girl who has a crush on an affluent American businessman and international playboy, Frank Flannagan (Cooper), with whom she has an affair based on her convincing him that, despite her young age, she has a long list of former lovers, basing her fictional accounts of these relationships on adaptations of the files her father has amassed as a private detective. Only after her father reveals his daughter's fabrications to Flannagan, that is, only when he assures Flannagan that her behavior demonstrated not her maturity but her childishness, can Flannagan recognize that he loves Ariane and propose marriage.

Hepburn thereby replicates the situation of Gigi, whom she had played six years earlier on the New York stage, enacting a plot that would be reprised the following year in the film *Gigi*. In *Love in the Afternoon,* as in *Gigi*, an extremely rich playboy finds himself attracted to a young woman but cannot commit to her because he is unable to reconcile her alleged (in Gigi's case, learned aura of) sexual experience with her endearing childlike qualities. Once he is convinced of her immaturity, he can opt to marry. Interestingly, in both films the proposal of marriage relegates the girl to silence. Also, interestingly, Maurice Chevalier

FIGURE 3-12 Honere thanks heaven for little girls.

follows *Love in the Afternoon* with *Gigi*, a film that allows his surrogate pederasty to burst into colorful song.

As Honere explains at *Gigi*'s conclusion, the miracle for which we "thank heaven" is that "little girls get bigger every day." A reprise, or more accurately a continuation, of the film's opening scene, "Thank Heaven for Little Girls" frames his Humbert-like narration, thus turning *Gigi* into the wet dream of this dirty old man. And yet, though 1950s readers found Humbert's confession prurient, 1950s audiences found *Gigi* "charming."[8]

A Generation of Vipers

Compare the love of little girls that charmed reviewers to the gothic discomfort evoked by Norma Desmond's relationship with Joe Gillis. Although the difference between Gillis's age and Norma's is less than the difference between Gaston's and Gigi's (and Joe and Norma are both well past the age of consent), Joe's submission nevertheless appears more coerced than Gigi's. In part this is because Gigi evokes Gaston's innocence, while Norma takes away Joe's. When Joe accidentally enters Norma's estate, he has in a manner of speaking found Shangri-La, a place where time has stopped and he may be eternally safe. And timelessness always suggests the Edenic. As Wallace Stevens asks in "Sunday Morning": "Is there no change of death in Paradise / Does ripe fruit never fall?"

But Eden, as Lundberg and Farnham implicitly warned, has a snake in the grass that is not intimidating but alluring. If Joe resembles an American Adam—from his roots in the heartland and his hard-boiled pragmatism to his self-deceptive innocence and inability to recognize genuine evil[9]—Norma is the Eve who seduces him and thus destroys them both. The alternative, Lundberg and Farnham made clear, is for women to accept their natural role, one that recognizes that self-satisfaction, as represented by feminism, is an obstacle to true satisfaction: "Psychologically, feminism had a single objective: the achievement of maleness by the female, or the nearest possible approach to it. Insofar as it was attained, it spelled only vast individual suffering for men as well as women, and much public disorder" (167).

The alternative to Norma Desmond can be found in the top award-winning movie of 1950, *All about Eve*, in which the central character, Margo Channing, starts off resembling Norma but, because of her interactions with Eve Harrington, comes to understand that true happiness will be found in subordinating her ambition to marriage and the needs of her husband. At the outset Margo, a major theater star, is past her prime and, like Norma, attempting to preserve her career by playing roles for which she is too old. Her lover, Bill Simpson (Gary Merrill), is a successful director who is thirty-two years old (the same age as William Holden when he plays Joe Gillis). Her run of Broadway hits has featured her in roles written by Lloyd Richards (Hugh Marlowe), the husband of her best friend, Karen Richards (Celeste Holm). Eve Harrington, a waif who idolizes Margo to the point of attending every one of her performances, hovers in the shadows of the stage door after each one. When Karen eventually introduces Eve to Margo, Eve quickly ingratiates herself and rapidly becomes Margo's personal assistant, but Margo, sensing the dimensions of Eve's ambitious intrusiveness, attempts to distance Eve from her personal and professional life. Eve, instead, ends up as Margo's understudy, and Karen, who is fond of Margo but irritated by her prima donna behavior, decides to drain the gas from their car while Eve is spending the weekend with her and her husband, so that Eve can go on when Margo misses her performance. Because Karen has tipped Eve off in advance, an array of critics, alerted to attend the performance, give Eve rave reviews that launch her stardom.

This stardom not only entails Eve's starring in Lloyd's next play (in a role that Margo, of her own accord, had decided she was too old to play), but also her having an affair with him. Her plans to take Lloyd away from Karen, however, are thwarted when Addison DeWitt (George Sanders), a prominent critic who had promoted Eve's career, blackmails Eve into, in effect, becoming his mistress, letting her know that he has uncovered all the fraudulent activities and statements that she has used to construct her alleged past. In the end Margo, married to Bill, and Karen, reunited with Lloyd, attend a prestigious awards ceremony, somewhat akin to the Tonys. While Eve is honored, Karen and Addison alternate in telling Eve's story, in the same way that Joe posthumously told Norma's. The story, in other words, like *Sunset Boulevard*, is a flashback narrated by those who have been affected by a ruthlessly ambitious woman, a point made by the critics who have linked the two films.

Margo's wit and her ability to see the evil in others enable her to recognize its potential in herself. Sternly rebuking both women for being ambitious, the film, Nora Sayre notes, renders Margo and Eve as "seething neurotics" (141). Because Eve so studiously and meticulously mirrors Margo, Margo can see a reflection of herself, which proves to be her salvation (see figure 3.13). But Eve is the heavy of the piece, as Peter Biskind points out: "She is the bad career woman because she actually wants a career" (264).

Margo's capacity, therefore, to separate stardom from happiness, a capacity absolutely absent in Lina and Norma, allows her to convert from Eve's mirror image to her mirror opposite. This conversion, I am arguing, reflects the historically specific conditions of a postwar America that marshals an array of powerful narratives to discipline women who wish to retain their prewar or wartime agency.

This is made strikingly clear when Margo renounces her ambition by articulating the informing principles of *Modern Woman: The Lost Sex*:

FIGURE 3-13 Margo can see a reflection of herself in Eve.

And what is [Margo] besides something spelled out in light bulbs, besides something called a temperament, which consists mostly of swooping about on a broomstick and screaming at the top of my voice. Infants behave the way I do, you know. They carry on and misbehave. They'd get drunk if they knew how, when they can't have what they want, when they feel unwanted or insecure, or unloved. . . .

Let's say I've been over-sensitive to [Eve], well to the fact that she's so young, so feminine and so helpless. To so many things I want to be for Bill. Funny business, a woman's career, the things you drop on your way up the ladder so you can move faster. You forget you'll need them again when you get back to being a woman. There's one career all females have in common, whether we like it or not: being a woman. Sooner or later, we've got to work at it, no matter how many other careers we've had or wanted. In the last analysis, nothing's any good unless you can look up just before dinner or turn around in bed—there he is. Without that, you're not a woman. You're something with a French Provincial office or a . . . a book full of clippings. But you're not a woman. Slow curtain. The End.

This speech, delivered with Margo stuck out in the cold, in a car that has run out of gas, announces her determination to abandon being a "modern" woman so that she can look for her lost sex, the one career for which she is genetically qualified. The speech occurs, moreover, at exactly the moment when understudy Eve will perform Margo's role. It less important that Eve replaces Margo than that Margo renounces what Eve is all about, the things about Margo upon which Eve modeled herself. If for Margo Eve represents the next generation, her behavior and her values join her name in making clear that, for the postwar viewer, it is a generation of vipers.

4

"What Starts Like a Scary Tale . . ."

The Right to Work *On the Waterfront*

Accompanying the opening credits of *The Court Jester* (1955), the song "Life Could Not Better Be" provides metacommentary on the action of the movie that follows: "Life could not better be, on a medieval spree. / Knights full of chivalry, villains full of villainy. / You'll see, as you suspect, maidens fair, silks bedecked, / each tried and true effect for the umptieth time we resurrect." Concluding with the verse, "What starts like a scary tale ends like a fairy tale," the song makes the medieval story an allegory for the decade following World War II. Emerging from the suffering of the Great Depression and the fears and sacrifices of world war, a joyful postwar America welcomed home its victorious army after 1945 with an unprecedented spectrum of benefits.

Accompanying this cornucopia, however, was much anxiety about returning to domestic life. Happy anticipation joined with apprehension about readjustment and concern over the specter of Fascism, the threat of Communism, and the fragility of postwar prosperity. Perhaps a decade after the war Americans were less dour than contemporary intellectual consensus tended to assert. By 1956 many hopes had been fulfilled: families had formed, private housing had expanded, and middle-class employment had proliferated. But did this transition create a lifestyle that made most people happy, or did the huge demographic changes merely refocus their discontent?

Although the lyrics "Life Could Not Better Be" imply the trajectory of increasing prosperity and security (as well as the decline of the Red Scare) consistent with the changes in American life from 1945 to 1955, the song and the film that it introduces may also express an emphatic bond, particularly characteristic of the 1950s, between fantasies of success and specters of catastrophe. Caught in the middle of these fantasy states was that new class of Americans: heavily suburban nuclear families with modern conveniences and decent (albeit rarely extraordinary) incomes. Along with purchasing power generally difficult to imagine before the war, they had financial credit and a modestly increasing amount of equity. Less identified by the nature of their work or the sources of their wealth than by the amount of their income, the postwar middle class comprised the exploding number of white collar, blue collar, service, and sales workers who shared comparable consumer potential and families of roughly the same age and size.

This demographic amalgamation, which informs the films I focus on in this chapter (*On the Waterfront, 1954*) and the next (*The Court Jester*), owed its variegated features—directly for many blue-collar workers or indirectly for many white-collar employees—to the significant growth of labor unions after the war. With the passage of the Wagner Act in 1935, workers acquired the right to organize and with it the ability to secure a living wage, sensible benefits, and reasonable security. Since the inception of the nation, in part because of the free labor of slavery and subsequently slavery by another name,[1] labor has been relatively inexpensive. Millennia of precedent in Western civilization, combining legal restrictions and informal practices, supported consistent undervaluing of work and pervasive overvaluing of property. In 1935, after half a century of exerted struggle, unions finally acquired meaningful legal protection, which enabled them in the later 1930s and the 1940s to expand their influence and leverage. As a result, by the 1950s organized labor had fomented a broad new demographic group crucial to the development of American prosperity at that time. As Michael Goldfield put it, "the social legislation of the 1930s successfully brought the United States out of the nineteenth century" (37).

The success of unions did more than improve the wages of the unionized; it enhanced the value of labor across a broad section of the economy. From a Cold War perspective, this prolific contribution to the imperative that Americans should live happier, more prosperous, and materially fulfilling lives made the labor movement, in effect, a cornerstone of the containment strategy. The appliances, gadgets, and media devices showcased in Moscow at Vice President Richard Nixon's 1959 "Kitchen Debate" with Soviet leader Nikita Khrushchev were exemplary versions of those available to an army of American workers who, thanks to the G.I. Bill, the Wagner Act, and the postwar industrial engine, were able to escape the physical and economic limitations of "proletarian" life (see figure 4.1).

About the model spaces in the American National Exhibition where Nixon and Khrushchev confronted one another, Kate Baldwin explains: "Masterminded by American architects hired by the United States Information Agency (USIA), the planned environment became the stage for the spectacle of everyday life in the United States. The goal was to showcase the 'American Way of Life' as superior in every respect to Soviet living conditions, and thus lure Soviet viewers away from their entrenchment in socialism. The American way, according

FIGURE 4-1 Richard Nixon's 1959 "Kitchen Debate" with Soviet leader Nikita Khrushchev.

to the exhibition's planners, was not only better, it was also available to anyone who lived under the sway of democracy" (1). Many Americans, to put it simply, could purchase new homes, late model cars, and state-of-the-art appliances because they were well paid for making them.

Threat of the Worker

Like so much of the postwar new normal, however, the success of the labor movement produced at least as much anxiety as satisfaction. Unions might be subversive. At worst they could be run by Soviet agents and at best they could be overly sympathetic to the idea of sharing the wealth. What kind of group, after all, more explicitly answered Marx's call for the workers of the world to unite? Unions thus evoked the kind of nativism that in earlier times had led Americans to fear papists or Freemasons. As much as successful unions helped confirm American Cold War propaganda, therefore, they also elicited from some quarters distrust or vilification. J. Edgar Hoover, testifying in 1947 before the HUAC, warned of Communist infiltration of organized labor: "I do fear, so long as the American labor groups are infiltrated, dominated, or saturated with the virus of communism. I do fear the palliation and weasel-worded gestures against communism indulged in by some of our labor leaders who should know better but who have become pawns in the hands of sinister but astute manipulations for the Communist cause" (Schrecker 133).

To deal with its fear of organized labor, a heavily Republican Congress passed the Taft-Hartley Act in 1947, which required union leaders to sign affidavits indicating that they were not members of the Communist Party. Because unions not complying with this requirement lost National Labor Relations Board protection, the NLRB (set up by the Wagner Act to safeguard the rights of organized labor) in effect contributed to pressure intended to undermine left-wing unions.

While this aspect of Taft-Hartley had the immediate effect of denying American Communists access to the workers whom they were pledged to unite, the long-term consequences of other provisions may have been even more pernicious, making it more difficult for unions to strike and/or to support other striking unions. In this way Taft-Hartley impeded organized labor from exerting the power over management and public policy that made unions attractive to American workers at the same time that the bill insidiously represented unions as obstructions to employment. In other words, the bill strongly contributed to a half century of propaganda that cast organized labor as impeding middle-class success by limiting opportunity, strangling profits, and undermining productivity. Thus, as rapidly as union membership expanded in the postwar period, so too did suspicion about its goals and benefits.

On the Waterfront can be read in this context as painfully negotiating postwar anxieties about the labor movement, which was portrayed in the American imaginary simultaneously as productive of middle-class living and inimical to middle-class values. This form of middle-class double consciousness, as we have seen, is central to C. Wright Mills's concern about the "little" people who make up the new middle class, what we might now call neoliberal subjects, constructing themselves not through solidarity with workers like themselves, but with the values of a power elite whose agenda is antithetical to the interests of little people. Because *On the Waterfront* presents a realist engagement with union corruption as a Christian morality tale, moreover, it puts material interests at odds with the possibility of redemption, such that organized labor obstructs the path to salvation.

The film advances this rhetorical position by representing the Hoboken International Longshoreman's Association local as implicitly analogous to a Communist cell and its rank-and-file members as the chief objects of the union's crimes. Turning those who oppose criminal activity into martyrs, it then equates fighting crime with renouncing the union's legitimacy. In the end, *On the Waterfront* overthrows the union not by voting out (or indicting) its corrupt leaders but by turning each longshoreman into a free agent who, in asserting his right to work, follows in the footsteps of Jesus.

Workers of God and Country Unite!

On the Waterfront is almost as famous for the issues surrounding its production as for its status as an icon of American realist cinema. Frequently viewed as director Elia Kazan's and author Bud Schulberg's attempt to vindicate themselves for "naming names" during the McCarthy era investigation of the film industry,[2] the film traces the decision of Terry Molloy (Marlon Brando) to break the code of silence along the docks by testifying before the Crime Commission, thereby exposing the corrupt, murderous leaders of the Hoboken longshoremen's local. Because in a film with extensive Christian imagery the inspiration for Terry's decision is the crusading Father Barry (Karl Malden), *On the Waterfront* has also been viewed as allegorizing a battle for the workers' souls, in which Terry figures as everyman or as a martyr.[3]

On the Waterfront's competing Christian and Communist allegories have their roots in the film's equally competitive production history. In 1951 Arthur Miller and Elia Kazan, who had directed Miller's first Broadway hit, *All My Sons*, began working on a film about corruption on the New York piers, for which Miller produced a screenplay called "The Hook," set in the Red Hook section of Brooklyn. The first version of Miller's screenplay focused on a failed attempt to overthrow mob control of the docks and the second version on the failed attempt of the hero to win the presidency of a union local in which mobsters had rigged the election. In 1951 Harry Cohn, head of Columbia Pictures, reflecting the pressure of HUAC's scrutiny of the motion picture industry, "told Miller and Kazan that, even though he liked the script he would only do it with FBI approval" (Braudy, 11). As Leo Braudy explains: "Miller was back in New York when Kazan called to tell him that [Roy Brewer, head of the International Alliance of Theatrical State Employees] had told Cohn that the script was all a lie, there was no gangster influence on the waterfront, and the union revolt should be against Communist leaders, not mobsters" (12). Cohn shortly thereafter sent Miller a telegram stating: "'ITS INTERESTING HOW THE MINUTE WE TRY TO MAKE THE SCRIPT PRO-AMERICAN YOU PULL OUT'" (quoted in Braudy 12).

Independently in 1950, Bud Schulberg had written a screenplay called "Crime on the Waterfront," inspired by an exposé of criminal activity on the docks written by journalist Malcolm Johnson, which was serialized in the *New York Sun*. In the process of researching his story, Schulberg became particularly interested in Father Corridan, a crusading Jesuit priest working at Xavier Labor School in Chelsea, opened by the Jesuits in 1936 "to combat the infiltration of local unions by communists" (Fisher xii). Corridan was active in fighting to improve conditions for longshoremen. As Leo Braudy explains, "Schulberg seems attracted to Corridan/Barry as a representative of a Christianity that, unlike the Communist Party he had rejected, was sincerely a supporter of social justice and a moral channel for the working-class vitality of longshoremen" (68).

In 1952, after Miller's script had been rejected by Cohn (among others) and Kazan had testified as a "friendly" HUAC witness, Kazan met Schulberg (another "friendly" witness) and read "Crime on the Waterfront." The most significant distinction, according to James T. Fisher, between Miller's screenplay and Schulberg's first version "was not between 'resisters' and 'rats' but between Popular Front Brooklyn and the 'spiritual front' politics Schulberg first imbibed from Corridan" (214). For this reason, it is not surprising that, as Fisher notes, "[M]any critics have understandably resorted to analyses of generically 'Christian' symbolism in the film: . . . they cite the passion/crucifixion/resurrection of Terry Malloy . . . or the shot of martyred longshoreman, Kayo Dugan's body ascending on a pallet accompanied by Pop Doyle and Father Barry" (273).

Working with Kazan, Schulberg subsequently produced drafts of the screenplay that balanced his story of Christian redemption with the heroism involved in testifying. Kazan has explained that the more he worked on the script, the more he realized "the fuel for it, the energy for it, came from the feeling that I was talking about myself" (quoted in Neve 30). When Terry shouts "that he is 'glad what I done,'" Brian Neve notes, "there is clearly a reference to the director's personal animus against particular individuals from the Communist Party" (31). If for both Kazan and Schulberg the film became, as Dan Georgakas puts it, "a morality play," the fact that it is "replete with Christian imagery" (49) reflects Schulberg's concerns more than those of Kazan (who claims to have hated religious overtones).[4]

Kazan's protestations notwithstanding, the two motifs are more cohesive than antithetical from the perspective of many "redeemed" Communists, in that saving one's soul, as a spiritual or secular activity, applied equally to rejecting Communism and to finding salvation. This is the informing principle of *The God That Failed* (1950), a collection of personal essays by intellectuals including Richard Wright, Arthur Koestler, and Andre Gide, who had rejected Communism because of its dogmatic practices. It is important to remember, in this regard, that testimony can be forensic or spiritual—that is, aimed at convincing a jury that is trying to discover the truth or addressing a deity who already knows it. While in the film the Crime Commission seeks forensic testimony, HUAC, as I have argued extensively in *Containment Culture*, actually sought spiritual testimony: a baring of one's soul in a ritual of loyalty to the state.[5] Thus the forensic testimony in *On the Waterfront*—as Father Barry makes clear—also serves a spiritual goal. Testifying served to cleanse Terry's soul, just as being a friendly HUAC witness did for Kazan. For this reason, Schulberg, despite his desire to focus on Father Barry, did not find that the insertion of the testimony theme was "unnatural" (Georgakas 45).

This "natural" conflation of forensic and spiritual testimony strongly reflected American Cold War ideology, which differentiated East from West as crucially on the difference between religious conviction and atheism as between private enterprise and state ownership. The Cold War slogan, "Better dead than Red," was shorthand for the idea that losing one's life was better than losing one's soul. Thus, to the extent that union officials represented Communists, faith was vital to their defeat.

The final version of the script, adopting this Cold War valance, became a battle for Terry's soul pitting Father Barry against the satanic union boss, Johnny Friendly (Lee J. Cobb). It recounts the story of a poorly educated longshoreman and former boxer who discovers, with the aid of a courageous priest and a saintly girlfriend, Edie Doyle (Eva Marie Saint), that he can defeat the mob by giving testimony. "Terry's behavior," Georgakas points out, "involves personal redemption, not political insurgency. Key to that redemption is the love of Edie Doyle . . . and the fervor of crusading Father Barry" (48).

Original Sin and the Initial Shape-up

At the film's outset, Terry does a favor for Friendly by enticing one of his coworkers, Joey Doyle, to meet him on the roof of his Hoboken tenement. There, Joey instead meets Friendly's thugs, who throw him off the roof to stop him from testifying about union corruption. Rewarded with money and a cushy job assignment, Terry reluctantly accepts the perks of having been a (somewhat unwitting) accomplice to Doyle's murder. At the same time, he rationalizes his involvement: "I figured the worst they were going to do was lean on him a little bit." *On the Waterfront*'s plot thus details the process by which Terry atones for his complicity in Doyle's murder by testifying in Joey's place and thereby becoming the focus of resistance to union corruption and the de facto champion of his fellow longshoremen.

Crucial in this process is Edie's relentless pressure. We first see Edie bent over her brother's dead body. When Father Barry tries to console her, she retorts angrily, "You're in the church if I need you? Did you ever hear of a saint hiding in a church?" At the docks the morning after her brother's murder, she stands next to Father Barry, looking nunlike in her dark coat. (In several other scenes, she wears a dark dress with a white collar; see figure 4.2.)

Returned from a Catholic college for women—we are told more than once that she was "with the sisters"—Edie is determined to penetrate the "D and D" (deaf and dumb) code of silence integral to the longshoreman community. Watching the shape-up, in which the union selects the men who will work that day, she teams with Father Barry to bring those responsible for her brother's death to justice.

Kazan, with a deft sense of dramatic unity—no doubt in part reflecting his experience directing for the stage—uses the shape-up to consolidate the film's central motifs: the workers fighting with the union for work, the Crime Commission pressuring the workers to abandon the code of silence in order to make

FIGURE 4-2 Edie looking nunlike.

the union more fair and to solve Joey's murder, Edie pressuring Father Barry to succeed where the Crime Commission was apparently failing, and Terry being attracted to Edie while also being favored by the union bosses for his complicity in her brother's death. Visually and thematically contextualizing all these conflicts, the shape-up epitomizes all corruption—spiritual, social, and legal—on the waterfront.

When the longshoremen gather for work, the hiring boss under Friendly's control distributes the necessary chits, of which there are fewer than there are men needing work. The inability of many longshoremen to get steady work is, indeed, a legitimate labor issue; conceivably, a good contract could eliminate chronic uncertainty about regular weekly (or annual) income. But the film precludes examination of that issue by eliminating management and owners. In the film, the union alone determines who will work, and it does so based on some form of conspiracy. A longshoreman receives a chit by signaling the hiring boss with a discreet gesture, such as touching his ear or hat brim, leaving those longshoremen without a secret signal to express their desire (usually unsuccessfully) with pleading faces (see figure 4.3). In this way, the film divides the rank-and-file workers into a generally disenfranchised mass and a covert in-group.

The world of *On the Waterfront* thus divorces employment from labor, such that Terry, among others, can be assigned a task that requires no work, suggesting that more people are hired than are needed. At the same time, the shape-up procedure suggests that the union is hoarding jobs. As the only injustice directly represented in the film, the shape-up identifies the union's distribution of employment as its chief crime. In the previous scene, Friendly

FIGURE 4-3 Longshoremen without a secret signal, pleading for work.

and his henchmen review an array of criminal activities—extorting shippers, loan-sharking—but only those that victimize union members are dramatized. In order to work, the longshoremen are forced to give kickbacks ($3 each) and to take loans at 10 percent interest a week. As Friendly boasts, "I got 2000 members in this local . . . that $72,000 a year legitimate. And when each one of them puts in a couple of bucks a day just to work steady: figure it out!" Although the union members are neither the chief source of Friendly's corrupt income nor, most likely, the chief concern of the Crime Commission, the film focuses on this form of exploitation. In a sleight of hand consistent with *On the Waterfront*'s more pervasive assault on organized labor, the union's discrimination against union members signifies quintessential criminality.

This is roughly the same kind of substitution used to criminalize the Communist Party. The rigidity of the American Communist Party has been well established, and ample evidence indicates that a small in-group in synergy with the Soviets often controlled decision making. Far from being illegal, however, towing a party line and/or associating with people who did so was protected by the First Amendment guarantee of free speech and assembly. Nevertheless, the party's unanimity and the extent to which it echoed Soviet positions caused many to view it as supporting "un-American" activities. Much of the postwar Red Scare, therefore, was motivated by the belief that American Communists were agents of a foreign government, many of them secret operatives who pretended not to be Communists so that they could infiltrate government agencies and independent groups, such as unions.

While the longshoremen await the shape-up, investigators for the Crime Commission unsuccessfully try to persuade them to provide information about Doyle's death. At the same time that this secular appeal takes place, off to the side, Father Barry accedes to Edie's spiritual demand, made the night before, that to solve Joey's murder he needed to bring the church to the docks rather than remain aloof from the workers. Father Barry's commitment to Edie and to the workers results in an evening meeting at the church with a few potentially dissident longshoremen, which is broken up by union thugs, who beat one longshoreman, Kayo Duggan, with clubs. While he is tending to Duggan, Father Barry asks if he is still D and D, to which Duggan responds:

DUGGAN: Are you on the level?

FATHER BARRY: What do you think?

DUGGAN: If I stick my neck out and they chop it off, will that be the end of it or are you willing to go all the way?

FATHER BARRY: All the way.

DUGGAN: They'll put the muscle on you too, turned around collar or no turned around collar.

FATHER BARRY: Wipe your face. Listen to me: You stand up and I'll stand up with you.

DUGGAN: Right down the wire?

FATHER BARRY: So help me, God.

Father Barry most dramatically fulfills that commitment with a powerful sermon over Duggan's corpse, when Duggan, after speaking to the Crime Commission, is "accidentally" killed in the hold of the ship (see figure 4.4). Barry's speech, which Schulberg initially felt to be the soul of the film, is based on a 1948 speech that Father Corridan gave before the Knights of Columbus in Jersey City.[6]

Even though some of the lines come directly from Corridan, and even though Corridan vehemently opposed the practice of the shape-up, Father Barry's sermon subtly shifts the emphasis away from corrupt unions to a repudiation of unionism. In the sermon, after acknowledging his promise to Duggan, Father Barry likens Duggan's death to the crucifixion:

> Some people think the crucifixion only took place on Calvary. They better wise up. Taking Joey Doyle's life to stop him from testifying is a crucifixion. And dropping slate on Kayo Duggan because he is ready to spill his guts tomorrow—That's a crucifixion. And every time the mob puts the pressure on a good man, tries to stop him from doing his duty as a citizen, it's a crucifixion. And anybody who sits around and lets it happen, keeps silent about something he knows has happened shares the guilt of it just as much as the Roman soldier who pierced the flesh of our Lord to see if he's dead.

FIGURE 4-4 Father Barry's "Christ in the Hold" speech.

When one of the longshoremen shouts, "Go back to your church!" Father Barry replies, "Boys! This is my church! And if you think Christ isn't down here on the waterfront, you've got another guess coming." Thus Father Barry's argument breaks down the distinction between the union bosses and the rank-and-file workers, as much as between the spiritual world of the church and the material world of the docks. The church subsumes the docks, making all activities subject to religious objectives. Testifying is not a legal obligation or a civic duty; it is a Christian imperative. In equating both the union bosses and the union members with the Romans who crucified Jesus, Father Barry is evoking a moment when, as the act of the crucifixion proved, civil law conflicted with God's law. And the longshoremen are being asked to choose, as Jesus and his followers did, spirit over flesh. They are exhorted to renounce the mob in favor of Jesus: "Every morning when the hiring boss blows his whistle, Jesus stands alongside you in the shape-up. He sees why some of you get picked and some of you get passed over. He sees the family men worried about getting their rent and getting food in the house for the wife and the kids."

And yet it is exactly that concern for feeding one's family that, according to Father Barry, the longshoremen must renounce, as doing otherwise incurs the recrimination of Jesus, who "sees you selling your souls to the mob for a day's pay." A union's concern—which is, to put it metonymically, "a day's pay"—is thus antithetical to salvation. Thus the goals of the labor movement, rather than the actions of a corrupt local, define corruption. This theme is reinforced by directing at the union bosses a charge usually applied to management, owners, and capitalists: that they profit from the labor of others. "What does Christ think of the easy money boys, who do none of the work and take all of the money, who wear $150^7 suits and diamond rings on your union dues and your kick-back money?" Certainly the union leaders in *On the Waterfront* benefit from the labor of the workers, but so do corporate profits, which are never mentioned by Father Barry or anyone else. Father Barry instead reinforces the notion that the mob revenue is extorted chiefly from its own members. As Father Barry moves from the particular to the general, moreover, he makes wanting a share of the longshoreman's pay synonymous with wanting a share of the employer's prof-its. *All* desire for money is damning: "You want to know what's wrong with our waterfront? It's the love of a lousy buck. It's making the love of a buck, the cushy job more important than the love of man. It's forgetting that every fellow down here is your brother in Christ." Although we see Friendly and his well-dressed assistants uncomfortably taking in this critique, it is important to remember that their discomfort emanates from the fact that the words are addressed to the longshoremen upon whom Friendly preys. Father Barry is telling the rank-and-file workers that *their* love of the lousy buck damns them. Because these longshoremen fear the scrutiny and retaliation of Friendly's mob, Father Barry reminds the longshoremen that they are subject to the scrutiny (and implicit retaliation?) of a higher power. In other words, if "every fellow down here is your brother in Christ," Christ himself is Big Brother: "But remember, Christ is always with you. Christ is in the shapeup; he's in the hatch . . . he's kneeling right here beside Duggan. And he's saying to all of you. 'If you do it to the least of mine, you do it to me.' And what they did to Joey and what they did to Dug-gan they're doing to you . . . and you . . . you . . . all of you! And only you, only you with God's help have the power to knock them out for good." Although faced with a secular problem (they don't have enough bucks), the rank-and-file longshoremen need God's help, which is earned by renouncing the love of bucks. By the end of the sermon, with work drained of its purpose, the right to work becomes a spiritual quest that requires rejecting the union's purpose: to improve the material conditions of its members. Unionism, in practice (limit-ing work through the shape-up) and in theory (making money more important than salvation) is the enemy of the working man.

As Terry's resolve to follow in the footsteps of Duggan and Doyle grows, his brother, Charlie (Rod Steiger), who is Johnny Friendly's lawyer, is sent either to dissuade Terry or to kill him. Failing to do the former and declining to do the latter, Charlie himself is killed. When Father Barry persuades Terry that revenge at gunpoint is neither as effective, nor as courageous, nor as virtuous as testify-ing, Terry exposes Friendly and his operation, for which Terry is vilified not only by the mobsters but also by the exploited longshoremen with whom he worked and by the neighborhood teenagers who had idolized him.

The film thus enacts a constant play of shifting allegiances. Although this is most dramatically represented by Terry's defection from Friendly to Father Barry, the story starts with Doyle's defection from the cult of silence, followed by Duggan's. In his refusal to kill Terry, Charlie also defects from the union bosses. Once Edie becomes Terry's girlfriend, she urges Terry not to testify, thus defecting from her pact with Father Barry. After Terry testifies, moreover, the other longshoremen turn on him for violating the code of silence. In another remarkable reversal of loyalty, the neighborhood teenagers—The Golden Warriors—enraged that Terry has broken that code, kill all the homing pigeons he had been raising on the roof of his tenement. This event underscores the pervasive unfairness with which Terry is treated for having the courage to stand up for the rights and interests of his fellow workers.

Waterfront Allegories and the Right to Work

Whether or not the film's Christian allegory and its Communist allegory rival or reinforce one another, they collaborate to obscure the seriously overlooked antilabor inflection effected by converting an exposé of corrupt unions into an attack on the labor movement in general. Father Barry's "Christ-in-the-Hold" sermon focuses the spiritual center of a generic antilabor argument, for which the shape-up provides a material instantiation. To understand how the shape-up functions in this way, we need to ask what evil, exactly, the Crime Commission is investigating. What crimes was Joey Doyle about to expose?

Beyond the murders of Doyle, Duggan, and Charlie, the only wrongdoing the film depicts, as I have noted, is the shape-up. This process of daily selecting workers by handing out chits is accurately portrayed as unfair, degrading, and corrupt. A somewhat common practice on some docks, "the shapeup endured into the early twentieth century as the dominant mode for hiring longshoremen in most waterfront labor markets around the globe" (Fisher 19). "In the Port of New York and New Jersey," James T. Fisher explains, "the 'shape' also performed a kind of ritual enactment of the local social order: it was grounded in forms of authority, benevolence, and deference that were exchanged face-to-face and left obligations undisguised. Everyone knew that a longshoreman sporting a toothpick behind his ear was in debt to a loan shark or bookmaker who worked in partnership with the hiring boss" (19). But by 1945 the shape-up was not the most common hiring practice, and the majority of longshoremen belonged to regular gangs with steady work on a given pier (94).

Even though Doyle's murder (as well as Duggan's and Charlie's) would have been unmotivated unless the union were engaged in a much wider range of crimes, it is important to underscore that the mob's only victims in the film are underemployed longshoremen who could not plausibly have enough resources to sustain a crime syndicate. No doubt the corruption on the docks that inspired *On the Waterfront* had more to do with smuggling, kickbacks, and shakedowns than with the exploitation of the dockworkers, who were actively or tacitly complicit in these enterprises. "In the 1930s," as Fisher points out, "waterfront entrepreneurs turned public loading from an optional service into a mandatory racket: truckers paid a steep loading fee whether they used the service or not" (10). "While the shapeup hiring system became the most notorious symbol of waterfront corruption," Fisher explains, "the loading racket was the port's uniquely insidious signature" (11).

Nevertheless, the film makes the shape-up the site of class conflict. Its depiction at the beginning and end of the film frames the action so as to provide the film's dramatic arc. At the opening shape-up, Terry is called to work first, and a hoard of longshoremen—a majority of those whom we see as individuals—are excluded. The final shape-up, the day after Terry testifies, reverses this pattern, when the hiring boss announces: "All right. Everybody works today." Everybody *but* Terry. Ostracized by the longshoremen and vilified by Friendly, he tells Friendly, "You're a cheap, lousy, dirty, stinking mug, and I'm glad what I done to you!" This leads to a fistfight between Terry and Friendly, who, aided by his henchmen, drags Terry behind the boathouse and brutally beats him. The confrontation fulfills Father Barry's prayers by turning Terry into a Christ figure on the docks who suffers for the sins of his fellow man, both those of the union bosses with whom he was complicit and those of the other D and D longshoremen, condemned by Father Barry for their complicity through silence. The impact of Terry's courage and suffering converts the other workers into followers who can now resist the temptation of the union. They stage a mini-strike, protesting that no one works until Terry does.

Although Terry is barely able to stand, Father Barry (displaying a startling absence of Christian compassion) commands the others not to help him, insisting that Terry walk unassisted up the boathouse ramp and across the yard to the warehouse. In his slow, painful climb, bleeding and limping, Terry seems to replicate the stages of the cross (see figure 4.5).

This symbolism is reinforced not only by his wearing a sacrificial robe—the jacket passed by Edie from her dead brother to Duggan to Terry—but also by Father Barry's implicit insistence that Terry's struggle serve the higher purpose of demonstrating that there is something more important than "the love of a lousy buck" (or getting medical attention for someone who may be bleeding internally). Thus, by refusing that for which they had previously been begging, the longshoremen in effect turn scarcity into abundance—their miracle of fishes and loaves—so that where formerly there was not enough work, now there is more than they want. Even more important, their appreciation of Terry's sacrifice enables them to reject the union's leadership for his.

FIGURE 4-5 Terry's Christlike climb.

The patriotic dimension of this conclusion is not lost on Biskind, who accurately explains that

America's confident sense of grace, its unembarrassed assurance that Americans were the chosen people, is evident in the film's lavish use of Christian iconography. . . . The figure who really brings Christian transcendence down to earth is, of course, Terry-the-Christ-figure. . . . In a democracy, in other words, power is not confronted with power but with Christian virtue. When Terry chooses to inform, spiritual values become immanent. In Christian terms, he assumes the role of the dove (the meek); in secular terms, he assumes the role of the stool pigeon (the informer), and the two become one. (178–179)

But Terry does not triumph over corruption; he defeats the concept of organized labor. As Georgakas notes, "Terry's victory involves personal redemption, not political insurgency" (48). "By the end of *On the Waterfront*, Terry has been maneuvered into more than betraying his pals; he has betrayed his class as well. The values that replace his old ones are mainstream, middle-class values, disguised as morality" (Biskind 182).

That morning Terry had arrived demanding "his right to work" (Chown 108), making *the right to work* his goal, rather than different union leaders or a new contract. This solution is particularly charged because perhaps the most insidious provision of Taft-Hartley was its protection of "right-to-work" laws, aimed at undermining union solidarity by permitting nonunion members to work in union shops, thereby making it possible for new employees, favorable to the employer, to vote out militant leaders or even the union itself.

By branding unions as obstacles to employment, right-to-work laws also provided antiunion forces with cogent propaganda. To the extent that Americans perceived work as a fundamental right, opposing right-to-work laws looked un-American and, to many people, supporting closed shops seemed elitist. If the spread of right-to-work laws has correlated to some degree with America's general decline in job security and real wages, advocacy of those laws has helped portray unions as protecting unreasonable advantages for incompetent workers at the expense of productivity, quality control, and public welfare. *On the Waterfront*'s portrayal of the union, therefore, as the sole source of all hiring decisions implicitly affirmed the tenets of Taft-Hartley.

But the truth is that people do not really want the right to work; they want the assurance they will be paid fairly for their labor. Although a union can offer to let everyone work, the payroll must come from management. Throughout *On the Waterfront*, however, because the union bosses are omnipresent and the corporate bosses absent, the union stands in for management and thereby bears the blame for the paucity of work. At the end of the final shape-up, someone who represents the owner of the warehouse intervenes and replaces the now ineffectual union hiring boss. He welcomes Terry at the doorway to the warehouse and shouts the film's final words: "All right. Let's go to work." In keeping with the spirit of Taft-Hartley, the right to work, attained when the workers renounce their love of a lousy buck, wins out over organized labor, making the right to work a victory for the worker, for Father Barry, and, if we believe the latter's speech, for Jesus. That is why Terry, denied his right to work at the beginning of the scene, earns it by becoming a martyr, and then stands erect at the entrance to the warehouse, before a Saint Peter–like owner, who happily admits him and all of his followers.

Edie's Victory and Domestic Security

Ostensibly, when the workers turn their backs on the satanic Friendly ("friendly," indeed; as Hamlet reminds us, the devil "hath the power to assume a pleasing shape") to follow Terry through the pearly gates of the warehouse, it is also a victory for Edie. At the outset she had been even more vehement than Father Barry that Christ belonged on the docks and that to save the longshoremen, he had to convince them to testify. In her devout commitment—"a woman with a mission," as James Harvey calls her (127)—she seems saintly, and in her courage protofeminist. Yet in the end she reverses herself. "Edie is changed profoundly by Terry's transformation," Lance Lee points out. "Her love turns her into a blind supporter of Terry once he turns on Johnny Friendly, one willing to flee before Terry's work is done for fear of its consequences to him" (79).

The film provides no explicit cause for her change of heart, made all the more startling in light of the way she helped motivate Father Barry's "Christ in the Hold" sermon. The only possible reason for Edie's change is not a loss of conviction but of maidenhood. Although the Motion Picture Production Code would prohibit any explicit sign of this change, her kissing Terry at night on the roof of the tenement, and later her clinch with Terry in the scene that employs the conventions of rape morphing into mutual passion, clearly signify this loss of virginity. "To contemporary audiences," Chown rightly notes, "sensitive to issues such as date rape, Terry kissing Edie, initially against her will, makes many uncomfortable" (116). Richard Schickel explicitly calls this "the violent scene in which Brando eventually takes her virginity" (301), although they are in fact immediately interrupted by calls from the thugs who have killed Charlie. Nevertheless, in the cinematic codes of the 1950s, it's safe to assume they did *it*, even if they first did *it* earlier, as Edie and Terry fade out when they start to kiss on the roof (see figure 4.6).

It would not be necessary to elaborate upon this point were "doing *it*" not seamlessly linked to Cold War gender roles, wherein doing it is either a step in the direction of domestic prudence or the initiation of a life of sin and decadence. Edie's virginity thus circulates in an economy of social and sexual concerns that require underscoring her love and commitment to marital partnership, a commitment that takes priority over her political concerns. Were this not the case, she would resemble the Communist atheists, who placed politics above family. Therefore, "Brando's sexuality," as Chown astutely explains, "is

FIGURE 4-6 Edie and Terry "kiss" on the roof.

used to recuperate her from her social activist position to a traditional, docile female role. . . . *On the Waterfront* flirts with having a feminist character, but ultimately ends up reinforcing the church, the family, and traditional gender roles" (116).

In this way, *On the Waterfront* further connects the right to work to the maintenance of Cold War gender roles, which "naturally" arrange for labor without the interference of unions. With Terry in the warehouse and Edie in the kitchen, both principals have attained the right to work at the tasks for which each is best suited.

5

"Life Could Not Better Be"

Disorganized Labor, the Little Man, and *The Court Jester*

If *On the Waterfront* (1954) engages the demographic angst of the blue-collar middle class by defining the free laborer as someone free *from* unions, *The Court Jester* (1955) valorizes the white-collar worker, whom C. Wright Mills aptly dubbed the "Little Man," by evoking the cultural narratives surrounding the baby boom and the social ethic of the corporation.

To understand how the film negotiates the anxieties produced by the booming households of the 1950s and the growing hoard of white-collar workers who headed them, we need to look at the middle class of that period as historically unique: a group defined more by its aspirations and status symbols, by its modes of consumption and sites of identification, than by its relationship to production, property, wealth. In 1956 that demographic group, for over a decade a relentless birth factory, lived chiefly in suburbia. During the 1950s, according to Landon Y. Jones, "No less than 83 percent of the total population growth of the United States . . . was in the suburbs, which were growing 15 times faster than any other segment of the country" (38–39).

Suburbia, as I have noted, distributed the middle-class population into geographic subdivisions based on income, which correlated to the square footage of the home, the size of the lot on which it stood, the number of cars its garage accommodated, and its distance from the metropolis (measured in minutes, not miles). Each town, and even each development within a township, mandated relative income homogeneity, which in turn converted a national composite of homogeneous suburban communities into the economically heterogeneous middle class of Cold War America.[1] In other words, the ability of postwar families to define themselves in nonmaterial ways enabled a perception called "the middle class" to become so widespread.[2]

As in the blue-collar world of *On the Waterfront*, the gender dynamics of this white, suburban middle class were organized to address the postwar masculinity crisis. "Advice writers," Elaine Tyler May explains, "urged women to be sensitive to the needs of the returning veterans, since the men's battles were not all behind them. Warning of the white-collar world in which many postwar men found their manliness at risk, *Photoplay* exhorted women to take responsibility for building up the male ego" (57).

In this context, *The Court Jester* does for the white-collar worker what *On the Waterfront* did for the blue-collar worker: it gives heroic status to his "right to work," a task made formidable by the baby boom, which shifted the domestic focus from the man of the house to the children at home. "Seldom has a generation transformed society while still in its infancy, but it is no exaggeration," Andrew Dunar aptly points out, "to suggest that the generation born in the period from 1946 to 1964 did so" (174). Although in the 1950s, as suburbia filled with first-time homeowners, the old adage, "a man's home is his castle," may have been iterated with alacrity, a more accurate turn of phrase might have been, "a man's home is his toddler's playpen."

The Infant King and the Royal Posterior

It is therefore significant that *The Court Jester*'s plot revolves around the fate of a baby. A farce set in medieval England, the film recounts the successful attempt of an outlaw called the Black Fox to restore to the throne the rightful heir, who is a toothless infant. It opens with a group of the king's men on horseback riding along the coast, while a voice-over narrator tells us: "This is the story of how the destiny of a nation was changed by a birthmark, a royal birthmark on the royal posterior of a royal infant child. Here returning to his castle is King Roderick, Roderick the tyrant, who some months before seized the throne by a massacre of the entire royal family. But uneasy lies Roderick's crown. For rumor hath it that an infant, the rightful heir to the throne, had survived the massacre, and even now was being cared for by a group in the forest, a group led by an elusive, dashing, outlaw known only as the Black Fox." The Fox, wearing a hood and mask, then appears in a tree's thick foliage with a bow and arrow and kills one of the king's men. Wrapped around the lethal arrow is the message: "The child lives. Death to the tyrant!" The action and mise-en-scène thus clearly embrace the Robin Hood genre. Even the casting of Basil Rathbone as the king's villainous advisor alludes to the similar role he played in *The Adventures of Robin Hood* (1938).

The Court Jester, however, crucially deviates from the genre. In the traditional tale, Robin Hood's band fights the abuses of King John until such time as the legitimate and (implicitly) just ruler, King Richard the Lionhearted, can return from the Crusades to reclaim his throne and end the tyranny. This assumes that legitimacy implies justice, that bloodlines define virtue. Although *The Court Jester*'s proper ruler is an infant and therefore unfit to govern, opposition to the baby's rule constitutes tyranny. The film, in other words, performs the cultural work of converting the oppression of the baby boom—which forced women to become housewives and men to become breadwinners—into a virtue. It extols the conditions by which families were pigeonholed in class ghettoes, where a television set provided their only meaningful conduit to a world of variety and opportunity.

The plot's premise—it is beneficial to replace one monarch with another—is an obvious joke (as even a glimpse at the current British royal family makes clear). But in addition to poking fun at the notion of monarchy, the premise satirizes the exalted place babies occupied in the 1950s. "Children," Jones explains, "were the whole point. This generation of Americans enshrined them. European visitors joked knowingly about how well American parents obeyed their children" (47).

The Court Jester thus engages whimsically the pervasive promotion of the family in the postwar period. "Along with the baby boom," May points out, "came an intense and widespread endorsement of pronatalism—the belief in the positive value of having several children. A major study conducted in 1957 found that most Americans believed that parenthood was the route to happiness. Childlessness was considered deviant, selfish, and pitiable" (121). At the same time, by showing accomplished outlaws, independent and daring, deft with sword and bow, bowing before "the royal birthmark on the royal posterior," the film highlights the absurdity of the idea that happiness comes from kissing the ass of the baby that rules your life (see figure 5.1).

Nevertheless, in *The Court Jester* the restoration of the rightful monarch serves the same purpose that the advent of the sound era does in *Singin' in the Rain*: to signify the postwar period as a return to normalcy, a time to be happy

FIGURE 5-1 The royal posterior.

again. If returning to normal produced happiness, what could be more normal than having a family and a nine-to-five job? Postwar prosperity, therefore, guaranteed men the right to go into work and women the right to go into labor.

By the end of 1946, 3.4 million babies had been born in the United States, an all-time annual high and an increase of 20 percent over the preceding year. Each of the following years helped maintain the high birth level, with 3.8 million in 1947, 3.9 million in 1952, and nearly 4 million each year from 1954 to 1964. By 1966, over 40 percent of all Americans had been born since the end of World War II. Although "demographers had predicted . . . that the boom was likely to end . . . after wartime parents finished having their welcome-home babies" (Jones 50), the initial spike in births was nonetheless heralded as a fortuitous quick fix for the perils of an economy no longer fueled by wartime spending. *Time* in 1948 gloated that the United States had gained "2,800,000 more *consumers* (quoted in Jones 36; emphasis added). Because the war effort had fueled recovery from the Depression, *Fortune*, viewing the exceptional birthrate as a safeguard against peacetime recession, wrote, "A civilian market growing by the size of Iowa every year ought to be able to absorb whatever production the military will eventually turn loose" (quoted in Jones 36). Even at the baby boom's inception the Cold War middle class was invested economically as well as psychologically in the infants upon whom their prosperity as well as their normality depended.

By 1956 the boom, rather than abating, seemed like a permanent feature of American life. The nation appeared to have tacitly succumbed to an invading army whose ranks continued to proliferate with troops led by commanding officers who could neither read nor cross the street alone nor, in many cases, talk. A dozen years after the war, with birthrates still booming, *The Court Jester* pits those who desire a nation free from the infant against those who are happy to be ruled by him. It enacts this as a struggle, moreover, between the classes that C. Wright Mills described as the "power elite" and the white-collar "Little Man."

Elite Power and Midgets

At Roderick's castle, which we enter in the film's first sustained scene, reside the aristocracy who epitomize what Mills' identified as

> those higher circles which make up the economic, the political, and the military elites. At the top of the economy, among the corporate rich, there are the chief executives; at the top of the political order, the members of the political directorate; at the top of the military establishment, the elite soldier-statesman clustered in and around the Joint Chiefs of Staff and the upper echelon. As each of these domains has coincided with the others, as decisions tend to become total in their consequences, the

leading men in each of the three domains of power—the warlords, the corporation chieftains, the political directorate—tend to come together, to form the power elite of America. (*Power Elite* 9)

Roderick, who makes absolute decisions, agrees with three of his lords that he should strengthen his power by marrying off his daughter, Gwendolyn (Angela Lansbury), to Griswald, a knight in the north with a significant army at his command. Such an alliance, while favored by three lords in the elite ranks of Roderick's court, threatens the king's chief adviser, Ravenhurst (Basil Rathbone). The plan is also unacceptable to Gwendolyn, who wants to marry for love rather than power, an idea put in her head by her adviser, Griselda (Mildred Natwick).

Everything in this scene exemplifies the power of the few over the welfare of the many and the sundry ways in which power can be exerted. The king plans to use his wealth and property (which includes his daughter) to bolster his military might. Ravenhurst demonstrates raw power by getting into an aborted duel with one of the other knights, and he also uses subterfuge, we later learn, by arranging for the assassination of his rivals. Griselda is a witch empowered by magic spells and potions. Roderick thus typifies one type of Mills's power elite: "Like any politician, especially when he is at or near the top of his hierarchy, the successful executive tries to win friends and make alliances, and he spends, one suspects, guessing about the cliques he thinks oppose him. He makes power-plays, and these seem part of the career of the managerial elite" (139).

The scene ends with a direct threat to Roderick's power—news that the royal infant is alive—and the command to assault the Fox's forest hideout: "Destroy forever this murderous fiend who calls himself . . . the Black Fox." This command is followed by a cut to a masked man in a Sherwood green outfit, who starts singing about the impossibility of outfoxing the Fox. Pulling up his mask (thereby revealing that he is played by Danny Kaye), he sings in the first person that his enemies can never find him. Restoring the mask, he concludes this portion of the song with: "They know that they'll never—I'm far too clever—they'll never out-fox the Fox."

The pulling down of the signature mask is done as if to reaffirm Kaye's identity as the Fox, but Kaye does so, it turns out, to embark on a second phase of the performance, which attributes his abilities less to ingenuity than to multiplicity: "The Fox, there's only one of me, til suddenly there's two of me; when two is what you see of me, gadzooks: three of me!" As he sings, similarly costumed masked men, of comparable height and build, appear from behind Kaye's cloak. Suddenly four "Foxes," who enact through dance the Fox's prowess, become seven—Kaye and six midgets—all dressed as the Fox (see figure 5.2).

Their masks up, they sing in unison as they join other little men dressed as the Fox and, finally, little men wearing peasant garb. Kaye, surrounded by six midgets, sings with them, "any one of us can be at any time the Fox," while

FIGURE 5-2 Kaye and six midgets, all dressed as the Fox.

he tears up the image of the Fox on a wanted poster and distributes the pieces to the midgets. He then sings, "but I tell you confidentially that I'm the Fox," again confirming his identity by pulling down his mask. The chorus of midgets responds, "no I'm, no I'm, no I'm the Fox." Then each singer parries individually with Kaye about which one of them is the Fox, until the number resolves with the proclamation: "No matter who's the Fox, they'll never, never, never, never-nevernevernevernevernever never out-fox the Fox!"

Significantly, the members of the last group of midgets with whom Kaye sings are not dressed as the Fox, so that the claim "I'm the Fox," initially associated with the stature of a hero and the costume of an outlaw, has been deployed to little men of every shape and guise. The frequent masking and unmasking of the performers, along with the groups' constant multiplication and division, make clear that in this world little people live in the tension between identification and anonymity. At various points Kaye seems to assert that he is the Fox by becoming anonymous—that is, by masking his face—just as at other moments he multiplies himself, to prove he is clever by demonstrating that he is not unique. In the end, the song supports the importance of being the Fox by asserting, paradoxically, that it doesn't matter who the Fox is.

But this musical number also demonstrates exactly the opposite. It creates a hierarchy organizing several substrata of would-be Foxes: those who share the Fox's dress and physique, those who have the body but not the costume, the costume but not the stature and, finally, neither size nor garb. The song's strangely egalitarian conclusion thus distinguishes all the little men from the bigger-than-life Black Fox, while at the same time allowing each little man a share of his heroism, in the same way that he received a share in the Fox's wanted poster and the permission to identify with his celebrity and prowess.

This capacity for vicarious identification with the elite is at the heart of Mills's concern about the class consciousness of white-collar little men, represented by Kaye and literalized by the midgets who would "do anything" for Kaye. This huge group of white-collar workers was in some ways even smaller—that is, more insignificant—than rank-and-file union members. In exchange for a secure place in the system, the little man had neither a stake in society's wealth nor a say in its practices. His classification as "middle," therefore, separated his "class" from property and the bourgeois prerogatives that accrue to ownership. In the early nineteenth century, "probably four-fifths of the occupied population were self-employed enterprisers; by 1870, only about one-third, and by 1940, only about one-fifth, were still in this old middle class. Many of the remaining four-fifths of the people who now earn a living do so by working for the 2 or 3 percent of the population who now own 40 or 50 percent of the private property in the United States. Among these workers are the members of the new middle class, white-collar people on salary" (Mills, *White Collar* 63).

Like the midgets in the forest, *White Collar*'s little man therefore had little authority or occupational autonomy. While in charge of finite tasks, the little man was rigidly delimited by an organizational chart that charged another little man with overseeing the performance of the little people within his purview. Clerks, payroll officers, and accounts payable personnel enabled bookkeepers to supply data to the clerical and supervisory staff of a central accounting department, data that were requisite to the organization's fiduciary responsibilities. Typists, secretaries, head secretaries, and private secretaries similarly produced and coordinated managerial documents.

Thus, in the same way that anyone could "be the Fox," the white-collar little man could, technically, be "management" rather than "labor." But his personal stake and managerial power were little, as was his significance in the large scheme of the organization or the small scope of his own life. Alienated not from the product of his labor, à la the Marxist model, but rather from an abstract organization, he could not fetishize what he had produced. Instead, he fetishized corporate power itself. Therefore, the little man, as an extension of a small power elite, overvalued authority per se, not by exercising it but by internalizing it.[3] He was not the beneficiary of power, merely its conduit. At the same time, Mills pointed out, the centralization of property, "has shifted the basis of economic security from property ownership to job holding; the power inherent in huge properties has jeopardized the old balance which gave political freedom. . . . For employees, freedom and security, both political and economic, can no longer rest upon individual independence in the old sense.

To be free and to be secure is to have an effective control over that which one is dependent: the job within the centralized enterprise" (58). Because the little man holds onto the right to work rather than what his work produces, he operates in a value system inimical to the interests of wage laborers. This value system, as Vance Packard explained in *The Status Seekers*, depends on having status, that is, the ability to emulate someone with power, to acquire signifiers of power's simulacra.

Organization and Status

Writing in 1959, Packard pointed out that despite the fact that it "is becoming more and more difficult to start at the bottom and reach the top" (6), "most white-collar people still aspire to rise, and this makes them poor prospects for unions. Many are caught up in a panic about their status and strain to demonstrate that they are different from the working class. Meanwhile many live lives of quiet conformity trying to live like—and to please—their superiors" (31). And yet, Packard noted, "while the boundary between white collar and blue collar is blurring, the boundary between lower and upper white collar groups is becoming sharp and formidable. . . . I has become the great dividing line in our society" (31).

The white-collar worker, therefore, shared a great deal with what William H. Whyte called "the organization man": "They are not workers, nor are they white-collar people in the usual, clerk sense of the word. These people only work for The Organization. The ones I am talking about *belong* to it as well. They are the ones of our middle class who have left home, spiritually as well as physically, to take the vows of organization life. . . . they are the staff as much as the line, and most are destined to live poised in a middle area that still awaits a satisfactory euphemism" (3). The tension that emerges for the little man, the mid-century organization man, the status seeker, is how to succeed in a normal way (a white-collar anxiety satirized by the 1962 Broadway show, *How to Succeed in Business without Really Trying*). The implicit dilemma of the1950s little man was how to maintain his individuality while suppressing creativity. That dilemma was mediated by what Whyte called a "Social Ethic": "The organization man seeks a redefinition of his place on earth—a faith that will satisfy him that what he must endure has a deeper meaning than appears on the surface. . . . almost imperceptibly, a body of thought has been coalescing that does that. . . . I am going to call it a Social Ethic" (6). By this, Whyte meant "that contemporary body of thought which makes morally legitimate the pressures of society against the individual. Its major propositions are three: a belief in the group as the source of creativity; a belief in 'belongingness' as the ultimate need of the individual; and a belief in the application of science to achieve the belongingness" (7). The organization man, like the little man, like a midget in the Fox's camp, just wanted to belong. The midgets make this clear when, at the end of the "Nobody Can Out-Fox the Fox" number, the real Fox suddenly arrives, rebukes Hawkins (the character Kaye actually plays) for wearing his outfit, and asks, "Who are these little people?" "They too would be part of our group, sir," Hawkins explains. "They feel strongly as we do about the tyranny and would join in our worthy cause."

This scene thus makes the Fox's band analogous to a corporation in which Hawkins and the other men, by replicating the Fox's appearance, become indistinguishable workers conforming to a singular corporate image. The only thing that differentiates them is their size. Some, like Hawkins, are as tall as the real Fox, albeit much lower in rank, while others are midgets. At the moment of the Fox's arrival, moreover, these Fox wannabes, as if to underscore their white-collar identities, form a human pyramid to literalize the corporate structure that Mills described (see figure 5.3): "The employees composing as new middle class. . . . have not emerged on a single horizontal level, but have been shuffled out simultaneously on the several levels of modern society; they now form, as it were, a new pyramid within the old pyramid of society at large" (Mills, *White Collar* 64).

The Fox, as played by Edward Ashley, moreover, looks more like a CEO than a dashing bandit. A British actor in his fifties who had worked in the United States since the beginning of World War II (in the 1950s and 1960s, chiefly on television), Ashley was never a leading man, but rather a working actor with a career of secondary roles. Nor does Ashley at any point demonstrate athleticism. Instead, despite his outlaw costume, he wears the demeanor of a business executive. With a dismissive grunt, for example, he ignores Hawkins's request for a promotion. Hawkins, formerly part of a carnival (which is where he befriended

FIGURE 5-3 A human pyramid literalizes the corporate structure.

the midgets), entertains the Fox's men while yearning for martial duties. He wants to be a fighter so that he can make a more meaningful contribution to the corporate effort and, in the process, affirm his masculinity.

About the latter, he feels particularly insecure, given that one of his jobs is to display the infant's royal birthmark—a purple pimpernel—to the Fox's new inductees, by lowering the infant's diaper, so that each new man can bow to the royal posterior. "Well, sir," Hawkins pleads, "you know I'd do anything for his majesty, but don't you think it would be better if a woman. . . ." The Fox shouts back at him, "Tend to your duty! And get out of my clothes," the latter command emphatically refuting the earlier claim that *anyone* can be the Fox. Again, while lowering the diaper, Hawkins says to the Fox, "Sir, don't you really think it would look better if this kind of thing were done by a woman?" The Fox condescendingly replies, "I've told you repeatedly, Hawkins, each one serves as best he can." But Hawkins presses for a more masculine role: "I know, sir, but when I ran away from the carnival, sir, and joined your group, I thought I'd be in the thick of it—robbing the rich and giving to the poor." This plea is interrupted by the arrival of a woman, Captain Jean (Glynnis Johns) who, representing yet a third challenge to Hawkins's manhood, is made his commanding officer when he is charged with taking the infant king to safe haven at a nearby abbey.

The Hero of the Baby Boom

By diminishing the capacity of the little man to play the role of the hero and by connecting that incapacity to child care, the film implicitly asks: What kind of man is best suited to be the "hero" in a society ruled by an infant? "Even as women's magazines celebrated motherhood, they often did so at the expense of men, portraying fathers as rather inept creatures who had to be manipulated by women in order to keep the household on a true course" (Dunar 194). The importance of providing an appropriately positive masculine role model at home, however, cannot be separated from the way in which the father's work affirms or undermines that role, an issue of great concern to the little man. His problem, as exemplified by Hawkins's place in the Fox's organization, is that he must demonstrate his masculine tendencies in the domestic setting despite their having been stripped away when he performs his nine-to-five role as breadwinner.

This is exactly the issue that Hawkins and Captain Jean confront while they are taking the infant king to safety. That night, when they take shelter from the rain in an abandoned farmhouse, Captain Jean, seeing Hawkins care for His Majesty, the baby, is struck by the tenderness with which Hawkins sings a lullaby. While Hawkins sings, Captain Jean alternates between gazing tenderly at the infant king and a bit lasciviously at Hawkins. After His Majesty falls asleep, she suggests to Hawkins that, because the roof leaks, they sleep together on a dry pile of sacks and hay. Implicitly because of possible impropriety, Hawkins hesitates, but Captain Jean stresses the importance of their both sleeping in the only dry part of the barn. "We can both lie there. If you get wet and ill you'll be no use to His Majesty." In order to squeeze into the narrow dry area, she further suggests that she cradle in his arm.

While clearly attracted to Jean, whom he continues to call "Captain," Hawkins remains unsure of himself. Even though Captain Jean's body language suggests romantic interest, Hawkins, thinking he may not be adequately masculine, fears he may be mistaking her cues. In keeping with the dicta of the 1950s, it becomes Captain Jean's job to help him over his insecurities. She starts by letting him know that she is not talking to him as his commanding officer, but as a woman:

JEAN: I'm sorry I spoke to you in the manner I did. I was wrong.

HAWKINS: Y-yes Captain.

JEAN: There's something else I would like to say.

HAWKINS: Yes.

JEAN: I *am* a woman. And I do have feelings.

Hawkins, as much nervous as enticed, still requires further reassurance. As he had told the Fox, he worries that his role in the organization undermines his manhood: "I find it hard to believe that the Captain could ever be fond of a man who . . . isn't a fighter." "Sometimes," Jean responds, "tenderness and kindness can also make a man, a very rare man." In this proclamation, Jean bolsters Hawkins's ego by indicating that his traits prove he is an exceptional man rather than a little man, in other words, by agreeing with him that "anyone can be the Fox." By equating nurturing to martial prowess, Jean reflects the consensus of 1950s experts and of the women's magazines that echoed their conventional wisdom. "Fatherhood," May notes, "became a new badge of masculinity and meaning for the postwar man, and Father's Day a holiday of major significance. Men began attending classes on marriage and family in unprecedented numbers" (129).

Jean's strategy evokes a proposal from Hawkins, which she accepts with a caveat: "Yes Hawkins, I think she could . . . and would . . . if things were different." Hawkins again becomes nervous, fearing that Jean may mean, "if only you weren't a little man." When, instead, she makes clear that she means the infant's assuming the throne, his demeanor becomes romantic. They speak in soft, breathy tones, as Hawkins runs his finger over her face and kisses her cheeks (see figure 5.4).

Jean's breathing becomes heavy, and, unable to restrain herself any longer, she kisses Hawkins passionately. Having seduced her man and gotten a commitment of marriage, she breaks his embrace with the excuse, "We daren't think of ourselves until our fight is won."

FIGURE 5-4 Hawkins runs his finger over Captain Jean's face.

At this point she has the idea that sets the film's complex plot in motion: someone must get into the castle and steal the key to the secret passage so that the Fox's men can sneak in, topple Roderick's regime, and enthrone the infant king. At that moment another man, also seeking shelter from the storm, joins them in the farmhouse. When they learn that he is Giacomo, "King of Jesters and Jester to Kings," bound for Roderick's court, Captain Jean knocks Giacomo out, so that the Fox can take him prisoner and Hawkins assume Giacomo's identity. Although complications too elaborate to summarize ensue, Kaye biographer Martin Gottfried deftly summarizes the general thrust of the story:

> While [Hawkins] is impersonating the bad king's new jester in order to restore the good king to the throne, the princess is smitten with him and commands her personal witch [Griselda] to help him.
>
> So Griselda hypnotizes [Hawkins] into believing he is a swashbuckler, and in that conviction he swings on ropes, leaps across parapets, and engages in swordplay. Unfortunately, this court jester can be brought in and out of the trance with a snap of the fingers, and fingers keep snapping, switching him instantly from daring-do to cowardice. (218–219)

As this summary indicates, Hawkins plays many roles, often marked by instantaneous transformations. His spectrum of abilities demonstrates the thematic tension when he sang that he could be the Fox and was then reminded that he could not. Hawkins also unknowingly plays additional parts: he impersonates Giacomo, without knowing that Giacomo is an assassin disguised as a jester, hired by Ravenhurst to dispense with his enemies in the court. In addition, although in effect betrothed to Captain Jean (who has also ended up in the castle and is fending off the advances of King Roderick), Hawkins, hypnotized by Griselda, is set to elope with Gwendolyn. When Ravenhurst discovers that Hawkins is not Giacomo, he arranges for him to be knighted so that he may joust with and thus be killed by Griswald. This requires a bogus process that truncates five years of training for knighthood into one day. To sum up, by the end of the film, Hawkins is a former carnival entertainer, a wannabe outlaw, a wine merchant (while transporting the king), a lullaby-singing nurturer, an imposter court jester, a secret assassin, a bogus knight, a potential bigamist, the leader of the little men, and the chief guardian of the royal posterior.

This array of characterizations was geared to show off Kaye's remarkable versatility.[4] But in so doing, it also exposes the impossible demands that the little man of Cold War America had to meet in order to support the baby boom. Fundamentally, the role of new fathers was crucial both to postwar normality and to maintaining the gender distinctions that, as we have seen, were deemed foundational to being happy again. Therefore, although the tenderness with which Hawkins sings his lullaby validates his parental role, it worries the gender distinctions upon which it was allegedly based.

Consider, for example, that 1950s fathers were charged with preventing their children from becoming "sissies," which meant, according to "Dr. Luther E. Woodward, psychologist and coordinator of the New York State Mental Health Commission . . . 'a boy (or girl) who gets too much satisfaction from what his mother does for him and not enough from what he does for himself [sic]'" (May 130). Dr. Benjamin Spock, whose classic *Baby and Child Care*, first published in 1946, became the boomer parents' Bible, *Farmer's Almanac*, and *Cliff's Notes* rolled into one, underscored gender roles in several ways, the most subtle and extensive being that Spock's generic child was implicitly male and, as it was for Dr. Woodward, only parenthetically female.

About handling a one-year-old, for example, Spock says, "There will always be a few things you will have to teach him to let alone," but, the doctor counsels, "you can't stop him by saying no, at least not in the beginning" (200). Although the chapter is devoted to the generic one-year-old, Spock's "him," as the following example makes clear, reflects not a grammatical convention, but a gender preference: "Don't say 'no' in a challenging voice from across the room. This gives him a choice. He says to himself, 'Shall I be a mouse and do as *she* says or be a *man* and grab the lamp cord.' Remember that his nature is egging him to try things and to balk at directions" (200; emphasis added)

Occasionally, albeit far less frequently, Spock's general advice applies to girls. In cautioning about "deliberate baby talk," he indicates he is thinking "for instance of the little girl with corkscrew curls and fancy clothes, who is the only child of a doting family. . . . They keep talking baby talk to her long after it is natural, and show her they love her best when she acts babyish and 'cute.' You can't blame her for playing up to them. But she will have a tough time when she gets around with children her own age, because they won't think she's cute; they'll think she's awful" (152).

Spock worries as well about how the gender of the parent affects upbringing. He fears, for example, that mothers can spoil a child, which happens "mostly if an older baby is fussed over when he doesn't need any attention" (98). Similarly, a "worrisome mother [can be] completely wrapped up in her baby. She has no outside interests or pleasures, doesn't keep up her friendships. She just hovers over the child. Every time he peeps, she jumps to see what's the matter" (98). A huge burden falls on the mother, whose every decision will affect the child for the rest of "his" life. During the first year, a mother who urges the child to eat "robs him of some of his positive feeling for life. . . . If mealtime becomes a struggle, feeding becomes something done *to* him, he goes on the defensive and builds up a balky, suspicious attitude toward life and toward people" (78; emphasis in original). And a mother's emotional state, Spock constantly warns, can be as detrimental as her behavior. "Mothers report that their children's stuttering is definitely worse when the mothers themselves are tense" (273).

This small sample of Spock's advice shows how much parents had to discipline their own behavior as much as their child's. The "permissive" attitude widely associated *with Baby and Child Care*, therefore, more accurately describes its view of the children, not their parents. Despite the prolific list of sanctioned behaviors and prohibited actions, Spock reminds parents—especially mom—to maintain a calm, positive attitude, lest the child incur serious, perhaps lifelong problems. The advice for dad is less extensive and less prohibitive. This attitude exemplifies May's point that in postwar parenting advice, "strict gender roles applied: it was as inappropriate for the man to protect the child as it was for the wife to encourage the adventure" (130). The father must take a role by not taking a role. This is how he can affirm his masculinity, his potential for being a hero, even though—or perhaps especially though—his situation as little man precludes any noticeably heroic behavior.

The Avatar of the Little Man

The problem that *The Court Jester* engages, established at the outset and hopelessly complicated by the impossible circumstances, is how to make the little man heroic rather than pathetic, how to turn his faults into virtues, his social limitations into valorized possessions. If, according to Kaye biographer David Koenig, the authors and producers, Norman Panama and Mel Frank, "agreed that the story's basic premise should be that Hawkins 'tries to be a hero and keeps falling on his ass'" (174), no performer in the 1950s was more perfectly suited for ennobling that premise than Danny Kaye, who might be considered the Cold War's equivalent to Charlie Chaplin.

Like Chaplin, Kaye was an autodidact whose abilities were diversified and prolific. Although he never had formal voice training, he sang in a nearly three-octave range, with a quality that would have allowed operatic training. He also had an acute ear for voices, sounds, and accents, such that he could credibly imitate an array of languages that he did not speak. An accomplished athlete, he displayed an extraordinary sense of movement and body control both in his broad dancing skills and in his stunts, which he performed himself. About the ballet number in his film *Knock on Wood* (1954), the *New York Times* dance critic wrote, "Mr. Kaye is not a ballet dancer; has, in fact, never had a lesson, it seems . . . [but he] is something of a genius. . . . [H]e would have made a superb ballet dancer had he been so inclined" (quoted in Gottfried 211). Similarly, Rathbone, known for his fencing ability, said about Kaye that, "he had never fenced before, but after a couple of weeks of instruction, Danny could completely outfight me. Even granting the difference in our ages, his reflexes were incredibly fast and nothing had to be shown to him a second time. His mind worked like a camera" (quoted in Koenig 178). His control of movement enabled him to move with aristocratic elegance and, with equal deftness, bumbling insecurity.

In this regard, he is one of the few screen actors who was Chaplin's equal, but there are more extensive similarities between them. Contrasting Kaye with the Little Tramp of *Modern Times* (1936) helps reveal common qualities of the two performers as well as the radically different cultural conditions that their performances negotiated. Whereas *The Court Jester* ultimately valorizes the social ethic that troubled Whyte, *Modern Times* demonstrates its bankruptcy by illustrating that being the organization's most compliant citizen was disastrous. At the outset of *Modern Times*, the Little Tramp, working on an assembly line, is so willing an accomplice to his organization that he virtually merges with the mechanical operation he facilitates. Even while breaking for lunch, his body continues to fulfill its mechanical obligations. The Little Tramp thus embodies the spirit of organizational productivity, manifest in a series of regular accelerations, mandated by the boss's voice, which is mechanically reproduced on loud speakers and television-like screens.

The totality of the Little Tramp's submission to the machine renders him an ideal subject to test the feeding machine, scientifically designed to let the worker ingest food with the same speed and efficiency with which he expresses effort on the assembly line. His merger with the anonymous flow of production therefore becomes most vivid when the feeding machine forces into his mouth a steel nut like those he tightens on the assembly line (see figure 5.5). It is almost as though the feeding machine were trying to eliminate the middleman by turning his digestive tract into one more assembly line that facilitates the nuts and bolts of manufacturing.

Surrendering to the organization's social ethic, however, causes a mental breakdown, manifest in the explosion of the Little Tramp's suppressed creativity.

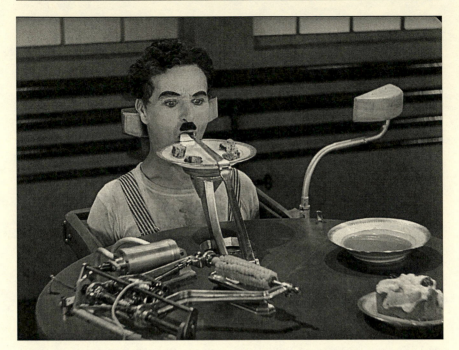

FIGURE 5-5 The feeding machine forces a steel nut into the Little Tramp's mouth.

Fluid, improvisational dance replaces mechanical gestures and twitches, as the Little Tramp creatively employs the workplace devices for the purpose of ludic invention: he turns the levers that regiment the pace of assembly into toys that disrupt its tempos of production, and he makes an oil can, intended to lubricate industrial flow, into a weapon that assaults the agents of the machine and blinds them with ejaculate (see figure 5.6).

This opening sequence launches a testament to the social and economic failure of the Depression, recounting the Little Tramp's repeated failures to be the ideal citizen of a dysfunctional society.

The Little Tramp and the Waif (Paulette Goddard) constantly struggle to find and hold jobs. For them, the prospect of owning a home is a shared fairy tale rather than their claim on a portion of the American Dream. The 1950s, however, accompanying the baby boom with a housing boom and an employment boom, were antithetical to the 1930s. The material conditions, at least for white Americans, of Cold War America extensively refute *Modern Times*'s Depression era critique of American capitalism. And indeed the same social ethic with which the Tramp, despite his most earnest efforts, found himself incompatible, in the postwar period seemed to embrace Americans, even, as Whyte suggested, to smother them in corporate group think and a normative suburban lifestyle. To put it another way, the same creativity that the social

FIGURE 5-6 The Little Tramp turns the oil can into a weapon.

ethic of *Modern Times* could not stifle was exacted from workers by the 1950s organization as the price of security.

In such an environment, Whyte underscored the importance of success on the personality tests that had become a regulating instrument of the organization. "The important thing to recognize" he explained, "is that you don't win with a good score: you avoid a bad one" (449). Safety on these tests "lies in getting a score somewhere between the 40th and 60th percentiles, which is to say, you should try to answer as if you were like everybody else is supposed to be" (449). Therefore, "when asked for word associations or comments about the world, give the most conventional, run-of-the-mill, pedestrian answer possible" (449).

The organization's enforced normality, as Packard saw it, did not incline postwar society toward classlessness so much as emphasize the need for status. Packard astutely noted that while the exploding middle of the middle class ostensibly diminished class distinctions, alternative class markers acquired increasingly greater importance. Packard identified six factors that "combined to establish the prestige ranking of any occupation. And this prestige rank of the breadwinner's occupation, in turn, . . . plays a major part in placing his family in the social-class system" (*Status Seekers* 82).

Status, because it relies on a relatively stable set of indicators, implies numerous codes of conformity, completely consistent with the emphasis on returning to normal and being happy again. Whyte's dilemma, therefore, was how to valorize creativity if, following the example of the Little Tramp, the failure to repress it represents an unacceptable challenge to norms. How does one articulate the dangers of success without disrupting the status quo or making success seem synonymous with failure? Whyte made clear, therefore, that his book "is not a plea for nonconformity. Such pleas have occasional therapeutic value, but as an abstraction, nonconformity is an empty goal, and rebellion against prevailing opinion merely because it is prevailing should no more be praised than acquiescence to it. . . . I am not, accordingly, addressing myself to the surface uniformities of U.S. life. . . . They are irrelevant to the main problem, and, furthermore, there's no harm in them" (11).

Nor did Whyte wish to decry the organization per se. The problem for the organization man "is not a case of whether he should fight against black tyranny or blaze a new trail against stupidity. The real issue is far more subtle. For it is not the evils of organization life that puzzle him, *but its very beneficence*. He is imprisoned in brotherhood. Because his area of maneuver seems so small and because the trapping so mundane, his fight lacks the heroic cast, but it is for all this as tough a fight as ever his predecessors had to fight" (13).

This is why Kaye's screen persona serves the Little Man so well. The bulk of Kaye's film canon, especially up to 1956, involved some form of dual identity. In *Wonder Man* (1945), he plays twin brothers, one a gregarious nightclub entertainer and the other his meek twin. In many other films he impersonates someone who is his antithesis. In *The Inspector General* (1949), for example, Kaye plays an illiterate shill for a traveling medicine man in nineteenth-century Russia, who is mistaken for the Inspector General, and in *On the Riviera* (1951), he is an entertainer who poses as a daring aviator. In three other films (*A Kid from Brooklyn*, 1946; *Knock on Wood*, 1954; and *Merry Andrew,* 1958), he is transformed into someone with a personality antithetical to his naturally gentle, insecure, or meek self. In the first film, a timid milkman is transformed into a prizefighter after accidentally knocking out a prominent heavyweight. In the second film he plays a ventriloquist with a dual personality, whose alternative dark side is expressed by his dummies. And in the third film, a shy English teacher becomes a circus clown. In *The Secret Life of Walter Mitty* (1947), the personality transformations, which proliferate, take place for the most part in Mitty/Kaye's mind.

What makes Kaye's roles particularly emblematic of the postwar period is that these are not ugly duckling stories. Instead of revealing hidden qualities that convert him from ordinary to exceptional, from passive to heroic, Kaye's plots resolve with the hero opting for the ordinary man over the exceptional one. But Kaye's films could repeatedly make everyman, *qua everyman*, the true hero exactly because Kaye had demonstrated he was not ordinary; he could appear dashing, suave, good-looking, and accomplished because he obviously was. Returning to ordinary life by choosing the life that the little man normally was forced to accept therefore became an ethical decision rather than a necessary default. Although this may be read as a false consciousness—the same sort that informed many 1950s television sitcoms—Kaye's characters seemed to relish renouncing privilege and to value being one of the little men, rather than the power elite. Epitomizing postwar Americans, his characters seem relieved, at last, to return to normal.

The Cold War Fairy Tale

Nothing makes clearer the contrast between Kaye's Cold War everyman and Chaplin's Depression era equivalent than the conclusion of *The Court Jester*, which exchanges the forlorn valor of the Little Tramp for the heroic value of the little man. Although the key to the secret tunnel has been successfully stolen and acquired by the Fox, a collapse in the tunnel makes it impassable by the Fox and his men. In consequence the Fox calls upon the midgets, who sneak into the castle to initiate the assault on Roderick.

In addition to lowering the drawbridge for the Fox's band, they take an active role in the battle with Roderick's men. First these gifted acrobats, on ropes hung from the rafters, swing down from the balconies behind large shields that topple Roderick's men. Then Hawkins uses one of the ropes to rotate a large chandelier in a regular motion, while a little man hanging from it clubs those of Roderick's men who are attempting to stand (see figure 5.7).

Other little men line up circus barrels, on which they roll the unconscious knights to the foot of the staircase. There, a little man lying on each step uses his feet to pass the unconscious knights up the stairs to the top of the castle wall, where a catapult awaits to toss them into the moat (see figure 5.8).

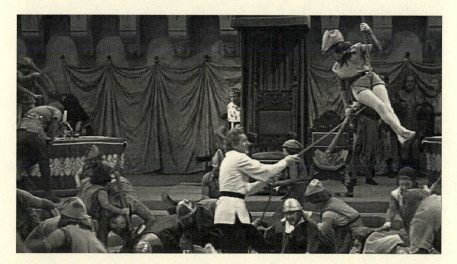

FIGURE 5-7 A little man clubs Roderick's men.

FIGURE 5-8 The little men form an assembly line.

The film's production schedule, as well it should, refers to this as the assembly line scene. The rhythmic motion, from clubbing to rolling to lifting to hurling, makes each of these little men an invaluable cog in the machine that converts the castle from Roderick's home into the royal infant's domain.

Making postwar production a heroic enterprise, *The Court Jester* provides the little men a chance to serve the nation by becoming interchangeable parts of the organization, conforming perfectly, even down to the medieval setting, to what Whyte described as the organization's "belongingness": "What [the social engineers] ask for is an environment in which everybody is tightly knit into a belongingness with one another; one in which there is no restless wandering but rather the deep emotional security that comes from total integration with the group. Radical? It is nothing so much as the Middle Ages" (36). Instead of suppressing their creativity, by becoming cogs these little men prove their ingenuity and demonstrate their dedication to the infant who rules them. As compliant parts of the organization, they at last demonstrate how anyone can be the Fox.

That claim, made in the forest, far from the power elite, preceded their plea for a small place in the organizational pyramid. But because the Fox failed to hire them, they had to return to the carnival, the place Hawkins had left to accept an entry-level position as entertainer in the forest. The film's hierarchy thus places the forest, where the struggle for the nation's welfare is being organized, above the carnival. Desiring a promotion in the forest structure from entertainer to fighter, Hawkins had recruited the little men to fill the vacancy his promotion would create. The story that began with the Fox turning down their promotion requests concludes with both Hawkins and the little men skipping a rung on the corporate ladder; the little men advance directly to fighters and Hawkins to commanding officer, with the little men as his cadre. The Fox's entire organization has advanced, moreover, from the secondary forest to the elite castle.

This rapid advancement also changes Hawkins's attitude. At the end, when Hawkins displays the royal posterior, those bowing are obeying a royal command executed by Hawkins, standing erect, proud, and joyful (see figure 5.9).

His victory, moreover, is not based on the skills he demonstrated as a world-class fencer or a world-renowned jester, but on his dignity as the nurturing and principled person he was at the outset. With the king on the throne and tyranny defeated, he can marry someone who loves his tenderness and suitability for fatherhood, traits that make him exceptional (to her!).

The human assembly line in *The Court Jester* operates, I believe, in direct dialogue with the dehumanizing assembly line in *Modern Times*, by validating, at last, the Little Tramp's aspirations. Converting the disasters of the Little Tramp into the triumphs of the little man, it demonstrates that postwar America has produced the possibilities for which the Little Tramp had yearned: to be a valued worker, to have a steady income, to buy a home, and (farther, perhaps, than the Little Tramp could allow himself to think) to devote himself to his child.

By reprising as the finale the opening song, "Life Could Not Better Be," the film underscores the values that have turned a scary tale into a fairy tale, those rewards available to all the little men who pay their modest mortgages and support their growing families: "The real king is on the throne. Jean is my very own." Therefore, as the entire chorus of outlaws, peasants, knights, royalty, and little men, singing in unison, attest, "life couldn't possibly, not even probably, life couldn't possibly better be."

FIGURE 5-9 Hawkins displaying His Majesty's posterior.

In 2002 Todd Haynes made *Far from Heaven*, a film that pulled off the remarkable feat of simultaneously being an homage to the Douglas Sirk women's weepies of the 1950s and to women who went to see those weepies. Julianne Moore plays an upper middle-class suburban housewife forced to live in the kind of devastatingly melodramatic story she had only encountered at the movie theater. The success of the film comes from Moore's ability to emulate Sirk's excessive characters while still portraying the excessively constrained woman who identified with them from the safe distance of the audience. Like Moore, Kaye can display exceptional talent while making it less important than the modest qualities of the people who watch his mastery. In 1935 William Empson's *Some Versions of Pastoral* argued that there was no true proletarian literature, because works about working-class people either cheered the protagonist's ability to escape proletarian life or celebrated working-class life as a form of pastoral, which Empson regarded as a conservative genre, aimed at preserving the status quo. *The Court Jester*, from that perspective, may be a version of pastoral that does to the white-collar worker what Empson felt much literature did to the proletariat. If so, the film still remains one of 1950s cinema's most elaborate and forceful attempts to address the angst that the 1950s organization and the baby boom created for the little men who produced the most prosperous middle class in the history of the world.

6

Citizens of the Free World Unite

International Tourism and Postwar Identity in *Roman Holiday, The Teahouse of the August Moon,* and *Sayonara*

If American unions, as compared to those in other nations, were neither the most progressive nor the most militant, they certainly were courageous enough to sustain decades of suffering, individual brutality, and mass violence to establish the dignity and value of human labor. While this did not end union busting or state-tolerated violence against strikers, it did initiate, as I have pointed out, a uniquely American class of people, proletarian, in that they sold their labor, but petit bourgeois in that they were paid relatively well for doing so. This group comprised the builders and buyers of automobiles, those who paved the national highways, and those who drove on them, the people who constructed suburbia and who inhabited it. In unprecedented numbers, they bought cars and homes, sent children to college, and acquired the wherewithal for leisure. From this group arose a new demographic, the middle-class tourist. Having some disposable income, the working middle class of postwar America, with the aid of guaranteed holidays, paid vacations, and a modicum of disposable income, acquired what had previously been the privilege of the elite: the capacity to travel. Those able to enjoy newly affordable and efficient transatlantic flights found that the power of the dollar made Europe a viable tourist destination. *Europe on $5 a Day* indeed!

Roman Holiday (1953), made a year before *On the Waterfront*, employs the practice of tourism to reformulate the image of Italy, consistent not with working-class values, but rather with American foreign policy and the international affiliations advanced by the State Department, the National Security Agency (NSA), and the CIA. Whether Churchill's "Iron Curtain" speech created or merely acknowledged incipient postwar alignments, his metaphorical curtain decorated a radically revised map of global loyalties. The complexity of this rearrangement arose from many factors, including the relationship between the free world's commitment to free nations and the commitment of the principal

US allies to restoring the hierarchies of their prewar colonialism. "The United States," Martin Walker explains, "was caught in a contradiction. American anti-colonial sympathies may have rested with the local nationals. . . . But America's crucial allies in Western Europe demanded American support in reasserting control over their old Asian empires. And increasingly as the Cold War deepened they were able to do so not in the name of the old imperialism but in the cause of the new anti-Communism" (61).

In reorganizing geopolitical Europe, Churchill's perspective initiated a process in the United States and Great Britain of befriending formerly demonized countries. Given the enmity that characterized that demonization and the destruction that World War II produced, the political viability of this conversion necessitated a reformation of the cultural imaginary. As parties to the 1949 NATO treaty, for example, Great Britain and Italy pledged mutual defense, despite the recent hostilities (at Anzio, for example) that ought to have rendered dubious in each country the political mandate for such a pledge.

Italy, however, was crucial and unique in the emergence of the Cold War. Central to both Europe and the Mediterranean, it formed a geographical hub in the competition between East and West for the economic, political, military, and philosophical domination of Europe and, potentially, North Africa and the Middle East. Its importance to the United States was further enhanced by the fact that 6 million Italian Americans still had ties to Italy and that the Vatican was the source of spiritual authority for over 30 million American Catholics. In addition, there was a history of American investment in Italy that antedated the war and had increased with the rise of Fascism.[1] At the same time, Italy's unstable government, its active Communist Party, and that party's relationship with the Italian labor movement made it difficult to reimagine postwar Italy as neither Fascist nor Communist, a problem the US government exacerbated through active attempts to undermine the Italian labor movement.

Direct interference with the internal processes of independent countries, however, was one way the United States, apparently with no sense of irony, fulfilled its role as "leader" of that new demographic group, the "free world," a self-named coalition with a self-appointed leader. At the same time, it employed several forms of indirect or "soft" influence, including cultural exchanges and tourism, which was seen as important to Americans' acceptance of Italians as fellow citizens of the free world. This perspective was well articulated by Pan Am Airline's president, Jaun Trippe, who also served as chairman of the Committee on Foreign Travel. As Christopher Endy explains, Trippe often "merged one-world themes with more Cold War-oriented calls for U.S. leadership of the free world. . . . 'We are a democracy,' Trippe pronounced in a 1951 speech. 'Our leaders move no faster than the average American voter believes they should. Thus, foreign travel is no longer a luxury. It is a necessity. . . . Our people must become world minded if our nation is to well discharge its new responsibilities as leader of the free world'" (42).

William Nichols, editor of *This Week*, "used his publishing connections to assemble a 1952 guidebook that emphasized travel's Cold War meanings. If each American made one friend in Europe, the guidebook calculated, 'then it would not be long before the North American Community would be as real and as closely knit a community as your own home town'" (Endy 118). Consistent with the mandate of Cold War objectives, *Roman Holiday*'s travelogue qualities promoted tourism for those Americans who could afford it and served vicariously for those who could not.

(Cold War) Marriage Italian Style

Postwar Italy had the strongest Communist party in Western Europe, and the United States feared that Communist success in the April 1948 Italian elections would sharply set back the strategy of containment. In addition to spreading the sphere of Soviet influence into the heart of Western Europe, it might encourage the radicalization of the (much more moderate) American labor movement. With all the major anti-Fascist Italian political parties having, as Ronald L. Filippelli explains, "formed a unitary labor confederation . . . establishing trade union unity [that] had given control of the labor movement to the Communists" (35), the United States began a combination of direct and sub rosa activities to defeat the Italian Communists in the national elections; "from the spring of 1947, the activity of the AFL abroad, and to a lesser degree the CIO, became indistinguishable from that of the American government" (106). Late in 1947, moreover, one of the first clandestine activities of the newly created CIA was its help in financing anti-Communist Italian unions.[2] "The extraordinary self-assurance and scope of AFL activities, emanating as they did from a private American institution with no official role in foreign policy, could have come only from the AFL's privileged position as a quasi-official partner of the American intelligence services" (115).

The US government also pressured private companies, most notable among them being the movie industry, to influence Italian political attitudes. Given that "in 1949 [American films] accounted for 73 percent of [Italian] box office takings" (Gundle 45), it is not surprising that, as Tony Shaw notes, "film inevitably played a central role in the massive 'state-private' American propaganda campaign to mobilise voters against the communist-militant-socialist coalition at the polls" (25). "In the months leading up to the April 1948 election, the ten leading American film distributors in Italy formed a consortium and cooperated with US government information officials in giving the widest possible dissemination to selected American feature and documentary films on a non-profit basis" (25).

Heavily promoted was *Ninotchka* (1939), which MGM had re-released in 1947 to capitalize on Cold War anti-Communist sentiment. The film, Shaw points out,

> was perfectly suited to the US government's propaganda campaign, a campaign that avoided allegations of American interference in Italian affairs and that reduced the issues before the Italian people to a series of simple choices: democracy or totalitarianism, abundance or starvation, happiness or misery. . . .
>
> The 1948 Italian election results were in all likelihood due more to the Vatican's political mobilization than to outside aide, but were read in Washington as proof of America's ability to influence the domestic affairs of other nations through the use of unconventional instruments, including film propaganda. (26)

Seeing film as an insidious instrument of persuasion was, as HUAC investigations evidenced, a tenet of American political paranoia. In its infamous 1947 hearings, HUAC treated movies as if "un-American" writers and directors could infuse them with messages powerful enough to subvert the audience, yet subtle enough to escape the scrutiny of producers, studio heads, and the hypervigilant Production Code Association. Although the hearings successfully led to the blacklisting of nine writers and one director, HUAC never proved its premise (and in a second round of hearings in 1951 abandoned it completely, concentrating instead on how Hollywood might be using its money and influence to promote subversive causes). Many of the blacklisted writers continued to work using fronts, including Dalton Trumbo, the highest paid writer in Hollywood at the time of his blacklisting. In fact, he won an unattributed "Best Story" Oscar for *Roman Holiday*.[3]

Whatever those who blacklisted Trumbo may have feared, the story seems to promote a relationship with postwar Europe consistent with the US agenda regarding Italian labor. It recounts the romance that develops between a European monarch, Princess Ann (Audrey Hepburn), and an American journalist, Joe Bradley (Gregory Peck), during the two days when she slips out of her (unnamed) country's embassy and experiences Rome incognito, in the company of Joe. These days when she is officially missing interrupt her diplomatic tour of Europe, devoted to promoting the economic and political interests of her country. Joe is broke, eager to return to the United States, and not on good terms with his editor. Having recognized Princess Ann, he believes an exposé of her delinquency will provide him with the story that will restore his economic and professional fortunes. Labor, in other words, is a central issue in the film, in that Princess Ann and Joe both have to decide whether they will do their jobs or take a holiday. Work interferes with their romance and their holiday enables it, so although they are both in Rome to work, they discover it is a venue for play.

Drawing on the heiress-incognito theme credited with initiating the screwball genre in *It Happened One Night* (1934), *Roman Holiday* alludes to the genre,

FIGURE 6-1 Joe finds Princess Ann on a bench.

but like *You Gotta Stay Happy* (1948), it does so in order to renounce it. In this instance, Princess Ann, rebelling against the rigors of her role and her treatment by her authoritarian "advisers," sneaks out of her embassy just shortly before the sedative with which she has been injected takes effect. In consequence, she ends up drowsy and penniless on the streets of Rome.

Joe, finding her on a bench (figure 6.1), attempts to be a Good Samaritan and help her to her home or hotel, but he is unable to glean enough information from the semiconscious princess, so he reluctantly takes her to his small apartment. He sees her photo the next day at his office, replicating the situation of *It Happened One Night*, wherein a working-class journalist seeks to make his fortune by writing about a missing aristocrat. In the course of that adventure, the couple fall in love and, in the end, marry, their union made possible because he will not have to give up his job, and she has none to abandon.

In *Roman Holiday*, however, the aristocratic woman has an important job, as the glimpses at the outset of the film of her whirlwind tour make clear. By promoting trade, she is restoring postwar Europe to an economic vitality that implicitly will insulate it from Communist seduction. For this reason, she must be exempted—in the way that Margo Channing, Lina Lamont, Edie Doyle, and Captain Jean are not—from prioritizing domesticity over professional obligations. Near the end of the film, after she has kissed Joe and wishes to make breakfast for him, she says, "I have to get myself a place with a kitchen," indicating that she would rather be a middle-class wife than a royal princess. Accepting her offer to share a kitchen with him, Joe quickly says, "Yes," even though he knows her true identity. While this potential marriage—placing the princess happily in the kitchen, as *You Gotta Stay Happy* did for the heiress—affirms Cold War gender codes, the principals must nonetheless disavow it. "At the same time," as Rebecca Bell-Metereau reminds us, that "women receive a side lesson on the desirability of domestic bliss over any career, even that of princess" (101), Princess Ann's recognition that personal happiness is subordinate to national interests brings Joe to the same realization.

To facilitate its undermining of screwball conventions, the film invokes the far less threatening representation of female agency found in the fairy tale. Figuratively anticipating *The Court Jester* (1955), *Roman Holiday* in effect says that what starts as a scary screwball tale ends as a Cold War fairy tale. In a formal ball at the beginning of the film, Princess Ann, while hosting dignitaries from throughout the Western world, loses her slipper, à la Cinderella.[4] But in *Roman Holiday*, the young woman is both Cinderella (the captive of evil godparents) and the princess she dreams of becoming. Later, awakened by her prince charming, she also plays Sleeping Beauty, but instead of waking up to her beloved, she ultimately opens her eyes to the work of promoting free trade. Matching her sacrifice, Joe gives her the photographs of their scandalous Roman holiday, thereby making the free market more important than the free press.

In this context, the "holiday" of the title does not mean a ritual festivity (a "holy day"), but rather a secular day off. Joe pretends to be on holiday while actually using Princess Ann's holiday to do his job. In the process, the film seems to demonstrate, he educates an aristocrat about the pleasures of working-class tourism and, by implication, the virtues of democracy. But the pleasures that make her want to be a housewife with her own kitchen are those gleaned by treating the Italians as consumables, characters who facilitate and enhance the way she takes in Rome. By making Rome available to her in this way, Joe shares the subject position of the tourist, rather than that of the working Italians whose living depends on tourist trade. When Joe finally jeopardizes his job by abandoning his article, he completes the process initiated when he pretended to be on holiday, that of subordinating the necessity of earning a living to the needs of Her Highness.

As in *On the Waterfront*, spiritual values trump material interests: she must go back to her work as monarch because she is ordained, and he must temporarily abandon his work for the same reason. Even more important, the Italian worker is as inconsequential in *Roman Holiday* as management is invisible in *On the Waterfront*. In Rome, the site of love, play, and empire, an American may love a European whose charm emanates from lineage that antedates Fascism. Her Highness permits leisure at the expense of work, rather than as the reward for it. In this way, Joe imitates US intervention in postwar Italy, which, as Filippelli explains, "allied the United States with the Vatican and the traditional Italian ruling class, which had been disgraced by the defeat of fascism" (xi). Princess Ann's photos, safely in Ann's hands, become travel souvenirs, the product of

FIGURE 6-2 The photos of Rome, safely in Ann's hands.

vacationing in an American tourist venue: Italy of the Roman Empire and the Renaissance (see figure 6.2).

The Cold War Tourist on Holiday

Tourism, a multifarious instrument of Cold War containment, augmented the Marshall Plan with private dollars and personal bonds. For this reason, the government "dedicated a section of the Marshall plan to arrange group tours, lobby for cheaper ship and air fare, and provide free marketing services to travel companies" (Endy 33). Speaking about the role of American tourism in postwar France, Christopher Endy describes a set of objectives that applied as well to Italy: "During the Cold War, major issues in U.S.-French relations included France's postwar reconstruction, the building of an anti-Communist 'Atlantic Community,' and often acrimonious negotiations on political, cultural, and economic levels over United States powerful influence in Western Europe. Tourism . . . affected all these Cold War issues" (3). Discussing the period's "romantic travel films," James A. Clapp notes that "the beautiful setting of Italian cities . . . hold out to the traveler and moviegoer the promise of romance" (55). Citing *Roman Holiday* specifically, he underscores that in addition to the principals, "the Eternal City had a part to play, as the couple got to know each other in and around many of its famous cites" (55). By accessing Rome for American moviegoers, Joe serves as an informal tour guide for America as much as for Princess Ann. The movie camera itself voraciously consumes Roman locales, just as the

FIGURE 6-3 The princess surreptitiously consuming Rome as a tourist.

camera of Joe's photojournalist partner, Irving (Eddie Albert), surreptitiously consumes the surreptitious princess surreptitiously consuming Rome in the guise of a tourist (see figure 6.3).

In so doing, the camera creates the foundation for American cultural imperialism by bringing home the pleasures of Rome forged by an American workingman for the pleasure of a European aristocrat. The logic of the film thus promotes a startling role reversal, wherein an American introduces Europe to a European, who is discovering Rome on the kind of shoestring budget typical of a first-time American tourist. In this way, Princess Ann can see Rome through American eyes, in exchange for which Joe gives up his income to shore up her national economy: a fair trade agreement.

As Dina Smith astutely points out,

The American film viewer desires unlimited access to foreign markets and consumables but also a distinct Rome or Europe to consume. A Rome and/or a Paris cannot remain unique once it has become an American tourist mecca, once its markets have been absorbed.

Roman Holiday comments on this conundrum when it rhetorically mimes a tourist documentary and thereby reminds us of the relationship between film consumership and tourism. As we follow Hepburn and Peck's characters through the city, Rome becomes yet another European destination, a two-hour stop for tourists (with the same ticky-tacky shops that could be in any city, anywhere). (47)

The film ends with Princess Ann, returned to her regal role, greeting the press in a section of her embassy. Seeing Joe amid the gathered reporters, she realizes for the first time that the prospect of their marriage was based on *mutual* deception. She also discovers what the audience has known from the outset: the amount of power an American workingman can hold over European royalty. By sacrificing the photos, therefore, he is submitting himself to the tradition of European aristocracy by converting his workday into a holiday, in the secular sense, which the ceremonial gathering in the Vatican-like setting of the embassy transforms into a "holy day" (see figure 6.4).

A few years earlier, this merger of holiday and holy day in the interest of tourism had occurred when, "teaming with the Vatican, Italian officials had

FIGURE 6-4 The Vatican-like setting of the embassy.

declared 1950 a 'Holy Year' and benefited from thousands of American and foreign tourists" (Endy 108). *Roman Holiday* thus does some of the same cultural
work as the Roman epic films of the period, such as *Quo Vadis*, which similarly
reject Fascist Rome by converting Rome into a holy city, a conversion effected in
Roman Holiday, as in *On the Waterfront*, through the working class's renunciation
of material interests.

The terms of endearment that the film negotiates, ordained by the prerogatives of American tourists and sanctified by the authority of the Vatican, also
served the important Cold War effort of forging a (Western) bloc out of diverse
states, whose relations only a few years earlier had been characterized by enmity
rather than affiliation. As part of the Cold War reimagining of friend and foe,
the United States embraced Great Britain, despite the UK's philosophy of social
welfare, which typified the kind of economic agenda HUAC wished to combat.

Giving a Lift to the Germans

If American movies, as surrogate tourists, facilitated citizenship in the free
world, constructing a congenial space in American thought for the most vilified Axis countries, Germany and Japan, was more difficult. The enmity that
characterized more than a decade of German and Japanese demonization, com-
pounded by the postwar revelation of atrocities, demanded a radical reformation of the American cultural imaginary.

The first test of this reformation was the Berlin Airlift. On July 24, 1948, the
Soviet occupying forces blockaded all roads leading from West Germany to West
Berlin, creating what has been called the first confrontation of the Cold War.
Rather than cede Berlin to the Soviets, the United States mounted an airlift. "In
the traditional narratives of the Early Cold War," Carolyn Eisenberg explains, "the
East-West confrontation appears to be the defining moment. According to these
accounts, Stalin had chosen to starve the city into submission but the courageous Western powers, spearheaded by the United States, reacted fiercely. . . .
Truman had sent the planes: huge C54s landing on the outskirts of Berlin every
two minutes. The action is immortalized in the still distributed photographs of
hungry Berliners looking to the sky as the planes swooped into Tempelhof airport,
carrying food and fuel to get them through the winter" (176).[5] This remarkable
expenditure of money and effort, certainly not anticipated by Stalin, lasted eleven
months and ended with Stalin's reopening of the Western arteries to Berlin.

What makes the airlift so striking was that Americans began rescuing Germans at the same time that the United States was condemning them in the
last of the Nuremberg War Trials. On October 16, 1946, ten Germans convicted
by an international tribunal were hanged in Nuremberg for their war crimes.
These executions, the result of a trial that lasted over ten months, were followed
by a dozen lower profile trials, averaging eight months each, resulting in 142

convictions and 13 additional executions. The last trials ended on April 13, 1949, 257 days after the beginning of the Berlin Airlift. For nine months, therefore, the American public received news of German atrocities at the same time that it sent German children candy bars and prayed for Berliners to survive the winter.

One narrative aimed at the postwar American audience, including millions who had fought in Germany (and some who had seen concentration camps first-hand), converts the occupation of Germany into a rescue operation, in which the Germans have the opportunity to prove themselves worthy of that rescue. (Over the course of the next four decades, as West Germany became increasingly important to American geopolitics, American films increasingly minimized the percentage of German "bad apples"; the generation of German filmmakers who emerged in the 1980s were far less forgiving about the actions of their parents.)

The Big Lift (1950) illustrates well how early Cold War films, by reconstruct-ing German-American enmity as the effect of divisions within the German population, used the rescue motif to negotiate changing the demographic cat-egory "German" from demonic enemy to valued ally. Against the background of the 1948 Berlin Airlift, it pits Germans open to the possibilities of democracy against those exploiting the Americans attempting to instill it. Filmed in a rav-aged Berlin, the movie complements the *Trummerfilme* (rubble film) produced in non-Soviet Germany, chiefly between 1945 and 1949, that "tended to portray ordinary Germans as victims, and that offered hope for a cheerful, ideology-free new beginning" (Brockman 195). The ubiquity of atrocities in these films defrays culpability by making them seem universal,[6] an approach antithetical to the East German films of the period, which conscientiously condemned Hit-ler and Fascism.

While combining a documentary paean to American technology and deter-mination with a story of love and deception, *The Big Lift* emphatically under-scores its veracity. "This picture," the opening title reads "was made in occupied Germany. All scenes were photographed in the exact locale associated with the story, including episodes in the American, French, British, and Russian sectors of Berlin. With the exception of Montgomery Clift and Paul Douglas, all military personnel appearing in this film are actual members of the U.S. Armed Services on duty in Germany." In laudatory fashion, the film presents actual Americans, in actual Germany, performing the actual tasks of an actual rescue mission. At numerous points the film presents detailed descriptions of cutting-edge tech-nological advances: how to land in fog, how radar is used for air guidance, and how massive supply loads are conveyed and distributed.

In this real setting, two airmen, Danny MacCullough (Montgomery Clift) and Hank Kowalski (Paul Douglas), start to date German women. Kowalski, who had been brutally abused in a German POW camp, is hostile to all the Germans he meets and verbally abusive to his German girlfriend, Gerda (Bruni Lobel). Danny, on the other hand, eagerly learns German, befriends Germans, and tries to understand their customs and circumstances. He falls in love with a war widow, Frederica (Cornell Borchers), who tells Danny that her husband was drafted during the war and that her father was a professor who disappeared after standing up to the Nazis. As the story progresses, however, Danny learns that Frederica's husband was actually in the SS and that her father was neither a professor nor an opponent of Nazism. Her explanation that she had lied out of shame about what her country had done evokes Danny's compassion, and he decides he wants to marry her. The marriage falls through, however, when Frederica's neighbor, Stieber (O. E. Hasse) discovers and discloses to Danny that Frederica's husband is alive and living in St. Louis. A letter to the husband, which Stieber steals, reveals that she is marrying Danny only to be reunited with her Nazi husband, hiding in the United States. At the same time, Gerda, dating Kowalski chiefly for rations and cigarettes, becomes obsessed with understanding American democracy, something she eventually comprehends with enough authority to stand up to Kowalski's abuse.

In the end, the imperfections of the US rescue produce a self-purifying process. Because Nazi-loving Frederica is an unsuitable Cold War ally, her attempt to exploit American freedom, rather than support the objectives of the free world, is thwarted by the "good" Germans. Gerda, on the other hand, having grasped the concept of democracy, decides she wants to help make Germany worthy of inclusion in the free world. In this way, Gerda also educates Kowalski. When Kowalski first arrived in Germany, despite speaking German he refused to acknowledge the language or to treat those who spoke it with common courtesy. At one particularly ugly moment, having recognized one of his former prison guards, Kowalski pursues and brutally beats him. But Gerda's questioning, at first naive and later pointed, combined with her ability to assert her own rights, makes Kowalski realize that he is replicating the storm trooper behavior that he had fought to defeat. Gerda's ability to epitomize American values thus challenges Kowalski to do the same, so that at the end of the film he speaks German warmly to the several workers expressing passionate gratitude for the airlift. He also extends his stay in Germany (explicitly to help break in some new equipment, but implicitly to stay with Gerda), and most important, he cautions Danny not to let his experience with Frederica prejudice him against all Germans.

The film's biggest lift is its elevation of Germans in the eyes of America. By recusing them from wartime propaganda and postwar revelations, it saves Americans from the belief, inimical to uniting the free world, that all Germans are bad. Of all the Germans with whom Danny and Kowalski interact, in fact, only Frederica and the former prison guard are condemnable. The rest are friendly, appreciative, and in many cases very helpful, despite their meager circumstances. In one episode, a woman on the subway attempts to smuggle coffee into the Russian sector. While the Russian soldiers, one of whom smells the coffee, are inspecting the train passengers, a German man tells the woman to hide the coffee in her hat, but when the Russian soldier returns, he reveals where the coffee is hidden, so that the soldier can confiscate it.

By 1950 the perfidious, authoritarian German had become a cinematic cliché. After the Russian soldiers leave, however, the man reveals a dozen bags of coffee hidden under his overcoat and gives two to the woman who had her bag confiscated. If the man exploited the German stereotype in order to trick the Russians, the film does the same thing in order to rescue the Germans from their stereotype. In this reversal, the Russians act like Nazis, and the Germans (former Nazis?) stand in for all those Europeans who endured Nazi occupation.

This episode is part of a motif exemplified by Frederica's neighbor, Stieber. Living very close to the airport, Stieber works as a Russian spy, charged with counting the American rescue planes taking part in the airlift (see figure 6.5). He does so with the approval of the American authorities, who want the Soviets to know that the airlift is extensive and effective. Bewildered, Danny points out, "The official figures on the Airlift are printed in the paper every day. The Russians must see it," but Stieber explains: "Russians believe nothing they see, only what other Russians say. . . . Russians don't believe papers. And so I say sometimes less. That Russians believe. Make them very happy."

Like the man on the subway who employs the German stereotype to undermine the Russians, Stieber also deceives the Russians by playing on their

FIGURE 6-5 Stieber as a Russian spy, counting the American rescue planes.

perverse presumptions. But recognizing that Danny's intentions are beneficent, Stieber has no interest in seeing Danny duped. His spying on Frederica, therefore, differs from his spying for the Russians, because his audience is different. When Stieber tells the truth, the suspicious Soviets are deceived, but the trusting American is undeceived.

Stieber not only exemplifies another "good" German, but unlike Nazis, he uses good judgment. If the Nazis were only following orders, they should have known that they were following the wrong orders. Like the man on the subway, Stieber in his relationship with the Russians satirizes the "good" Nazi by following orders in such a way as to undermine the objectives of the people giving them. He understands that Russian orders are no better than Nazi orders, and he grasps the difference between the Russians, who have incentivized deceit, and the Americans, who have sacrificed to earn loyalty. He rescues Danny, therefore, in recognition that the airlift rescued Berliners: from starvation, from Russian control, and from their own past.

The Teahouse of the August Moon, Sayonara, and The Reopening of Japan

Overcoming the racial prejudice toward the Japanese, which proliferated as part of the US war effort, posed another cogent free world problem. The internment of Japanese Americans, but not German or Italian Americans, illustrates the racial hierarchy implicit in the US war effort. Two popular mid-1950s films, *The Teahouse of the August Moon* (1956) and *Sayonara* (1957), both of which indicate how Japan must reject its traditions in order to be accepted by the West, provide clear examples of the template, in America, for a successful reopening of Japan.

In 1951, when General Douglas MacArthur was relieved of his duties by President Truman, the general testified before a joint session of Congress that Japan, whose occupation he had been directing, was radically different from Germany. "If the Anglo-Saxon was say 45 years of age in his development, in the sciences, the arts, divinity, culture, the Germans were quite as mature. The Japanese, however . . . were in a very tuitionary condition. Measured by the standards of modern civilization, they would be like a boy of twelve as compared with our development of 45 years" (Dower 550–551). John Dower underscores, however, that MacArthur's comments were made in a complimentary context, as a way of absolving the Japanese of culpability for an array of heinous war crimes. MacArthur's intention was to argue that the Japanese could be trusted more than the Germans because the Germans, as "adults," understood the difference between right and wrong, but ignored it. This act of MacArthurism was, I think, less in the spirit of general beneficence than in the strategic interests of the free world.

Charles Willoughby, a German-born, sometimes monocle-wearing major general, who had emigrated to the United States in 1910 as Adolf August Weidenbach, was throughout the war one of General MacArthur's chief aides. (MacArthur used to refer to him as "my pet Fascist," a particularly apt phrase, given that after his retirement from the army in 1951, Willoughby served as an advisor to and lobbyist for Francisco Franco.) Willoughby's extensive involvement with the Japanese occupation helped architect postwar Japan's anti-Communist state. Immediately after the surrender, he formed a rapport with his Japanese counterpart, Lieutenant General Arisue, who had at one point been Japan's liaison with Mussolini. Their bond, based on the fact that both admired the dead Italian Fascist, helped Willoughby construct a strong Japanese anti-Communist intelligence agency sympathetic to the US Cold War agenda. Because they both spoke German, moreover, Willoughby and Arisue could communicate in secret, which facilitated Willoughby's recruiting Arisue to assist in operating a spy network within the Occupation General Staff, which allowed Willoughby contact with former officials of the Japanese secret police, enabling him to gather intelligence imbued with the secret police's anti-Communist bias and to compile information on "undesirable" activities of occupation officials, which he forwarded to HUAC, where the information was used to remove New Dealers from the occupation.

The work of MacArthur's pet Fascist was the first step in what, in 1947, became a sharp reverse course in occupation objectives and priorities. As noted occupation historian John Dower describes it:

> Radical trends in the labour movement were quashed. Plans to bring additional accused top-level war criminals to trial were abandoned. Antitrust policies . . . were jettisoned . . . The purge apparatus that had been used to deny public office to individuals associated with militaristic and ultra-nationalist organizations was turned against the political left . . . This "Red Purge" in the private as well as the public sector . . . swept more than 20,000 union members, teacher, journalists, broadcasters, filmmakers and the like out of their jobs. By 1950 . . . individuals formerly purged for their wartime associations began to be "depurged" and returned to public life. In this milieu, the civilian Old Guard . . . soon consolidated its position as America's new Cold War subalterns in Japan— and, indeed, Asia. (xxi–xxii)

Although Willoughby and Arisue were philosophically well suited to spearhead this agenda for incorporating Japan into the free world, the United States also needed to enlist support for its new alliances from Americans who did not happen to admire Mussolini or speak German. Even at the highest levels of the State Department, the Japanese were regarded with intense racial suspicion. George Kennan "considered the suspiciousness and inscrutability of Soviet diplomats and leaders 'the results of centuries-long contact with Asian hordes'" and John Foster Dulles indicated in 1951 that "the Oriental mind, particularly that of the Japanese, was always more devious than that of the occidental mind" (Borstelmann 51).

Rescuing the Japanese Character

The problematic, confused, and often confusing image of Japan and the Japanese in American popular imagination in the decade following World War II is exemplified by a September 10, 1951, article in *Life Magazine*, "The Birth of a New Japan," occasioned by the drafting of a treaty that would end the US occupation. Announcing that "now, in 1951, Japan has been rescued from the worst consequences of its aggression and defeat" (Gibney 134), the article treats Japan's World War II defeat as a form of Japanese victory and thus turns Hiroshima and Nagasaki into an American rescue mission. As the article, in an unmistakably self-congratulatory context, states, "No other people but Americans—optimistic, expansive, equally confident of their political institutions and their machines—would have attempted to remake another nation in their own likeness" (144). The article subsequently praises Japan's staunch anti-Communism as indicating the positive influence of the occupation. The impetus of the rhetoric, therefore, is to rescue the *image* of Japan, allowing Americans to favor rather than fear Japan's imminent return to independence.

The article thus identifies profound flaws in Japanese tradition and character. It highlights, especially, Japanese inability to distinguish right from wrong, as that blindness, the *Life* reporter feels, disposes the Japanese to America's influence. For example, about the manners and customs exercised on entering a Japanese farmer's home—removing shoes, squatting on clean mats, not acknowledging the host until greeted, accepting tea, and admiring the home's floral arrangements—which typify traditional behavior, the reporter explains: "Here . . . is the old Japanese life, graceful to watch but *dangerous to pursue*" (Gibney 137; emphasis added). Instead of explaining why this behavior is "dangerous," the reporter instead describes Japanese militarism in the preceding decade, implying an obvious connection: the roots of Pearl Harbor lay in the customs of traditional Japanese life. At the same time, the article argues, those customs were at odds with the true nature of the Japanese people, whose embrace of the occupation and of American GIs was "the normal and honest reaction of an extraordinary national character" (137).

That "extraordinary character," however, is systemically amoral, marked by "pragmatic worship of pure success [and] substitution of a maze of contractual obligations for a definitive notion of right and wrong" (Gibney 137). What the article describes as a "steel web" of obligations, commitments, and loyalties replaces, in Japanese culture, any sense of absolute values, as exemplified by Plato or Christianity, such that the rigid web of obligations, "taut enough to achieve a precarious equilibrium" (138), renders the Japanese model citizens "often *appallingly* polite" (138; emphasis added). Away from home, however, the Japanese man "can be brutal and dangerous. With no moral codes to restrain him, released by his superiors from his bonds, the thousand lifetime frustrations of the repressed little soldier boil over. In Nanking he rapes and pillages in the streets. At Bataan and in Manila he kills Filipino babies and bayonets help-less American captives. This is what happens when a Japanese is 'taken out of context'" (141). While the author clearly avoids one implication of his argu-ment—that amorality predisposes people to capitalism—he does outline a set of cultural narratives that reflect the path to reinventing Japan and the Japanese in the American imaginary: historically and culturally the Japanese are morally inferior to Americans, but that inferiority allows adaptability, as the reporter's wartime anecdote proves: "On Okinawa, I watched a captured artillery captain obligingly direct American fire on the position which he had just left. Another prisoner . . . voluntarily worked for U.S. Marine intelligence officers, explaining the locations and compositions of his own forces. Neither of these men thought of himself as a traitor, for there was nothing left to betray. After capture, they instinctively felt that their only hope was to fit themselves into some new pat-tern of loyalties and obligations" (141).

Thus amorality, a product of ensconced culture and tradition, equips the Japanese well to abandon culture and tradition. The test of the occupation, therefore, is the extent to which it can draw on Japanese traditions in order to say *sayonara* to them. The success of this American operation depends on the Japanese proving themselves capable of being rescued from their history, their culture, and their identity. The article thus contributed to a large postwar media effect aimed at convincing Americans to accept a theretofore vilified Japan on the basis that its people were demonstrating they were worthy of rescue.

An *Atlantic* magazine article written in August 1956, the bulk of which dis-parages every aspect of Japan's work ethic, initiative, and productivity, places in a business context the competing narratives that informed the American popular image of Japan in the mid-1950s:

> Japan's great pact of cheap and surplus labor is a disadvantage, for it leads to a lack of interest and efficiency. . . . In all walks of Japanese soci-ety raises are awarded mainly according to seniority rather than merit; and generally speaking, it is more important to age than to think.
>
> A worker expects his employer, or substitute father, to take care of him for life, and hiring a worker is closer to adoption of a child than to fitting the right worker to the right job. ("Atlantic Report on . . . Japan" 19)

As in the *Life Magazine* article four years earlier, Japan seems socially, eco-nomically, and even emotionally retarded. In this way, the rhetoric evokes what is referred to in American history books as the nineteenth-century "Opening of Japan," by which is meant both its accessibility to Western markets and prin-ciples and its emergence into the industrial age, as defined by Euro-American economy and production. In this context, the postwar occupation merely restages the earlier rescue operation: once again an infantile people are being shown a way out of their regressive state into one of psychological as well as economic self-sufficiency.

This infantilization of the Asian forms a central motif of the extremely successful film *The King and I*, nominated for Best Picture in 1956. In this film the British governess hired to take care of the royal children of the king of Siam eventually educates him, as she does his children, by gently instructing all of them in Western manners and morals.[7] *The King and I* thus exemplifies a Western narrative practice spanning several centuries, which Traise Yamamoto describes as the "feminization of Japan": "An ideological trajectory that includes the civilizing missions of the Jesuits in the sixteenth century, the influx of Christian missionaries in the early twentieth century, and the disciplinary rise of Japan studies in the mid-twentieth century. In each instance, Japan has been positioned as the site of instruction and an object of knowledge subject to the West's ideological gaze" (12).

Levittown of the August Moon

Like the film musical *The King and I*, *The Teahouse of the August Moon*, a film comedy made the same year, set on Okinawa during the US occupation, represents the Asians in every aspect of their behavior as identical to their depiction in the *Atlantic* article, at the same time that it makes Okinawa synonymous with Japan. For 1950s American audiences the important distinctions between Okinawa and Japan would have been moot; most of the film's American viewers would have regarded Okinawa as a specific place-name within the generic setting of "occupied Japan." A short promotional film about the making of *Teahouse* in fact treats the film as though it were set in Japan: "Operation Teahouse," the narrator explains, "utilized all the technical and physical facilities offered by modern Japan. But equally important was the natural scenic beauty of old Japan." Therefore, the film was shot in Nara, an "ancient capital of old Nippon," and the film short shows the Nara "local citizens who will portray the inhabitants of our story's Tobiki village" (on Okinawa).

In *Teahouse*, Marlon Brando plays the "Japanese" interpreter, Sakini, as childish and lazy, unable to keep his socks up or understand fundamental instructions from Colonel Purdy, the commanding officer of the occupation post (see figure 6.6). Despite insisting that he is "most eager to be educated by our conqueror," Sakini's inability to distinguish figurative from literal commands, combined with a childish demeanor, render him incorrigible, in consequence of which he is sent to the southern tip of the island to help the incompetent but well-intentioned Captain Fisby (Glen Ford) modernize Sakini's home village. In every way the village's economic savvy and sense of marketing conform to the *Atlantic* description: "Japanese industry is also weak in manufacturing practices, both in finding out whether there is any consumer demand for a given product,

FIGURE 6-6 Marlon Brando as Sakini.

and in selling the product once it has been manufactured" (20). Thus, at the insistence of Fisby, the villagers attempt to sell handmade sandals and cricket cages, for which there is no demand and which cost much more to make than mass-produced alternatives.

In the film, however, these poor marketing decisions that, according to *Atlantic*, characterize the Japanese, are made by the US military. This would resonate well with the audience, given that over 20 million American men had served in the American armed services between 1942 and 1956. Typically, these ex-GIs had returned to civilian life with almost comic disdain for military procedures, supported by a prolific array of anecdotes. A popular saying of the 1950s, cited by Leon Slater in his memoir, *Not in Vain: A Rifleman Remembers World War Two*, was "there were three ways of doing things, the right way, the wrong way, and the army way" (54).[8] Fisby's commanding officer, Colonel Purdy, relentlessly exemplifies the army approach by, for example, ordering pointless signs, such as those differentiating officers' clotheslines from enlisted men's, so as to segregate laundry by rank. Each day Purdy counts the laundry in French, because the army taught him French in preparation for the invasion of Europe, then assigned him to Okinawa. Giving Fisby "Plan B," a book produced in Washington "pertaining to the welfare and recovery of these villages," Purdy tells Fisby: "You don't even have to think, Captain. This document relieves you of that responsibility." Having been in the paper box business before the war, Purdy admits to Fisby that he knew nothing about foreigners, but "my job is to teach them democracy, and they're gonna learn democracy if I have to shoot every one of them." The US military in this film is everything that the occupation did *not* desire the Japanese to become: it is not competent, and it is not democratic.

The village starts to prosper, therefore, not when Fisby follows Plan B, but when he is seduced by Japanese manners. Instead of building a schoolhouse with the materials supplied by the military, he builds a teahouse (see figure 6.7), which he populates with the village women who, rather than abandon their Japanese traditions, epitomize them by learning to become geishas (see figure 6.8).

The villagers facilitate their conversion from impoverished peasants to those enjoying the lifestyle associated with teahouses and geishas by selling to army bases the moonshine the village has for centuries produced for its own consumption. When Colonel Purdy uncovers these practices, he orders the teahouse and the whisky still to be destroyed, only to discover that US congressmen about to arrive at the village regard its conversion as a model of successful

FIGURE 6-7 Teahouse built with the materials supplied by the military.

FIGURE 6-8 The village women learning to become geishas.

occupation. Standing on the site of the demolished teahouse, with the arrival of the congressmen immanent, Purdy believes his career is over, when he is informed by Sakini that the stills were not destroyed but hidden, and that the teahouse was disassembled but not demolished, as proven by the fact that, in a matter of minutes, the villagers reassemble it (see figure 6.9).

This scene is extremely revelatory in several ways. First, it illustrates that the Japanese are efficient and productive workers. The reconstruction of the teahouse, moreover, replicates in microcosm the Levittown-like, assembly-line production of housing that made possible postwar America's affordable suburban lifestyle, suggesting how much the Japanese are actually like the Americans (see figure 6.10).

FIGURE 6-9 The villagers reassembling the teahouse.

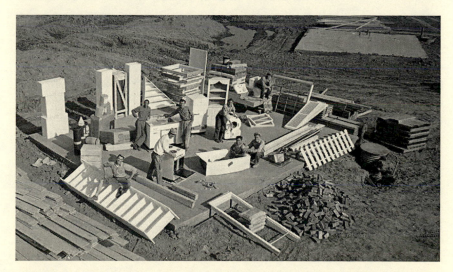

FIGURE 6-10 The reconstruction replicates the Levittown-like, assembly-line production.

Finally, the fact that this Japanese village prospers from leisure activities allays anxiety over the possibility that a democratic Japan will be an industrial rival to the United States, in the way that it had been a formidable military rival in the preceding decade. Following the implicit prescription for rescue outlined in *Life Magazine*, traditional Japanese amorality and duplicity are channeled into a production line and lifestyle for which the postwar, American middle class serves as the model.

Thus, in the process of deprecating Japanese business practices, the *Atlantic* article mentions that "some companies keep as many as three sets of books: one for themselves, one for their investors, and one for the government" (20), a practice actually indicating a shrewd business sense, one exactly analogous to the villagers' action, in *Teahouse*, of officially destroying the stills while secretly hiding them. That is one example among many demonstrating the villagers' ingenuity, cunningly disguised as the incompetence that Sakini, especially from the perspective of Colonel Purdy, appears to manifest.

Even more telling is the *Atlantic* article's attempt to disguise the success of Japanese business that belies the article's pervasive critique: "For the Japanese cannot continue to expect to increase annual exports to America by 62 per cent, as they did last year . . . without making concessions in return. An example is the marked increase in exports of Japanese sewing machines to America—100 per cent in one recent *month*—while at the same time the Japanese vigorously deny American sewing machine companies an entry into the Japanese market" (22; emphasis added).

The complaint here relates to the superiority of Japanese business and the way that Japanese trade policies place the United States in the supplicant position, a reversal rather than a restaging of Perry's "Opening of Japan." The complaint, moreover, would be meaningless if the article's pervasive critique of Japanese business practices were valid. To reconcile this contradiction, the article, as does *Teahouse*, evokes the term "democracy": "It is not likely that Japan can make further improvements in Japanese industrial production without introducing industrial democracy and a more truly competitive pattern of life" ("Atlantic Report on . . . Japan" 22). The Japanese, in other words, should compete with one another rather than with the United States. In the Cold War model, democracy means following the self-proclaimed "Leader of the Free World," not competing with it. And in the parlance of containment, about which I have written extensively, the battle to defeat Communism was waged not only at the economic, military, and geopolitical levels, but at the lifestyle level as well.[9] "Baseball," Ian Buruma points out, "was encouraged [during the Occupation] as an intrinsically democratic game" (134). The *Life Magazine* article similarly points out in regard to the occupation, "Baseball was of course democratic" (Gibney 147).

Geishas of the Free World: Unite!

A *Time magazine* article thus praises the Japanese for developing housing structures along the Western model: "The apartment house has become not only a place to live but also a new way of life" ("Life with a Key" 42). This new way of life, connected to a government-sponsored housing program and headed by a seventy-two-year-old banker, Hishaakira Kano, includes central heating, gas stoves, stainless steel sinks, and tables with legs. The apartment doors have Western-style locks with "Yale-type keys." Kano tells *Time* "This flat piece of metal is wonderful. It gives us privacy and security" (42). "Adds waspish Banker [sic] Kano: 'The key will emancipate wives. Their husbands will now have no good excuses for leaving them at home and going off alone to the geisha house'" (42).

This fascinating conclusion to the article conflates social and economic progress in Japan, defining the amalgam in terms of postwar American middle-class domestic values. People with a rudimentary understanding of technology (amazed by the wonders of the "flat piece of metal" called a "door key") and with a commensurately dubious sense of family values (by Western standards), under the leadership of a wasp-like capitalist, can learn to relate the ability to protect one's property to the superiority of the nuclear family, which privileges togetherness over socially and spatially divided gender activities. Lynn Spigel notes, "In 1954, *McCall's Magazine* coined the term 'togetherness'," pointing out that the term "shows the importance attached to family unity during the postwar years" and that "[H]ome magazines primarily discussed family life in language organized around spatial imagery. . . . In fact, the spatial organization of the home was presented as a set of scientific laws through which family relationships could be calculated and controlled" (37). In adopting the spatial arrangements and the incumbent controls that such arrangements impel, Japan takes another step away from tradition and toward democracy. As the *Life Magazine* article (Gibney) made clear, Japan's capacity for democracy depends on changing its culture and lifestyle.

The cultural work being performed by *The Teahouse of the August Moon* interestingly coalesces its merger of technology, capitalism, and white, middle-class Western morality around the problematic figure of the geisha, a person whose alleged allure is chiefly to people who eat on the floor and are amazed by door keys. Yet the basic point that *Teahouse* makes is that the geisha and the Japanese lifestyle are alluring rather than retrograde. Fisby does not instruct the Japanese, but rather the Japanese instruct him; democracy does not mean eliminating the geisha, but making her services accessible to more men and making her appearance and performance skills accessible to more women.

The embrace of the geisha's fashion and talents therefore entails rejecting her profession, which makes her role discrete from that of the wife. If wives

FIGURE 6-11 The lush travelogue highlighting Japanese performance arts.

learn to perform as geishas, then as the geisha becomes democratized, the geisha profession becomes obsolete. In *Teahouse*, therefore, when the village housewives demand to learn the geisha's skills, they are following the rescue plan outlined by *Life Magazine*, that is, celebrating their tradition by eliminating it. Rejection of the professional geisha and the sexual license she provided Japanese men not only democratized the housewife, to the extent that the 1950s American housewife typified democracy, but also removed the threat that the geisha lifestyle posed to 1950s American masculinity, which was circumscribed by the puritanical norms of Cold War America, for the gendered narrative that placed Japan in the feminine position was, as Yamamoto points out, central to the West's acceptance of Japan: "[T]he feminization Japan functions in relation to the masculinized West in the same was as the stereotype of the Japanese woman functions in relation to the white Western male. Both relations are inscribed by overdetermined patterns of submission and domination in which race and gender difference mark the boundaries of the orientalized other in a manner that both "invites" access and allows erasure of the threatening Japanese other gendered as male" (22).

The sexual dynamics of this relationship are paramount, as underscored by the way they connect *Teahouse* to Brando's next film, named, ironically, with the word he speaks to conclude *Teahouse*: "Sayonara." The 1958 film *Sayonara*, a serious melodrama, was at the time the fifteenth highest grossing film in the history of American cinema. This film, also about the seductive power of the Japanese performing artist, focuses on the US military's prohibition against marrying Japanese women, a regulation that was in place in 1950, the moment in which the film is set, but had long been rescinded by 1958, when the film was made. In effect, it is about what kinds of negotiations are necessary, by 1958, to make the Japanese acceptable partners, given that they had become invaluable Cold War allies. Hence, it is not surprising that both films attend extensively to lifestyle and sexual freedom. *Sayonara* uses the panoramic widescreen to set the melodrama against a lush travelogue, highlighting especially Japanese performance arts (see figure 6.11).

You Say "Sayonara," I Say "Hello"

A point I developed at length in *Containment Culture* was that the Cold War was a courtship narrative staged between rival suitors, the United States and the Communists, in which it was impossible to keep the genders straight.[10] In *Sayonara*, Major Gruver (Brando), who seems to lack adequate libidinous drive when in the presence of his American fiancée, Eileen, becomes rapt by his first sight of the Japanese performer, Hana-ogi. From both a racial and a gender perspective, his response is transgressive. As the star in an all-female theater company, Hana-ogi, who plays both male and female roles, is initially distinguished by her androgynous appearance. When Gruver first sees her on stage she is playing a man, and later when he sees her walking with the other women in her troupe, all of whom wear kimonos, she is wearing white pants, shirt, and hat (a look that would be echoed in the following decade by Candace Bergen, playing the explicitly lesbian Lakey in the 1966 film *The Group*). By simultaneously epitomizing a Japanese tradition and violating it, Hana-Ogi functions in *Sayonara* as the housewife-geishas do in *Teahouse*. Just as the democratizing of the geisha mollifies concerns over the sexual license of Japanese men, so the Japanese tradition of same-sex theater safely contextualizes American Cold War homophobia.[11]

Gruver's attraction to Hana-Ogi also invokes issues of miscegenation, strongly resonant with American audiences at a time when the desegregation of American society was causing widespread, often violent conflict. There can be no doubt that Brando's insistence on playing Gruver with a thick southern accent underscored allusions to racial conflict in the United States, of which anti-Japanese racism at the time was a typical, albeit not pervasive, example. "The concentration on racial difference in the film can only serve to comment on internal American politics and the race laws of the time" (McIlroy 134). While calling attention to racism, the casting nonetheless adheres to the racial prohibitions of US history and culture, which tacitly recognized male relations with nonwhites, as evidenced by the open acknowledgment of slaves fathered by their owners, but vilified sexual relations between black males and white females to such an extent that, even as late as the 1950s, a black male could put his life in jeopardy simply by looking at a white woman in a manner deemed "improper."

In this regard, *Sayonara* adheres to the standard pattern of 1950s race casting: Gruver and Joe Kelly (Red Buttons), an enlisted man in his unit, are white actors playing men who love Asian women. In the (less explicit) relationship between Eileen, played by British actress Patricia Owens, and Nakamura, the star of the all-male Kabuki theater, Nakamura is not played by a Japanese man, but by white actor Ricardo Montalban.[12] In the same way that the casting of Nakamura avoids violating racial taboos, the script avoids gender transgressions. While Nakamura, like Hana-ogi, could evoke homophobia because he plays cross-gendered roles in a single-sex theater company (see figure 6.12), he explicitly affirms his heterosexuality by expressing his attraction to Marilyn Monroe.

Costume is very important in both *Teahouse* and *Sayonara* because the Asian outfit, which Brando dons (along with the customs of taking off his shoes and of sitting on the floor) in the same way that Fisby does in *Teahouse*, serves as the exotic alternative to the occupying military uniform. Thus the allure of the Asian focuses the erotics of transgression evoked but also strictly prohibited in the homosocial environment of the US military. These echoes of homoerotics and homophobia frame the way the film establishes the conditions under which one may succumb to the transgressive attraction of Japan. In contradistinction to Gruver, Kelly marries a Japanese woman and adopts the Japanese

FIGURE 6-12 Nakamura playing cross-gendered roles in a single-sex theater company.

lifestyle, so much so that when he is ordered back to the United States without his bride, Kelly and his wife, Katsumi (Myoshi Umeki), commit suicide, replicating the theme of a Japanese puppet show they had attended. At the puppet show, Kelly objects to the story of the two lovers committing suicide, but Katsumi explains that it means they will be together for eternity, a proposition he apparently comes to accept.

In this way Kelly, instead of helping to democratize Japan, gives up his life to endorse prewar Japanese beliefs associated with practices of hara-kiri and kamikaze. The difference in Japanese and Western attitudes toward the value of human life, which suicide signified, was often evoked in the United States to justify the use of atomic bombs on Hiroshima and Nagasaki. In a logic of self-justification, the use of nuclear weapons was not the product of Western indifference to Asian life, but rather the logical extension of Asian attitudes and beliefs. Because these beliefs were inimical to democracy, Kelly and Katsumi by committing suicide in effect join those killed in the war's extensive bombing—nuclear and conventional—as victims of Japan's suicidal tradition.

Among those victims of tradition and/or bombing was Hana-ogi's father, which had caused her to hate Americans, but as she explains to Gruver, while he has been (obsessively) watching her, she has also been watching him; realizing that he does "not look like a savage," she asks his forgiveness. By looking at him, in other words, she comes to understand that her anger about her father's death is actually guilt about her prejudice toward Americans, a guilt not caused by the white man's appearance, but rather dispelled by it. The ameliorative quality of whiteness is consistent with the idea that the war was a rescue operation, one that requires a reevaluation of Japanese traditions, something of which Hana-ogi is uniquely capable. Through her array of costumes, on stage, among her theater troupe, and with Gruver, Hana-ogi demonstrates that she is not bound by tradition. As Brian McIlroy points out, "as such costume changes suggest, she is—like

Japan itself—both old and new, in constant flux, a prize for the Americans to capture and control" (133). Gruver thus can couple his proposal to Hana-ogi with her rejection of the traditions that connect her family honor to remaining a permanent, unmarried member of the Mitsubayashi opera company, conditions that she at first rejects and then accepts, whereupon the film comes to an abrupt ending with Gruver, pressed by journalists for a quote, saying "Sayonara."

Our Holiday Vacation Complete, We Bid a Fond Farewell to Old Japan

When we couple the endings of these two films, made back to back by Brando, we see that he says farewell to Japanese tradition from both the subject position of the occupied and of the occupier, in both cases acknowledging admiration for Japan in exchange for Japan's farewell, in its own words, to its own past: "Sayonara."

7

Expedient Exaggeration
and the Scale of Cold War Farce
in *North by Northwest*

*N*orth by Northwest (1959) contains a stunning and also frustrating God's-eye-view of Roger Thornhill fleeing the UN building, immediately after he has been photographed standing, with a bloody knife in his hand, over the corpse of Lester Townsend. In a compilation of confusions typical of bedroom farce, Thornhill has by this relatively early point in the film been misrecognized, misunderstood, or disbelieved by almost everyone he has encountered, from the thugs working for Vandamm (the head of an international espionage ring), to the Glen Cove police, to the room service staff at the Plaza Hotel, to his own mother.

In the tradition of classic farce, the film generates momentum from the mounting frustration produced by the collision between what perception confirms and memory denies. Thornhill remembers being kidnapped, being force-fed a bottle of bourbon at the Townsend estate, and being forced to drive an automobile with nearly fatal consequences. The ostensible Mrs. Townsend, when questioned by the police the next day, confirms Thornhill's memory of the Townsend estate, but insists he was an intoxicated dinner guest who left early, in the same way that Vandamm, as the ostensible Mr. Townsend, had insisted the night before that Thornhill "remember" he is CIA operative George Kaplan.

Comedy and Madness

As many have noted—associating it with black humor or, following Stanley Cavell, a comedy of remarriage—*North by Northwest* has a strong comic component.[1] None of these discussions, however, has pointed out more specifically that *North by Northwest* is a *farce*. Dating from antiquity, farce is one of the most enduring forms of comic drama. It relies on misconceptions, mistaken identities, and the mayhem endemic to a world that seems to have lost its mind, for which reason, honesty, or morality provide no antidotes. Rather, farce functions much like the Derridian *pharmakon*, its own internal logic mandating toxic behavior as the only remedy for a toxified reality. Thus farce becomes, in Maurice Charney's words, "a comedy with an extravagant plot in which anything can happen" (97). This is because farce, as Albert Bermel explains, "deals with the unreal, the worst one can dream or dread. Farce is cruel, often brutal, even murderous" (21). In its efforts to forestall the cruel, the brutal, or the murderous, "the conventional device for creating farcical instability is a profusion of stage exits and entrances, swiftly executed" (33); therefore the character in a farce, John Dennis Hurrell notes, "is barely conscious that he is a moral creature; he is always conscious that he is a thinking, devising creature" (214). "One might argue," Hurrell explains "that farce, with its temporary reversal of the well-ordered and morally directed world, is a kind of assertion of man's continual capacity for setting his house in order through the ingenious use of his capacity to make practical, rather than ethical decisions" (214).

But in a farce those "practical" decisions are made in the process of dealing with a world that seems to have gone mad. The central character, therefore, resembles Hamlet when he utters the phrase to which *North by Northwest*'s title alludes: "I am but mad north-north-west. When the wind is southerly I know a hawk from a hand-saw" (act 2, sc. 2). Doubting the sanity of the world into which he has been plunged by a ghost appearing to be his father, Hamlet forestalls making an ethical decision by making the practical decision to feign madness, lest he be deceived by a case of mistaken identity. ("The spirit that I have seen/ May be a devil," he states, "and the devil hath power/ T'assume a pleasing shape" [act 2, sc. 2].) [2]

That the devil in *North by Northwest* has that power is certainly exemplified by the casting of the handsome, suave James Mason to play the role of the demonic Vandamm. His calm self-assurance perfectly sets the pitch for the farcical opening episode of the film, in which, true to the ethos of farce, everyone is a victim. Advertising executive Roger Thornhill, during a business meeting in a cocktail lounge at the Plaza Hotel, attempts to signal the bellboy so that he can send a telegram. He makes the signal, however, at exactly the moment that the boy is paging a "George Kaplan." This leads two thugs to mistake Thornhill for Kaplan and therefore to kidnap him. They take him to the Glen Cove estate of Lester Townsend. There Vandamm, whom we later learn traffics in espionage, demands to know what "Kaplan" knows about Vandamm's operation; but he makes that demand of Thornhill, who knows nothing about the operation or about Kaplan. Were Thornhill aware of Kaplan's operation, he would know that his identity was created because the CIA didn't know enough about Vandamm's operation. In other words, when Thornhill tells Vandamm that he doesn't know anything, this is more or less true, whether he is speaking for himself or for Kaplan, but a premise of farce is that the conditions that circumscribe speech render truth unreliable. The fiction of Kaplan, we later learn, must be maintained (even posthumously) because, as the Professor who directs the CIA's unit following Vandamm explains, "we don't know enough about [Vandamm's] operation." But when Vandamm hears this truth from the man he presumes to be Kaplan, he is certain the utterance is fictitious.

If these events exemplify pure farce, more generally farce could be viewed as the quintessential Hitchcock genre, especially in the way that "farce brings together the direct and wild fantasies and the everyday and drab realities" (Bently 203). After all, almost all of Hitchcock's films involve some way in which the wrong man is mistaken for the right one, not just as an initiating plot mechanism, but repeatedly, and by everyone. If Hanay, in *The 39 Steps* (1935), is taken for a murderer or mistaken for a politician or, by the Scottish farmer, for the seducer of his wife, Hanay also misperceives others. With nearly fatal consequences, for example, he takes the Professor for the man who will exonerate him, rather than a villain who would kill him. Charlie, in *Shadow of a Doubt* (1943), mistakes her uncle Charlie for her savior, and initially he makes the same mistake about his niece. *Notorious* (1946) is an encyclopedia of misconceptions and mistaken identities organized around Devlin's and Alicia's misperceptions of one another, misperceptions echoed equally by the CIA and by Alicia's husband, Alex, as well as by Alex's overt household (himself, his mother, his servants) and his covert household (the spy ring). In fact, it would be difficult to find a Hitchcock film that did not have moments of classic farce. (Think, for example, of all the bedroom and identity switching in *The Lady Vanishes* [1938] both in the Balkan inn and later on the train, or the fatal farce that ensues when Bruno, a stranger on a train, mistakes Guy for his compliant co-conspirator. What about the problems with mistaken identity that lead to so many bedroom doors being burst open or slammed by the Bates family? And what is the trouble with Harry?)

In *North by Northwest*, however, farce is more sustained and more integral to the film's thematics, I think, than in any other Hitchcock work. (As Louis Phillips notes, "Lies, impersonations, and deceptions. What an unholy trinity governs the textures of Alfred Hitchcock's *North by Northwest*"; 255]). In other words, I am arguing that Hitchcock is using farce not just to reflect the human condition (at least as experienced by the creatures of his worlds), but also to construct a sustained commentary on the historically specific circumstances of the Cold War and the fictitious residence of George Kaplan, known as "the free world."

National and International Farce

Much *North by Northwest* criticism understandably underscores the film's Americanness. Richard Meola calls it "a particularly rich consideration of American artifice and identity confusion" (122), and Richard Millington has discussed it as the exploration of an American character, focusing more specifically on Thornhill's ultimate rediscovery of that character and its triumph over the arbitrary

Cold War allegiances that undermine selfhood. Millington views the triumph of the romance plot as "Hitchcock's answer to the question of whether—and how—American character might be rescued from the constraints the film so richly describes" (143).

Similarly, Steven Cohan, in *Masked Men,* has shown that Thornhill/Grant represents an examination of the American character in crisis. The poster for the film, he points out, which shows a man in free fall, provides a disoriented exemplar of the mid-century professional class, as much dislodged from the film's diegesis as is the character Thornhill from his customary routines or the actor Grant from the masculine image that his screen persona had come to signify. In this context, I suggest that Thornhill's adventure also throws into question the fundamental meaning of allegiance that the concept of the double—be it the double agent, the Communist cell member, or the closeted homosexual—constantly worries within the demographic scheme of Cold War binaries.

Foregrounding the regulatory systems of the 1950s, Robert Corber reads Thornhill's engagement with the CIA, through the persona of George Kaplan, as the process whereby Thornhill serves his country. Thornhill does so by learning to regulate his unruly and disorganized character in a manner consistent with what Corber calls "the cold war settlement," which politicized the regulation of private life as much as it sexualized the political identity of American citizens. "When Thornhill agrees to impersonate Kaplan," Corber accurately points out, "he demonstrates his maturity as an American citizen" (201). Thus "when Eve shoots Thornhill with blank bullets, she 'kills' Kaplan, the man Thornhill has been impersonating, and enables Thornhill to return to being himself. Because Thornhill has shown he is willing to perform his patriotic duty, he no longer needs to assume Kaplan's identity and can act independently without the Professor's supervision" (201).

If the Cold War, as Corber demonstrates, explains a great deal about Thornhill, Thornhill and *North by Northwest* also say a great deal about the Cold War, which, as I have detailed extensively elsewhere, projected a politically bifurcated world as a courtship narrative, in which America figured the Soviets both as seductresses and as rival suitors, reflecting an inescapable duality in ostensibly monolithic blocs.[3] Framed by the trope of courtship, every state was always already potential partner and potential rival for other couplings.

Nothing exemplifies better the failed attempt to mask the dualities of Cold War international rivalries than the UN Charter, written in 1945.[4] "The Organization is based on the principle of the sovereign equality of all its Members" the Charter emphatically states in Article 2, Item 1, in the spirit of which, the Charter empowers the General Assembly to admit states that comply with UN principles and exclude those that do not, the chief criterion for acceptance being that the states be "peace-loving" (article 4, item 1). Therefore, UN members, according to article 1, pledge themselves to the goal of taking "effective collective measures for the prevention and removal of the threats to peace." At the same time, in the same initial article of the charter, the members also accept the UN's role in the "*suppression* of acts of aggression or breaches of the peace" (emphasis added). Thus, while "all members shall settle their international disputes by peaceful means in such a manner that international peace and security, and justice, are not endangered" (article 2, item 2), the member states must also agree "to make available to the Security Council, on its call and in accordance with a special agreement or agreements, armed forces, assistance and facilities, including right of passage, necessary for the purpose of maintaining international peace and security" (article 43, item 1), for the Security Council may decide to "take such action by air, sea, or land forces as may be necessary to maintain or restore international peace and security" (article 42).

The decision to "take such action" is in theory equally binding on equal members, all equally pledged to international peace and equally obliged to pursue that goal. The manner of compliance, however, is determined by a body structured to preserve the *inequality* of its members. Of all member states, only fifteen serve on the Security Council; of those fifteen, only five are permanent. Even among the privileged permanent members, a structural inequality enables one member to veto decisions made not just by the majority of Security Council members, who are elected by a majority of the member states, but also decisions made by a majority or supermajority of the four other permanent Security Council members. In other words, in the interest of achieving a world peace based on the equality of nations, those equal nations must submit to an inequitable distribution of power, so that if all sovereign states, à la the UN Charter, are equal, some states, à la *Animal Farm*, are more equal than others.

Identifying the inherent problem facing an organization of "united nations," E. B. White wrote about the 1945 United Nations Conference in San Francisco: "It is an awkward paradox that the first stirrings of internationalism seem to tend toward, rather than away from, nationalism. Almost everything you see and hear in San Francisco is an affirmation of the absolute state, a denial of the world community—the flags, the martial music, the uniforms, the secret parlay, the delicate balance, the firm position, the diplomatic retreat. Ninety per cent of the talk is not how people shall be brought together but of the fascinating details of how they shall be kept apart. And under all of this is the steady throbbing of the engines: sovereignty, sovereignty, sovereignty" (81).

If the charter's conflation of sovereignty and inequality and the promotion of world peace through the authority to mandate armed action seem paradoxical, they may appear less so in light of the fact that one of the people most instrumental in shaping the preamble to the charter was Jan Smuts, at the time premier of apartheid South Africa. As Mark Mazower has meticulously detailed, Smuts's input in the shaping of the UN used the language of self-determination to reinscribe colonial hierarchies and maintain the primacy of white, Euro-American interests and values through mechanisms of control over the potential postwar autonomy of nonwhite people. Challenging the idea that the UN was primarily an American instrument, Mazower argues that "it was essentially a further chapter in the history of world organization inaugurated by the League [of Nations] and linked through that to . . . the questions of Empire and the vision of global order that emerged out of the British Empire in its final decades" (14). "With the rise of the Cold War," Jessica Wang explains, "the United States turned away from the commitment to international law and international institutions that had been part of American political culture throughout the first half of the twentieth century. Within the Truman administration, early enthusiasm for the UN as a prelude to a new kind of politics gave way to the projection of American power in the face of the Soviet threat" (211).

Hence, the United States exploited its influence over member states and its loose interpretation of UN rules to subordinate UN decisions to US objectives. "Given the weight of numbers, the United States rarely appeared in open defiance of the United Nations during early decades of the Cold War. Despite this overwhelming influence, however, the United States consistently dismissed the United Nations and its mechanisms for promoting international peace and stability, turning instead to American-centered means to wage the Cold War" (Wang 213).

International Farce and Expedient Exaggeration

In light of this background it may be apt that the backdrop for the only successful murder in *North by Northwest*—ultimately the film's only successful covert activity of any sort—is the site constructed to maintain world peace. "In a film in which international relations are seen as conducted in terms of the blackjack machinations of rival cliques of spies," George Wilson notes, "the usual symbolism of the United Nations appears more than ordinarily bizarre" (1163).

In the macabre and, I think, intentionally political structure of the film, Hitchcock makes this political irony—the murder of Townsend at the UN—the logical extension of the bedroom farce at the Plaza where, for Thornhill, the farcical energy of all the initial mistakes, misconceptions, and misrepresentations had, a short time earlier, culminated in overt laughter. Having gotten access to Kaplan's room, Thornhill, in front of his skeptical mother, interviews the chamber maid and the valet, each of whom confirms—in scenes echoing Shakespeare's farce *A Comedy of Errors*—that he is indeed George Kaplan, although he has no knowledge of being Kaplan.[5] Then the phone rings, and Thornhill answers it, in effect confirming to his callers what he continues to deny to his mother. Who else but Kaplan, the callers rightfully reason, would be answering the phone in Kaplan's hotel room? Thornhill has thus simultaneously identified and located Kaplan for the callers, and they head up from the hotel lobby to complete their homicidal mission, while Thornhill, like the man in a French farce unjustly pursued by an angry cuckold, flees before the circumstances that incorrectly prove his guilt actually result in his death.

Because split-second timing is the essential lubricant of farce, Thornhill and his mother enter the crowded descending elevator exactly one second after the potential assailants exit the adjacent ascending one, allowing the two thugs to join Thornhill and his mother. When Thornhill signals his mother that these are his pursuers, she asks, loudly, "You gentlemen aren't really trying to kill my son, are you?" The villains disguise their discomfort with laughter that, starting out nervously, grows stronger and becomes contagious, leaving Thornhill the awkwardly unamused butt of a joke, illustrating that, as Bermel points out, farce "has two main laughter-releasing mechanisms: characters who are only partially engaging, and improbable situations in which they are caught up" (22). The scene in the elevator thus intersects two forms of hysteria—the hilarity of farce and the immobility of fear—such that the laughter proves a release valve for the incipient violence, and comedy trumps terror.

Or rather, as we find out in the next scene, simply defers it. The Plaza episode illustrates that farce, as Eric Bently notes, "is a conception that bristles with menace" (206), a bristling that virtually spills out of the Plaza's bedroom and into the UN Secretariat. Once again all the confusion of mistaken identity and the anxiety of escalating danger play out when Thornhill, in meeting the real Lester Townsend at the UN, replicates the previous night's scene in Townsend's Glen Cove estate, where Vandamm, playing the role of Townsend, refuses to believe that Thronhill is actually Thornhill. Now Thornhill, playing the role of George Kaplan, similarly refuses to believe that Townsend is Townsend. Thornhill's misconception, however, gets an innocent man killed; Thornhill succeeds, in other words, where Vandamm had failed. The moment is pure farce: Thornhill went to the UN because the police exonerated the fake Townsend from the attempted murder of Thornhill, which precipitates the murder of the real Townsend at the command of the fake Townsend, who had attempted to kill George Kaplan, whom he thought was the fake Roger Thornhill. But Thornhill, by being blamed for the murder of the real Townsend, in effect ends up exonerating the fake Townsend once more.

At the UN—and this is very important for my argument—the hilarity in the Plaza elevator is replaced by the violence it has forestalled. By transferring its energy from the hotel to the UN, the film graphs the potential violence of bedroom farce to the actual violence of international espionage. In so doing, Hitchcock brokers an unholy marriage, one suggesting that the Cold War is not only a courtship narrative but one in which even the most innocent ad men cannot keep the blood off their hands, the whole thing—the myth of nationalism and the myth of internationalism, the covertness of covert action or the overt objectives of it, the relentless auctioning of allegiance and the transparency of puppet states, the arbitrary relationship between legitimacy and demonization, the fundamental distinction between hot and cold wars—is pure farce writ grotesquely large.

Perhaps the first indication that the UN was a farcical double agent was the Berlin Airlift of 1948–1949, a tactic actually aimed at thwarting the Soviet goal of German reunification rather than saving Berliners from starvation. Thus, as Carolyn Eisenberg explains, "the success of the airlift obviated the need for further diplomacy" (183) that would have allowed West Berliners to receive supplies from the Eastern Sector. In order further to obstruct negotiations with the Soviets—a strategy agreed upon by the United States, England, and France—Secretary of State George Marshall opted to turn the matter over to the UN, and when President Truman attempted to reopen talks, he was forced to back down in the face of the charge that "he was 'playing politics' and had undermined United Nations diplomacy" (183). As a result, Truman allowed "the State department [to turn] to the United Nations as a means of . . . *avoiding* a diplomatic solution" (183–184; emphasis added). However, when the UN seriously sought "a means of reconciling competing interests, United States policy-makers could see little value in the proceedings. Once the UN moved beyond a simple condemnation of the Soviets, its operations became a threat rather than an opportunity" (188).

The God's-view shot of Thornhill fleeing the UN, which reduces him to an ant (see figure 7.1), shows us how utterly unimportant he is from the perspective of global politics, underwritten throughout the Cold War by an array of actions, often involving UN soldiers.

The individual UN member states, moreover, were simultaneously engaged in multilayered competitions with one another—armed conflicts, as in Korea;

FIGURE 7-1 The God's-view shot of Thornhill fleeing the UN.

counterinsurgency, as in Vietnam; and armed intervention, as in Hungary—as well as covert operations by the United States, the Soviet Union, and their numerous cohorts and subsidiary states, throughout Africa and Latin America. In addition, an intelligence war, commencing with the multinational scramble for postwar German secrets and scientists, persisted unabated for over forty years, organized primarily along the polarities of the Cold War axes.

Perhaps nothing made the farcical relationship between the UN and the free world more visible in the late 1950s than the 1956 Suez Crisis, which began when Egyptian president Gamal Nasser used support for the construction of the Aswan Dam to play rival suitors, the United States and the Soviet Union, off against one another. Nasser decided to turn down the Soviet overture, however, only to discover that Secretary of State John Foster Dulles had retracted the American offer. Like a spurned lover, Nasser vengefully nationalized the Suez Canal, which had been under British and French control and was crucial to their energy needs. In the next three months of diplomatic activity, President Dwight D. Eisenhower, resembling the typical dupe in a French farce, "oblivious to his own administration's confusing signals, sought a peaceful resolution to the crisis, while [England and France] not quite sure what to do, mainly sought a *pretext* for a military solution" (Meisler 102; emphasis added). Instead of finding the pretext, England and France enlisted Egypt's rival, Israel, as their co-conspirator. In secret, the French and the British concocted an excuse—combatting terrorism—for Israel to attack Egypt, but in the process of combatting Egyptian terrorism, Israel happened to seize the Suez Canal. The British and French, as "surprised" as the Egyptians by the Israeli attack, found to their "dismay" that because the hostilities involved the canal, the conflict threatened their national interests. France, posing as a neutral party, wanting only to keep the canal open, ordered both Egypt and Israel to retreat. Although France knew that when Egypt declined this ultimatum, it would have an excuse to take the canal by military force, the plan required France to act as if its ultimatum were made in earnest. Thus, it needed to wait for Egypt's reply, by which time Israeli forces had taken Gaza and most of the Sinai peninsula. This was preceded by the French and British initiation of "a charade . . . at U.N. headquarters in New York" (103), and it was followed by an array of farcical collusions, betrayals, and misrepresentations, entailing, among other things, America's controlling the flow of Latin American oil to Europe, UN Secretary-General Dag Hammarskjold's intervention (with Eisenhower's support), and Dulles's bringing forward a UN resolution to withdraw all forces. "Dulles insisted that the United Nations would be rendered impotent if nations followed the lead of Britain, France, and Israel, and 'took into their own hands the remedying of what they believe to be injustices'" (109).

In all of this, however, the UN was more a pawn than a force, transparently so. Mired in its own contradictions, it had no clear way to reconcile conflicts among the powers whose interests it was created to protect. Replete with spurned partners, secret liaisons, jealous conspirators, and multiple adulterers, the prolific infidelity of the Suez Crisis made the UN the site of cuckoldry and revenge writ large, so that in the end all parties were caught with their proverbial pants down.[6]

In attempting to resolve the conflict, moreover, the UN instead transformed from mediator to peacekeeper. Many were aware that this new role compromised the UN's primary purpose, not by violating its charter but rather by exposing the charter's incoherence. Inherently, the concept of "UN peacekeeper" was self-contradictory, as noted by Brian Urquhart, who as Under Secretary-General created that UN function: "The real strength of a peacekeeping operation lies not in its capacity to use force, but precisely in its *not* using force and thereby remaining above the conflict and preserving its unique position and prestige. The moment a peacekeeping force starts killing people, it becomes a part of the conflict it supposed to be controlling, and therefore part of the problem" (quoted in Wang 222).

Expedient Exaggeration

The recognition that the UN was operating at cross purposes is implied by the stunning Saul Bass opening credit sequence of *North by Northwest*, which presents a series of vertical lines, intersected not horizontally but by lines skewed at 30 degrees to the horizontal axis, suggesting that the film is as much about misalignment as about alignment, especially in that the actual credits follow the skewed lines rather than paralleling the implicit horizontal border (see figure 7.2).

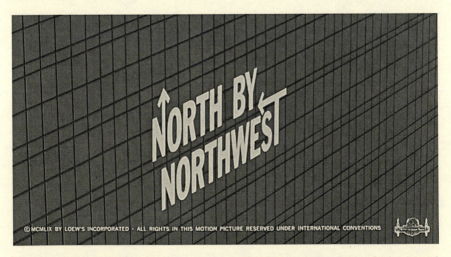

FIGURE 7-2 The credits follow the skewed lines rather than paralleling the horizontal border.

As these credits appear, the green background transforms into the side of a large glass office building, with a façade that resembles that of the UN. As in the shot of Thornhill fleeing the UN, we are high up, in this instance not looking directly down but rather from an angle that gives us a distorted reflection of the traffic of daily life below, the life belonging to individual citizens rather than to that demographic abstraction, world citizen. A shift to a ground-level shot of those individuals provides the final credit shot and the opening action to which it segues: Roger Thornhill rushing out of an elevator of a busy midtown office building while dictating to his secretary.

Even though he is only a few blocks from the Plaza, she urges him to take a cab, and he secures one by telling the people who are about to enter it that he is with a sick woman. Inside the cab, his secretary chides him, "You knew you were lying." "In the world of advertising," he responds, "there's no such thing as a lie. There's only expedient exaggeration." The phrase "expedient exaggeration" importantly connects a convention of farce to the issues of scale implied by the cut from the lofty skyscraper to the traffic of anonymous pedestrians. The sequence's simultaneous transition from the stars named in the credits to the ordinary characters they play similarly signals two registers of scale important to the film. In addition, Thornhill's quip associates him with the character he is about to become, George Kaplan, the CIA's expedient exaggeration.

"Expedient exaggeration" is also a good way to describe the UN's mandate to secure world peace. "The UN's later embrace of anti-colonialism" Mazower explains, "has tended to obscure the awkward fact that like the League it was the product of empire and indeed, at least at the outset, regarded by those with colonies to keep as a more than adequate mechanism" (17). "For Smuts, the Great War showed just how easily the old alliance politics inside Europe could disrupt Europe's civilizing task outside of it" (36). "Nationalism [in Smuts's view] was a real force in the world, and—in his view—a good one in the African context where it brought whites together and promoted their civilizing mission in the Dark Continent" (34).

Furthermore, nationalism requires the same expedient exaggeration as does an organization devoted to international cooperation, because nations need informing myths to unify a large, multifarious population. One has only to consider the quotations from Chairman Mao Tse-tung, Joseph Stalin's revisionist history, or the proliferation of adult westerns on American television in the 1950s to recognize the zeal with which the Cold War employed the principle of expedient exaggeration.[7] Perhaps nothing more grotesquely literalizes this aspect of American mytho-historical hagiography than the heads carved into Mount Rushmore. "Iconic jest," Brigitte Peucker rightly calls the film's concluding scramble across the stone figures (149).

Vandamm, who proves to be in many ways Thornhill's kindred spirit, articulates Thornhill's proclivity toward expedient exaggeration when, at the auction in the middle of the film, he accuses Thornhill of "overplaying" his part. This is another way, among several, that Vandamm doubles Thornhill. Like Vandamm (an anagrammatic echo of "ad man"), Thornhill sells ideas, and like him, Thornhill is amoral. Late in the film, Thornhill arranges for the murder of Kaplan, the man he is impersonating, in order to keep secret the identity of another operative. In order to keep secret his identity as an international operative, Vandamm, similarly, had arranged for the murder of Lester Townsend, the man whom *he* impersonated.

But Vandamm and Thornhill most obviously double one another as Eve's lovers, both of whom are unaware of her double identity and both of whom put her in mortal danger. Unlike the Professor, who lured Eve into becoming a double agent by appealing to principle, Thornhill seduced her, as did Vandamm, with charm, in part no doubt owing, for each man as played by Grant and Mason, to an ersatz accent that converted a signifier of British nationality into a geographically unspecifiable cosmopolitanism. As I have noted, this is exactly the work that the UN Charter performed of masking nationalism through vague, contradictory allusions to globalism. Similarly, the film's spectrum of duplicitous courtships—involving, in sundry pairings, Eve, the Professor, Thornhill, Vandamm, and Vandamm's assistant, Leonard—replicates the play of partnerships surrounding Suez.

Cold War Stars

Because stars, as my attention to accents illustrates, impart to a film an array of associations beyond the film's narrative and the roles the actors play in it, the star is larger than his or her character, at times even arguably larger than the film itself. Hitchcock's use of stars thus constitutes another important issue of scale in *North by Northwest*, a film in which stars abound.[8] These include not just Grant, Mason, and Eva Marie Saint (who at age thirty-four had already been nominated for two Emmys and won several film awards in the United States and abroad, including an Oscar), but also Leo G. Carroll, who had become a minor star on American television (see figure 7.3).

In the doubling that proliferates in *North by Northwest*, these four stars in the end compete for screen space with four of American history's greatest stars, the Mount Rushmore presidents.

Carroll also doubles Grant and Mason in that he too was a British actor who developed a distinctive manner of speaking by tweaking his accent, such that he could have a successful career in America playing Americans. This similarity clues us to the largely overlooked fact that the Professor is as much a rival for Eve as are Thornhill and Vandamm. On one level, the film presents three British actors vying to play the American Adam to Eva's Eve. Furthermore, the character Carroll plays is as perplexing as those of his male rivals, as some critics

FIGURE 7-3 Leo G. Carroll as the Professor.

have noted, underscoring the amorality of the Professor.[9] As Wilson points out, in the film "there is no salient distinction between American and Enemy spies" (1168). But despite the fact that *North by Northwest* has been connected with *The 39 Steps*,[10] no one has pointed out that the Professor's namesake in *The 39 Steps* is one of the most heinously cold-blooded villains in Hitchcock's canon. Perhaps this allusion is downplayed because in *North by Northwest* the Professor is on "our" side in the Cold War and therefore we tend to assume, as did Eve (and as did Hanay in *The 39 Steps*), that the Professor is virtuous.

Just as Carroll's stardom is overshadowed by that of the leading actors, so too is the Professor's role in the film's events. Dispassionately, he facilitates attempts to kill both Thornhill and Eve (and with equal dispassion has Vandamm's close associate, Leonard, shot). This typified, however, the way the CIA actually worked, as it was not populated with flashy, debonair operatives, figures like Cary Grant (Grant turned down the role of James Bond before it was offered to Sean Connery), but with inconspicuous bureaucrats like Leo G. Carroll.[11] Equally inconspicuous was the way it operated, through involvement with a vast number of American businesses, agencies, and organizations that fronted for it, including, infamously, the National Student Association.[12] In regard to foreign policy, the CIA worked covertly, often in direct contradiction to explicit US policy. For example, Secretary of State Dulles made it appear that the United States was not involved in the internal affairs of other countries, while the CIA, run by his brother, Allen Dulles, was the architect of regime changes. When these regimes fell, the United States, with John as its spokesman, played the benign albeit enthusiastic observer.[13] Officially, in other words, the United States abided by the UN Charter, while in effect it turned it into a farce. "The physical resemblance of actor Carroll to the Dulles brothers," according to Donald Spoto, "is startling, and his role, if not modeled on a composite of the two, is at least oddly apposite" (340).

One reason Carroll's performance masked the Professor's ruthlessness was the persona Carroll had made familiar in an iconic 1950s television show, *Topper*. In the title role, Carroll played a good-natured if slightly awkward banker who finds himself the owner of a home haunted by a young couple killed in an avalanche. Topper, the only one able to see or communicate with the ghosts, is regularly forced into an expedient exaggeration of his bumbling nature, so that he can hide the identity of his friendly spooks or perform damage control regarding their unruly plots. Like Topper, the Professor makes an art of covering up misdeeds, in other words, serving to provide cover for US global designs (sometimes, as with the Korean "police action," very transparent cover), exactly as the UN did in the 1950s.

Lest *North by Northwest*'s connection with *Topper* seem fortuitous, it is important to note that the television series was based on the very successful 1937 film *Topper*, starring Cary Grant in the role that initiated the skyrocketing of his career, the debonair and casually alcoholic ghost George *Kerby*. In the film, a drunken Kerby dies in a car crash similar to the one Vandamm tries to orchestrate for the drunken Thornhill, or rather for George *Kaplan*, spook Kirby's latter-day incarnation. (The name was intentionally changed to George Kaplan; in earlier versions of the screenplay it was George Rubin.)

If the "slow dissolve from Grant's face to the face of Mount Rushmore" denotes for William Rothman that "Grant is an authentic American hero" (244), it is because, I think, Rothman has fallen for Hitchcock's trick. Grant, like all the rivals in the film for Eva's Eve, is only disguised as an American. In the dissolve that Rothman praises, Hitchcock establishes the authenticity not of Grant but of George Kaplan, the ghost of George Kerby, who launched the Grant star persona on one of the greatest trajectories in American film history. Like Mount Rushmore, Grant is an allusion to an illusion, a blank space revealed, as so many have noted, by the "O" at the center of Roger Thornhill's logo (see figure 7.4); Thornhill himself stands for nothing.

The "O" also turns his name to "ROT," thereby evoking the usual negative connotations associated with ad men. Cavell also points out that Thornhill's trademark suggests "Hamlet's sense that something is rotten," but Cavell's truncating of the quote from Shakespeare typifies the superficiality of his reading. The full line reads, "something is rotten in the state of Denmark" (*Hamlet* act I, sc. 4). Shakespeare is not commenting on *Hamlet* but on the state. In other words, reading Thornhill's monogram through the film's extensive allusions to *Hamlet* suggests that the state is rotten. Should it be any surprise, therefore, that the name in *The 39 Steps* identifying Hitchcock's quintessential villain now has been given to a CIA unit head.

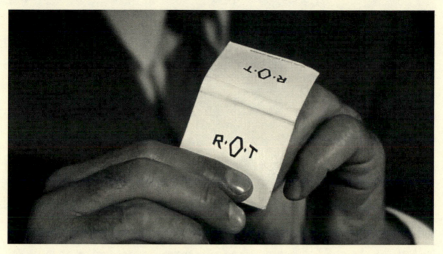

FIGURE 7-4 The "O" at the center of Roger Thornhill's logo.

The mélange of contradictory identities and the tricks they play with the loyalties of the characters and the assumptions of the audience make clear that Wilson is correct when he says that, in *North by Northwest*, "the field of action is filled with a parade of performers who bear a problematic relation to their roles" (1169). But I think this is not because, as Wilson contends, they constitute a metacommentary on the art of filmmaking, but rather because they compete generically under the global auspices of the UN and the duplicity that the free world both masks and signifies.

The commonality of the four principals consolidates at the auction scene, the only time when all four share the same space. The scene is shot by Hitchcock as a relentless array of courtship triangles, emulating the Cold War competition for partners among the member nations, only ostensibly united by their common goals and interests. Grant and Mason, both in grey suits, white shirts, and grey ties, square off against each other in perfect profile, with Eve directly between them (see figure 7.5).

This visual and verbal love triangle is preceded by a series of other triangulations, including one among Eve, Vandamm, and his homosexual secretary, Leonard, and one among Vandamm, Thornhill, and the Professor. The most important triangle for the purposes of this discussion, however, is among Vandamm, the visual track (which shows Eve as the figure of his affection),[14] and the audio track (which features the figurine as the object of his desire; see figure 7.6).

The desire for the figurine identifies Vandamm with the UN's world of international espionage, because it contains the microfilm, whose secrets render microscopic Thornhill's personal affections or well-being, in the same way that the God's-view shot from the top of the UN did.

FIGURE 7-5 Grant and Mason, with Eva/Eve between them, square off against each other in perfect profile.

FIGURE 7-6 The figurine as the object of Vandamm's desire.

The Scale of the Cold War

These shots and the political perspectives they represent contribute to the film's organization around issues of scale: Our attention is twice called to Eve's tiny razor (see figure 7.7), and Thornhill locked in the upper birth of Eve's train compartment compares himself to a sardine.

When Thornhill is deposited on the road cutting through the expanse of western Indiana cornfields, long shots emphasize the disproportion between his stature and the vast, flat landscape (see figure 7.8). The refrigerator in the back of the pickup truck Thornhill steals to get back to Chicago seems disproportionate to its conveyance, and even more so when parked on a city street.

Even the early shots in which Thornhill and then Vandamm first enter Townsend's library suggest that something about the scale is slightly off, in that they show Thornhill's and then Vandamm's full bodies, a portion of the floor, and a significant expanse of the wall above, instead of the more conventional Hollywood shot from the knees up. In the film, Hitchcock's "conflation of cinematic subjects" (the "small" and the "big"), as Jonathan Auerbach and Lisa Gitelman insightfully note, "corrupts the spectator's intuitive sense of scale" (745).

This corruption is an issue of intimacy, because intimacy is a dynamic of scale, in that closeness renders large, as it does a tiny razor, what from another perspective might seem very small, in the same way that a man on the street would from the top of the UN building. Thus, cinema's capacity for the close-up has, virtually since its inception, rendered it an intimate medium. "With the close-up," Bela Balazs wrote in 1924, "the new territory this new art opens up" (38).

In the two-dimensional space of the cinematic medium, moreover, size and distance share a common code, so that being larger makes things closer. Thus

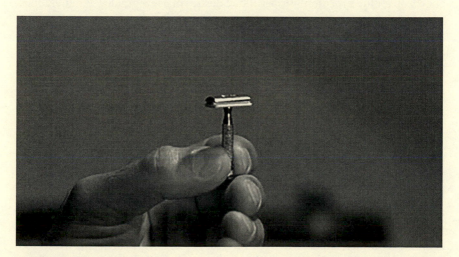

FIGURE 7-7 Eve's tiny razor.

FIGURE 7-8 The disproportion between Thornhill's stature and the vast, flat landscape.

the national and international agendas that loom large at the UN render the lives of particular citizens distant, that is, microscopic, like Thornhill in the God's-view shot with which I started.

The point I am making is that in terms of national issues, intimacy is symbolic and romance is metonymic. One's love of country is by definition only possible as a member of an impersonal mass, while one's love of an individual is only possible by making that individual distinct from and larger than the general populace. Politics and (hot or cold) warfare subordinate the individual to the greater good, to the "big picture," while romance turns the big picture into a backdrop for the expediently exaggerated desires of a few privileged individuals. The romantic couple represents metonymically all the true lovers in the population, while the nation represents symbolically a love greater than individual desires. As Rick says to Ilsa on an airfield of French-occupied North Africa, at the moment in *Casablanca* (1942) when nationalism—American and French— trumps romance, "it doesn't take much to see that the problems of three little people don't amount to a hill of beans in this crazy world." They will always have Paris, in other words, only if the Germans do not.

On the imaginary chart of scale relations that I have just sketched, with nationalism at one end and romance at the other, farce becomes a radical extreme: the intimacy of romance exaggerated to grotesque proportions, in that farce requires a population of individuals with such inflated drives that everything *but* the problems of three little people amounts to a hill of beans. Thus by putting farce and espionage in conflict, Hitchcock is forcing us to view the same characters through opposite ends of a telescope, rendering them alternately too distant and too intimate.

But this too is the way we regard stars. When they are on screen, they are not just characters, but also everything that draws audiences to them independent of the characters they are portraying.[15] In the same way that the optics of the telescope, operating in two directions, allows two antithetical interpretations of scale, stars both fill the roles of their characters and also exceed them. Stars bring to films an *a priori* intimacy with their audience; stardom creates an aura of grandness and a concomitant sense of closeness, both effects dependent on the close-up. "With the formation of a star system heavily dependent upon the maintenance of the aura," Mary Ann Doane reminds us, "the close-up became an important means of establishing the recognizability of each star" (46).

In terms of the issues of scale at work in *North by Northwest*, stars make large the people who, from the international perspective of the UN, would otherwise be reduced to dots. The fate of Eve and Roger is minuscule compared to that of the tiny microfilm. Thus the parallel characters, Thornhill and Vandamm, underscored by the star personae of Grant and Mason, replicate the competition between national and romantic objects by internalizing them. In this sense, we can see Vandamm's conflict as his having to decide through which end of the telescope he should view Eve. Although he eventually decides to regard her as distant and small—his final plan is to throw her into the ocean—his hesitation leads to his undoing. The same holds true in reverse for Thornhill, who despite all the demands that his stardom be invested in a nationalist ethos, cannot resist seeing Eve as the inflated object of a beloved gaze.

These issues of scale, intimacy, romance, and nationalism are powerfully represented in the scene at the auction when the auras of the two stars are pitted against one another. Importantly, in that scene the small figurine, in terms of national security, is larger than anything in the room, except the even smaller microfilm it contains. The very peculiar and very brilliant framing in the scene makes vivid the interpersonal and international conflicts at stake in these issues of scale. In addition, it indicates how both issues reflect courtship narratives.

In a number of the shots we see only the very top of Eve's blonde head at the very bottom of a frame that features the heads and upper torsos of Thornhill, Vandamm, and Leonard. Such framing is usually considered verboten, especially in the classical Hollywood style that attempts to present characters as whole and to obscure the viewer's cognizance of the frame. The appearance of the top of a cut-off head at the bottom of the screen would almost certainly indicate an error accidentally overlooked when the daily rushes were reviewed. But because the top of Eve's head appears in several shots—fourteen discrete shots in a ninety-second sequence—it is clear that Hitchcock is using this transgression as a motif. As the shots change, moreover, that blond head-top shifts back and forth along the bottom border of the frame (see figure 7.9), so that the audio auction for large espionage secrets competes with a parallel "auction" over Eve.

FIGURE 7-9 The shots with the top of Eve's head moving back and forth across the bottom of the frame.

The men, oriented and reoriented above Eve's head, also trope (or are troped by) the final chase over the heads on Mt. Rushmore, again, albeit inversely, for possession of the two "objects" at the auction, the statue and Eve. If the shot from the top of the UN makes Thornhill look microscopic, the shots on Mount Rushmore make the national icons look grotesque, suggesting that in this second struggle the significance of the two key objects has been radically redefined by a world of pervasive personal duality: the two Kaplans, the two Townsends, and the double agent, Eve. The dual scales at work in the film—and in any concept of nations united internationally—are perhaps best represented by the sequence Hitchcock was not allowed to film: "What I wanted to do," Hitchcock told Arthur Knight, "and was prevented from doing, was to have

Cary Grant slide down Lincoln's nose and hide in the nostril. Then, I wanted Grant to have a sneezing fit" (Gottlieb 85), thus evoking an unavoidable contrast between Lincoln's monumental, immobile nose and Thornhill's tiny, animate one, a contrast between the small spontaneity of human agency and the overwhelming rigidity of national symbolism.

Again, as Farce

This takes me to one more parallel. Like the UN episode, the sequence immediately following, at the CIA headquarters, concludes with a God's-view shot, this one also used to mark Thornhill's insignificance on the stage of global politics. The Professor's staff has figured out the events culminating in Townsend's murder, their farcical quality acknowledged by one assistant when he says, "So horribly sad . . . somehow I feel like laughing." The Professor then concludes they should do nothing to save Thornhill, and Hitchcock cuts to a shot from above of the entire board table, while another assistant, the only woman in the group, announces: "Goodbye, Mr. Thornhill, wherever you are."[16]

The concluding God's-view shots of these two successive episodes suggest that the CIA, like the UN, plays God. The shot from the UN visually deprives Thornhill of all identity, making his life worthless; the shot at the CIA, through the sound track, weds him to a false identity that makes his life expendable. In two successive scenes, first the visual and then the audio register renders Thornhill negligible, as devoid of meaning as the middle initial in his logo. Viewed from on high, Kaplan is just another US front, and the farcical hotel bedroom his puppet state. Thornhill, therefore, will serve as well as any one of the interchangeable figureheads upon whom the United States has conferred bogus identities, just as in the end he will climb over a monumental set of American figureheads, scrambling for a small figurine, with even smaller figures on microfilm, in order to return his identity to the human scale of the bedroom farce, the marriage plot, the courtship narrative, shorn of its Cold War alignments and misalignments, consummated in the small upper birth in a sleeping compartment of a train thrusting itself into a dark tunnel.

Hitchcock has acknowledged—as has just about everyone else—the symbolic consummation projected by the final shot. If it is Hitchcock's joke on the censors, it is writ awfully large. It is difficult to imagine that even a full-frontal carving of Lincoln, going all the way to the base of Mount Rushmore, could produce a phallus as huge as the Twentieth Century Limited. At the same time, the tunnel also returns Thornhill to the dark hole, that zero at the center of his constructed logo. Robert Stam identifies that "O" with the arbitrariness of Hitchcock's plot devices: "The espionage of *North-by-Northwest* forms a Hitchcockian McGuffin. . . . The purpose of the spies, like those of the CIA, remains obscure, hollow like the 'O' in Roger Thornhill's name that 'stands for nothing'" (21).

But perhaps more accurately the *microfilm* is the film's McGuffin and espionage its theme, the central intelligence whose agency is thematized by all the intersecting narratives: the Oedipal story (a quintessential espionage narrative), the romance story, the advertising/propaganda story, and the international rivalry story. Espionage is a subversive activity, one relying on untrustworthy allegiances, divided loyalties, and malleable identities. To the extent that those critics who argue that Thornhill actually is Kaplan are right, perhaps it is because this is a Cold War film. Its unity comes not from disdain of historical specificity but from engagement with it. In this regard, Hitchcock seems to be citing Marx, who wrote: "Hegel remarks somewhere that all great events and characters of world history occur, so to speak, twice. He forgot to add: the first time as tragedy, the second as farce" (146).

8

Defiant Desegregation
with No (Liberal) Way Out

In addition to overcoming a catalog of international farces (with very unfunny consequences), America's construction of the free world faced another formidable obstacle, owing to the status of that unique demographic group, African Americans. Race relations created what Gunnar Myrdal in 1944 correctly labeled "The American Dilemma." That dilemma made it impossible, as Mary Dudziak and Thomas Borstelmann have extensively shown, to disentangle, at the height of the Cold War, citizenship in the free world from American racial demographics.

Thus we return to the UN, where the collision between national and individual interests discussed in the last chapter reveals their racial dynamics. Suez, as Borstelmann notes, "confronted the Eisenhower administration with an international crisis that played out along racial lines. . . . Eisenhower told his advisors not to over emphasize the role of Nasser, as the British had, because the Egyptian president merely embodied the broader desire of Arab peoples for full independence and for 'slapping the white man down'" (102).

This racial attitude typified the Truman administration as well. George Kennan, Truman's architect of containment, had a "personal dislike and even loathing for peoples of Africa, Asia, the Middle East, and Latin America. He tended to lump them together as impulsive, fanatical, ignorant, lazy unhappy, and prone to mental disorders and other biological deficiencies" (Borstelmann 50). No better were the Dulles brothers, who headed the CIA and the State Department under Eisenhower. "Descendants of South Carolina slave owners [they] showed little interest in racial matters, [and] FBI Director J. Edgar Hoover viewed the mere advocacy of racial equality as a subversive act" (88).

The allegiance of nonwhites was nevertheless vital to the free world's strategy for containing Communism, so that actual demographic groups—African Americans and Africans—could not be disentangled from that imaginary demographic, the free world. Nor could the real populations of the free world be logically aligned within a field of concerns that included decolonization, deseg- regation, anti-Communism, European free world allies, Asian relationships, and democratic electoral politics.

Even though anti-Communism was both a global strategy and a domes- tic policy, it mandated domestic actions often at odds with US international positions. Breaking with Truman over the issue of civil rights, the States Rights ("Dixiecrat") Party ran Strom Thurmond, at the time governor of South Caro- lina, against Truman in 1948. Linking civil rights with Communism, the Dixie- crats represented states' rights and protection of segregation as quintessentially anti-Communist. If Truman increasingly described demands for decoloniza- tion as Communist influenced, "Dixiecrats, and other white Southern leaders," as Borstelmann explains, "brought that argument home to their own region, attributing efforts at racial reform there to Communist agents" (65). In 1955, a few days before the Supreme Court issued its follow-up to *Brown v. Board of Edu- cation of Topeka* (1954), Mississippi senator James Eastland gave a speech assert- ing that the court was basing it desegregation decisions "on the writings and teachings of pro-communist agitators and other enemies of the American form of government."[1]

African Americans, however, seeing an inherent connection between colo- nialism and racism, stressed the importance of supporting decolonization, even though the free world's success relied on the Western European nations that were attempting to preserve their eroding colonial empires. The strategy of containment, therefore, needed to retain the support of the colonizers while recruiting the loyalty of the formerly colonized. This meant that in the inter- est of fighting Communism, the United States had to court newly independent nations appalled by the racial policies supported explicitly by some strong anti- Communist factions in the United States, implicitly by America's most powerful allies and privately by Truman's policy makers, including all three of Truman's secretaries of state.

The first, James Byrnes, was a southern segregationist who, after leaving the Truman administration, succeeded Thurmond as governor of segregated South Carolina. Byrnes was followed by George Marshall, a "white Virginian whose career in a segregated army inclined him to discount the abilities of African Americans" (Borstelmann 51). Dean Acheson, Truman's most influential secre- tary of state, supported South African apartheid and in 1969 "rued the failure of the United Nations to be housed in a serene city like Geneva or Copenhagen, regretting that it wound up instead in New York, 'a crowded city of conflicting races and nationalities'" (quoted in Borstelmann 52).

For many the UN focused angst about the role that racial demographics would play in the postwar "return" to normality, as it did for Acheson. The US delegation at the founding of the UN was divided regarding the charter's stand on colonialism, with Dulles (who in 1953 would succeed Acheson) fearing that the charter's human rights clause might lead to an investigation of the race situation in America. "The elemental problem for America's first Cold Warriors was their inability to wall off white America's racial attitudes and practices from the rest of the world and its nonwhite majority" (Borstelmann 76). If, as we have seen, the UN Charter did not successfully negotiate the conflict between universal rights and sovereign prerogatives, that failure surfaced vividly in regard to global race relations. As Dudziak succinctly puts it, "lynching and racial segregation provoked international outrage, and by 1949 race in America was a principal Soviet propaganda theme" (15).

With the advent of the Cold War, therefore, as Dudziak has proven, the practice of segregation became an untenable liability for the United States; its demise was a question of when, rather than whether, and certain to be sooner rather than later. Despite prolonged court battles, filibusters (in the 1950s used infrequently but to debilitating effect), vigorous assertions of states' rights, and the active and vocal resistance of white southerners, it was clear by 1950, no matter how vociferously denied, that legalized segregation in the United States was over. This meant that both South and North were anticipating more racial integration than had characterized prewar America, a place where it was tacitly accepted that communities, unions, hotels, and clubs could with impunity bar Jews as well as blacks. (It is often forgotten that the anti-Semitic practices of "restricted" clubs were the referent for Groucho Marx's oft-quoted quip, "I don't want to belong to any club that would have me as a member.")

There was no way out of the prospect that Cold War imperatives would reconfigure American racial demographics, nor any way of explaining the paucity of Hollywood films made between 1946 to 1962 dealing directly with African American issues, fewer than 1 out of every 400. The casting and the themes of television shows in the black-and-white television era, as I have demonstrated in detail elsewhere, were even more uniformly Caucasian.[2] Rod Serling was asked to develop a television drama based on the Emmitt Till incident. Till, a fourteen-year old black boy from Chicago, was visiting relatives in Mississippi in August 1955 when he allegedly whistled (or at least leered inappropriately) at a white woman. That evening he was kidnapped, tortured, and killed. The murder drew international attention, in part because his mother insisted on having an open casket at his funeral. However, by the time Serling finished revising his script to comply with the producer and the network, the story was no longer set in the South, and the victim was no longer black.[3]

The titles of two of the most significant 1950s films dealing with white anxiety about changing racial demographics, *No Way Out* (1950) and *The Defiant Ones* (1958), reveal troubling confusion about the prospect of integration. No way out of *what*? for *whom*? And what exactly *are* "the defiant ones" defying? Both film titles suggest an injustice in search of a perpetrator, a condition that accurately reflects the ambivalence surrounding racism and integration in the 1950s. In the late 1940s the South underwent a rapid transformation from an antination- alist region to a hypernationalist one, something typified by the Cold War rheto- ric of Thurmond's Dixiecrat presidential campaign. Thurmond suggested that America could win the Cold War only by adopting the ideals of southern society. This position provided no way out, in that the goals of the Cold War rhetoric at the heart of Dixiecrat nationalism also required reforming southern racial prac- tices, a reformation the Dixiecrats unabashedly defied. Both *No Way Out* and *The Defiant Ones* deal with this dilemma by displacing the defiance and desperation. Instead of assailing southern racial discrimination, the films represent racism as a function of class and gender, as understood within the parameters of 1950s social codes.

(Not) Showing Racial Prejudice in 1950

No Way Out, made four years before *Brown v. Board of Education*, relentlessly links overt white racism to crime and promiscuity. When Ray Biddle (Richard Widmark) and his brother Johnny are both wounded while attempting to rob a gas station, Ray, believing that Dr. Luther Brooks (Sidney Poitier), the "nig- ger" doctor who treats them, has intentionally killed his brother, enlists the brother's wife, Edie (Linda Darnell), who is also Ray's adulterous lover, to help him argue for Luther's dismissal or prosecution. The irrational vehemence of Ray's charges ultimately foments a race riot by stirring up the fear and prejudice of the lower-class community, "Beaver Canal," from which Edie and Ray come. Their upbringing in this white neighborhood, where crime, promiscuity, adul- tery, and racial hatred fester, is the cause of their anger and immorality and that of their cohorts. Because Beaver Canal names the contaminated corridor of the city, the lewd pun evoked by its name—suggesting Yeats's famous poetic asser- tion that "love pitched its tent in excrement"—seems intentional and pointed.

Because Edie, as Johnny's widow, can allow the autopsy that could exoner- ate the black doctor, Ray pressures her not to cooperate. Responding to Ray's appeal, based on his sexual relationship with her and Edie's loyalty to her race, she complies, while blaming her moral weakness on being trapped by that dirty place, Beaver Canal. She starts to become Luther's ally, therefore, when his supervisor and mentor, Doctor Wharton (Stephan McNally), persuades her that she can escape. *No Way Out*, like many of the films I have discussed, thus pres- ents entering the postwar middle class as redemptive, because doing so prom- ises economic opportunity and provides a repository of moral and psychological stability. It stands for normality; it is the postwar norm.

In the middle of the film, while Dr. Wharton is working through the night, Edie stays at his house, cared for by his black housekeeper, Gladys (Amanda Rudolph).[4] At breakfast, when Edie asks Gladys what she does on her day off, she replies that she sits in the park or goes to church or to a movie, but "come supper time I go somewhere and cook." She fixes her friends "a good supper." Making clear that she has passed the age when she is interested in men, Gladys relishes a maternal role.

Although Edie questions whether cooking for friends constitutes a genuine day off, Gladys says, "I like it. I'm a good cook. Something I can do better than other people. It makes me a somebody." This response underscores Gladys's racial identity by deflecting it. The issue framing her discussion with Edie, the reason Edie is in Dr. Wharton's house, is Edie's complicity (or her reconsideration of it) in allowing Luther to been seen as a black man when he should be seen as a doctor. Like Luther, Gladys wants to be recognized for her accomplishments rather than the color of her skin. That she excels in the domestic sphere, moreover, functions as a message to Edie about how to be happy. Being a good cook and using that skill to take care of others, Gladys explains, "gives me a reason to be alive. Everybody got to have that." "Or a reason not to," Edie responds, indicating that sexual activity does not fulfill her in the way that domestic activity gratifies Gladys.

When not on her day off, Gladys directs her maternal instinct toward Dr. Wharton, as evidenced by her preoccupation with what he eats: he likes split pea soup, doesn't get home on time so it gets lumpy, doesn't like lumpy soup, only drinks milk when he's been up all night. When Dr. Wharton returns home, Gladys gently chastises him in a maternal way: "You're tired all right. That's what makes you so touchy." A little later, with a mother's stern affection she commands him to "drink your milk."

When Luther's wife, Cora (Mildred Joanne Smith), arrives at this breakfast gathering, she too becomes an implicit role model for Edie by demonstrating that a woman's way out of the lower social class is through a life built around domestic service, one that does not differentiate among marital, professional, and communal maternalism. This makes the film, in its historical moment, truly color-blind; in the postwar realignment of gender roles, women of all races and ethnicities, it asserts, are equally valorized by returning to the kitchen and recognizing that maternity, figurative or literal, provides true happiness. As we have seen, Lundberg and Farnham invoked both biological and Freudian "science" to argue that women harmed themselves by emulating men and that promiscuity was inimical to a woman's sexual satisfaction. (Only women embracing their maternal instinct by trying to conceive during sex, Farnham and Lundberg insisted, could achieve full orgasm.) Women without children, therefore, were too neurotic to teach children, as the *choice* not to have children *testified* to a woman's neurosis, just as the *inability* to have children would inevitably *cause* it.

In the breakfast scene, Wharton responds to Gladys like a prepubescent boy. Despite the fact that McNally is the tallest person in the room, the scene is shot to emphasize his subordinate role by having the top of his head lower than

FIGURE 8-1 The camera placement visually reduces Dr. Wharton's physical stature.

or roughly on a level with that of the women at his kitchen table. The camera placement thus visually reduces his physical stature (see figure 8.1) in the same way that Gladys has verbally diminished his authority.

Wharton's representation in this scene makes impossible Edie's conventional role in the classic Hollywood-style plot, that of Wharton's love interest. The scene thus provides an interesting turning point: Edie begins to abandon her prejudice not by redirecting her sexual desire toward an honorable, middle-class man, but by substituting maternal instincts for libidinal. Discovering the value of middle-class maternalism solidifies the earlier assurance that she can "get out of Beaver Canal," the ground zero of all her problems. The film thus defies both the conventions of the Hollywood plot and the expectations it specifically sets up: Edie is not saved by the love of a good man but by the potential of her instinctive maternalism.

Similarly, at the end of the film Hollywood convention dictates that Dr. Wharton arrive at his home in the proverbial nick of time to save Luther, who is being held at gunpoint by the homicidal, hysterical Ray. Instead Wharton's return is relegated to an unseen denouement. In a cinematic sense, he turns out to be neither lover nor hero, the two roles this type of Hollywood crime melodrama typically demands. All the physical and libidinal energy in the film by default emanates from Ray, who channels those energies into hysterically pitched racial hatred. In the final scene, although Luther is shot—albeit not seriously—while

FIGURE 8-2 Luther saving Ray's life by caring for the open wound in his leg.

disarming Ray, he nevertheless saves Ray's life (see figure 8.2), demonstrating that Luther's professional oath triumphs over the effects of racism.

The characters in this film repeatedly bemoan their inability to find a way out: for Edie out of her class and its immorality, for Luther out of the prejudices against a black doctor, for Ray and his siblings out of the empowerment of African Americans, and for Wharton out of the bureaucratic and political pressures that compromise good medical practices and fair administrative procedures. But all of them do find a way, even Ray (who in the end must recognize that Luther, by declining the option to let Ray die from his earlier wound, disproves Ray's prejudice).

The Way Out of the Issue and the Decade

If *No Way Out* demonstrates that defiance can provide a way out, *The Defiant Ones*, made four years after *Brown v. Board of Education* in a nation steeped in the violence that resistance to desegregation provoked, constructs a narrative from which, for several reasons, there is no way out. When two chain gang members, Joker (Tony Curtis), a white southern racist, and Cullen (Sidney Poitier), a southern black, manage to escape, still chained together, they learn to overcome their mutual distrust and hatred. Despite the injustice of their sentences, the cruelty of the chain gang, and the greater injustice of racism, of which they are both represented as victims, the Motion Picture Production Code, still in effect in 1958, prohibited their successful escape. Thus, at the same time that civil disobedience was becoming an effective civil rights tactic, a film attempting to portray heroes who defy racism was required to punish those heroes.

Since their punishment is inevitable, the politics of the film emerges in how it focuses the blame for their eventual return to the chain gang. As in *No Way Out*, it does so by concentrating its animus on a small number of characters, falling into the same demographic groups: generically lower-class whites (inhabitants of southern-style Beaver Canals) and sexually active women. The "white trash" element consists of the deputies on the manhunt who run the bloodhounds; these people with thick southern accents are out of control, care more about dogs than people (especially black people), and listen to loud rock 'n' roll music on loud transistor radios. The educated sheriff, Max Muller (Theodore Bikel), in contrast, is humane and liberal enough that he wonders whether being reelected (by pandering to a redneck constituency) is important. Although he eventually captures Joker and Cullen's escape is actually thwarted by an unnamed woman (Cara Williams), a suburban housewife (at least suburban in demeanor and appearance, complete with a mid-1950s perm and toreador pants) who is inexplicably living with her nine-year-old son, Billy, on a farm in the middle of the woods, somewhere in the deep South (see figure 8.3).

FIGURE 8-3 Billy's (nameless) mother, looking more suburban than rural.

Abandoned by her husband, without a working car or any apparent ability to do farm work, she spends her time decorating her house with kitsch, epitomized by her framed paint-by-number picture. Worst of all, in the canon of 1950s values, she is a bad mother, willing to abandon her son if Joker will take her to New Orleans.

Lest we miss how condemnation-worthy her lack of maternal instincts is, it is worth considering that Judge Kaufman's sentencing of Ethel Rosenberg to death was explicitly grounded in Rosenberg's failure as a mother:

> Let no mistake be made about the role his wife, Ethel Rosenberg, played in this conspiracy. Instead of deterring him from pursuing his ignoble cause, she encouraged and assisted the cause. She was a mature woman— almost three years older than her husband and almost seven years older than her younger brother. She was a full-fledged partner in this crime.
>
> Indeed the defendants . . . placed their devotion to their cause above their own personal safety and were conscious that they were sacrificing their own children, should their misdeeds be detected—all of which did not deter them from pursuing their course. Love for their cause dominated their lives—it was even greater than their love for their children. (quoted in Schrecker, *Age of McCarthyism* 167)

This reflects the general belief in the 1950s that bad mothers were a national menace. As Ellen Schrecker explains:

> The anticommunist literature contained a strong strain of misogyny that blamed domineering and overprotective moms for turning their sons (rarely daughters) into Communists, while at the same time, it also accused communist mothers of neglect. Ethel Rosenberg's allegedly cold and unemotional behavior was presumably a sign of her political indoctrination and showed that she deserved the penalty that she received. J. Edgar Hoover, who had originally opposed the death sentence because she was a mother, claimed that he had changed his mind after she had rejected her own mother's plea that she confess for the sake of her children. During the early fifties, there were actually cases in which judges refused custody to women accused of "Communist leanings." (*Crimes* 147)

Drawing on extant cultural narratives, tragically exemplified by Kaufman's rationalization for the state-sponsored murder of Ethel Rosenberg,[5] *The Defiant Ones* makes inappropriate female sexual desire, typical of the lower class, antithetical to appropriate maternal instincts and therefore responsible for many social ills, including racism. The middle-class world allows women to assume the "normal" role of housewife and, even more important, the "natural" role of mother. In this world, women can be happy and also achieve real sexual gratification rather than the illusionary sort that results from frequent sexual encounters, several partners, and birth control. A by-product of these nonmaternal values is that the unhappy women engage in other problematic social behaviors, such as supporting racism, engaging in espionage, and proliferating kitsch.

The importing of this promiscuous housewife—as a few years earlier *The Ten Commandments* (1956) had imported Nefretiri, the pharaoh's fictional wife who makes the pharaoh defy God's will—shows that women who do not understand their proper role, women who are bad wives and bad mothers, are the root cause of social problems. Like Edie, Billy's mother is the nominal and failed love interest in the film, although the nature of her failure is diametrically opposite to Edie's. The virtues of maternalism woo Edie away from sexual desire, which becomes synonymous with rejecting racial prejudice. Billy's mother, on the other hand, is wooed away from her maternal obligations by her sexual attraction to Joker. Williams nurses Joker, who is bedridden with a fever because of an infection caused by his shackle. Then (as the close-up of Joker followed by a fade-out conventionally suggests), she mounts him.

Whatever the morality of her sexual assault on a man in no position to say "no," her act of self-gratification apparently has curative powers, at least temporarily, in that Joker is his old self the next morning, fever-free and showing few if any effects of his wound. (One can only imagine the lives that might have been saved in Crimea had Florence Nightingale's cadre known this method for curing infection.) After Billy's mother has sex with Joker, she plans to leave her son with a neighbor so that she can go to New Orleans with Joker.

Billy's mother's racism is also palpable. From the moment Cullen enters her house, she treats him in overtly discriminatory ways, relenting a bit only at Joker's insistence. In the same way, moreover, that she discards her son, and for the same reason—her planned escape with Joker—she dispenses with Cullen, giving him incorrect information about the swamps, which dooms him either to capture or death. When Joker discovers the lie and runs off to save Cullen, she wounds Joker with her son's .22 rifle.

In the moral lexicon of both films, female promiscuity equates with racism and maternal instincts with virtue. Billy's mother, therefore, provides a morality test for Joker, one complicated by the fact that he must in effect decide whom he loves more, Billy's mother or Cullen. Joker's choice of Cullen is thus as much a rejection of the bad mother as it is a subordination of his own sexual desire, that is, desire for Billy's mother; in an era of rigid binaries, Joker's heterosexual encounter with Billy's mother at least superficially inoculates him against the charge of homoerotic desire and at least in theory removes any homophobic taint from the fact that he ends the film with his head in Cullen's arms.

Joker's decision to reject Billy's mother triggers an economy wherein she can inflict a new wound for the one that she had healed: she cures Joker because he is liberating her from motherhood and then injures him because he has chosen the black man over the white woman. By exchanging his freedom for

Cullen's safety, Joker implicitly obligates Cullen to give up his own freedom in repayment. Joker, like Edie in *No Way Out*, has saved his soul by trading places with the African American (in the same way that Terry Molloy saved his by donning the jacket of Doyle and Duggan in *On the Waterfront*).

From a Black Space to an Ambiguous Future

But here the differences in the pre- and post-*Brown v. Board of Education* films emerge. The endings of both films entail a crucial moment in which the viewer cannot see what actually happens, a graphic indication of the confusion and anxiety about representing a liberated black population.

In *No Way Out*, Ray is about to shoot Luther in Dr. Wharton's living room while Edie looks on. To save Luther, Edie flips the light switch so that both the room and the screen go completely black at the moment when Luther disarms Ray. While the film uses the word "nigger" prolifically, it seems unable to show a black man striking and overcoming a white one.

In *The Defiant Ones*, with the hounds close on their heels, Cullen and Joker have reached the train that will take them out of the state. Cullen has jumped on and is offering his outstretched hand to Joker, who is running alongside the train. Joker grabs Cullen's hand but, owing to the wrist infection and the rifle wound, lacks the strength to hold on. At exactly the moment that their hands separate, however, the film cuts to a shot from ground level, obscured by weeds, so that it is impossible to see, as both bodies tumble down the embankment, whether Cullen fell off the train while reaching for Joker or jumped off the train in order to be with him on the chain gang (see figure 8.4).

While the conclusions of both films depend on the behavior of an unjustly treated black man toward a wounded white man, in the earlier film the black man acts to prove he is better than the white man, and in the latter film to

FIGURE 8-4 The shot from the weeds obscures how Cullen's fall from the train occurred.

show that he forgives him, that he cares for him. The darkness in *No Way Out* indicates the film's inability to visualize black agency or black power, no matter how much the Cold War portends a shift in race relations, such that the film's title indicates no way out of the darkness before the proverbial dawn, which the blackout in the final scene literalizes. That we are not allowed to see the process by which the black man overcomes prejudice and oppression signifies the difficulty in 1950 of envisioning such a turn of events, no matter how forcefully global politics impelled it. To put it another way, the darkness in *No Way Out* is the aporia that *Brown v. Board of Education* will fill.

The landmark decision ending segregation in American schools was in the works in the 1940s, as the number of decisions and pending cases slowly grew. The *Brown* decision in fact applied to five separate cases consolidated under one ruling. (Perhaps the most significant earlier decision was issued in *Sweatt v. Painter*, a ruling prohibiting the University of Texas Law School from excluding African American students because the school could not demonstrate the existence in Texas of a separate black law school that was its equal.) Despite the path on which the postwar Supreme Court, full of Democratic appointees, had embarked, the process was neither sure nor swift. Under Chief Justice Vinson, the court heard arguments in 1952 but declined to render a decision, in part because the justices were so personally contentious and often openly disdainful of one another that there was likely to be as much disparity between concurring opinions as division between the pro- and anti-desegregation proponents.

While there seemed to be at least five votes to overturn the principle of separate but equal (established in *Plessy v. Ferguson, 1896*), even those likely to be on the winning side were loath to go forward. Daunted by the enormous task of implementing desegregation, those in favor of that position became nervous. A Justice Department official recalled that Justice Hugo Black, a southerner fully committed to voting against segregated schools, nonetheless warned "that many whites would fight school desegregation tooth and nail. 'The guys who talked nigger would be in charge' [the official] remembered Black saying. 'There would be riots, the Army might have to be called out'—he was scaring the shit out of the Justices, especially Frankfurter and Jackson, who didn't know how the Court would enforce a ruling against *Plessy*" (Patterson, *Brown* 54). The court therefore agreed to rehear the case argued in the fall of 1953. In the interim, Chief Justice Vinson died and was replaced by Earl Warren, whose genius lay in his ability to forge a consensus. Writing a decision that pleased none of them, he nonetheless crafted a document devoid of any argument so objectionable as to impel one dissent. As a piece of legal reasoning, Warren's opinion has been widely criticized, chiefly because it does not rely on any of the standard criteria for determining the law of the land: not legal precedent, nor historical understanding, nor rigorous legal logic. In fact, it explicitly throws out the first two principles and substitutes social science for the third. Never addressing the massive disparities between black schools and white (e.g., in per capita spending, facilities, class size, salaries, or teacher preparation), the ruling instead argues that black students by being separated from white students experience a sense of inferiority so psychologically damaging that it impairs their ability to function as productive citizens in a democracy. The converse—that white students separated from black students would be comparably damaged—was not considered or, I think one can safely say, even imagined by the justices. Ironically, the monumental decision overturning the centuries of American thought that had made "separate but equal" tenable would ban that principle from American education on a notion of white superiority: the tacit assumption that being separated from whites was a powerful deprivation.

Whatever it lacks as a legal argument, the decision in *Brown* nevertheless provides a vivid snapshot of the attitudes toward race, nation, and the Cold War that in 1954 found unanimous judicial assent. Segregated schools were un-American. While the decision filled in one blank, it openly acknowledged another: that it did not define the procedures to correct the wrong it had articulated. So profound was the court's quandary that it asked to hear arguments the following year about the method for implementing *Brown*. The result was a ruling on May 31, 1955, ordering the South to desegregate with "all deliberate speed," but providing no timetables and mandating no procedures. This decision—*Brown II*—opened the door to rampant local litigation and procedural or violent defiance, both often sanctioned or initiated by southern elected officials.

In the three years marked by the illegality of segregation and the absence of widespread integration, a set of practices were exposed nationally in all their ugliness. Rather than illuminating the future of race relations, this public exposure made that future painfully opaque, like the ambiguous camera angle and cutting in *The Defiant Ones*. The change in perspective at the moment Cullen sacrifices his escape demonstrates an inability to envision the disparity between the way that logic suggested African Americans would use their court-empowered agency and the way the liberal consensus hoped they would. James Baldwin said that he saw the film twice, intentionally: "When Sidney jumps off the train to rescue Tony Curtis. . . . I saw it twice, deliberately, in New York. I saw it downtown with a white liberal audience. There was a great sigh of relief and clapping: they felt that this was a very noble gesture on the part of a very noble black man. . . . Then I saw it uptown. When Sidney jumped off the train, there was a tremendous roar of *fury* from the audience" (Standley and Pratt 11–12).

That fury reflects both the revival of the civil rights movement and the frustration already starting to emerge about its ineffectiveness, or at least at the slow pace at which it was fomenting change. Ineffective implementation was offsetting the euphoria surrounding *Brown*, and instead of removing one bullet from the Soviet propaganda arsenal, as reports of the 1954 decision portended, resistance to integration illustrated globally the validity of Soviet charges. Many southern states refused to obey court orders or did so while actively or tacitly supporting "white citizen" violence that prevented their implementation. This violence was not limited to the physical surroundings of the schools or intimidation of the African American students attempting to enter them. As James Patterson explains: "White violence against blacks in the South had declined since its peak years between 1890 and 1920. Now, after 1954, it surged again, perhaps reflecting rising white anxiety about blacks getting 'uppity' in the aftermath of *Brown*. If they managed to get into white schools, there was no telling what might come next—perhaps competition for jobs. Between 1954 and 1959, there were 210 recorded acts of white violence against black people in the South, including six murders, twenty-nine assaults with firearms, forty-four beatings, and sixty bombings" (87).[6]

Direct violence was one aspect of a multifarious Southern resistance, which included organized campaigns, public pronouncements, legal challenges, bureaucratic delays, transparently token compliance, and extensive state and municipal counterlegislation. Georgia, for instance, made it illegal to spend public funds on desegregated schools (Patterson 99).

Although these acts to preserve white supremacy were widespread, the actions taken by Arkansas governor Orville Faubus to thwart integrating Little Rock schools came to epitomize the problem, so that "the name 'Little Rock' quickly became the foremost symbol of American racism, with hostile crowds in Venezuela chanting it as they attacked [Vice President] Nixon's motorcade in Caracas in 1958" (Borstelmann 104). Opposition to segregation provided Faubus with a convenient issue to carry him through a stiff reelection campaign. In September 1957, when nine black teenagers were to enter Central High, Faubus called out the National Guard in anticipation of violence that was not incipient, but quickly became a self-fulfilling prophesy. In the weeks that followed, angry white citizens and the National Guard made it impossible for the black students to enter the school. When the courts enjoined Faubus from barring the students, Faubus called off the National Guard, leaving the students "at the mercy of a howling, spitting mob" (Patterson 110). The spreading violence eventually forced President Eisenhower to call in the US Army, which permitted the black students to endure a brutally unpleasant school year, full of violence throughout the Little Rock community, including threats to kill the school superintendent and shots fired into the home of the Arkansas NAACP president. When the school board's argument that the violence necessitated delaying integration was unanimously and emphatically rejected by the Supreme Court, Faubus closed all the high schools in Little Rock for the entire 1958–1959 school year.

He did so with the entire world watching, at exactly the moment when newly formed nations of color were starting to parade into the UN. In a letter to Eisenhower, UN ambassador Henry Cabot Lodge wrote, "here at the United Nations I can see clearly the harm that the riots in Little Rock are doing to our foreign relations. More than two thirds of the world is non-white and the reactions of the representatives of these people is easy to see" (quoted in Dudziak 131). At the same time, the reactions of southern whites showed that *Brown* had struck a particularly sensitive nerve. "Desegregation of schools," Patterson explains, "always remained an extraordinarily problematic matter for white parents, and for emotionally powerful reasons: they wanted the very best education for their children, and they worried about social mixing, dating, and even marriage" (88).

Integrated Schools and Festering Delinquency

The incidents in Little Rock typified the intersection of anxiety about two emerging demographic groups: blacks in white classrooms and juvenile delinquents. If fears about both groups had been long cultivated in the American imaginary, the "deliberate speed" of integration ordered by the court and the rapid explosion of the teen population quickly produced racialization of delinquency. It is not surprising, therefore, that the *Reader's Guide to Periodic Literature* lists more articles on juvenile delinquency published from April 1953 to March 1961 (433) than in the prior twenty years (398), and nearly twice as many as in the subsequent eight years, 1961 to 1968 (233) (Gilbert 65).

The shift toward the racialization of delinquency is illustrated by two 1955 films, *Rebel without a Cause* and *Blackboard Jungle*. These films, released the year after *Brown* was decided and on the cusp of its implementation, illustrate the intertwining of race and delinquency, portending the transformation of the juvenile delinquent from the victim of a somewhat uncanny social disease to the effect of a racial problem.

Rebel, reflecting the "disease" model of juvenile delinquency, echoed the concerns of the 1940s and 1950s that an epidemic of delinquency was immanent, one that, like polio, ignored geographic and class distinctions. The "epidemic targeting defenseless children, grew to dramatic proportions," David Oshinsky explains, "in an increasingly suburban, family-oriented society preaching ever-higher standards of protection for the young. How ironic, how *unfair*, that polio seemed to target the world's most advanced nation, where new wonder drugs like penicillin were already available and consumers—mainly housewives—worked overtime to eliminate odors and germs" (*Polio* 4–5). This tinge of the uncanny, intensified exponentially by advertising and motivational research techniques, which had been perfected in the decades after the war, turned "a horrific but relatively uncommon disease into the most feared affliction of this time. . . . Polio hit without warning. There was no way of telling who would get it and who would be spared. It killed some of its victims and scarred others for life, leaving behind vivid reminders for all to see: wheelchairs, crutches, leg braces, breathing devices, deformed limbs" (*Polio* 5).

If the language of epidemiology, on the one hand, and of terror, on the other, applied equally to polio and delinquency, the rhetoric surrounding the dreaded delinquent, which made adolescence a virus, revealed a growing anxiety over the immanence of radical changes in American demographics. Undergoing a massive baby boom, the nation faced a youth population that it could neither envision nor comprehend. While Dr. Spock might reassuringly advise new parents of the 1940s and early 1950s about caring for infants and raising children, just as he did about polio, he seemed almost dumbfounded by teenagers. Just 6 of 500 pages in his book address puberty, and none are devoted to adolescents.

In the uncharted future for postwar parents, the mental stability of the baby boomers was particularly threatening because those boomers were bound to outnumber the authority figures charged with channeling their behavior into good citizenship. "The marriage and baby booms of the 1950s," Gilbert explains, "indicated rising—even unjustified—expectations for the family. The enormous demographic shifts following the war also changed the character of delinquency. Urbanization, suburbanization, and the westward tilt of migration shook the mixture of populations. This reflected in changing populations of in schools and other youth institutions" (*Cycle* 130).

A broad range of influences endangered the upbringing of these children, destined as they were to move largely unmediated through a world saturated with visual and audio stimulation. Televisions brought them images and narratives from around the world. By the late 1950s the radio, in the 1930s an immobile piece of furniture, had become a portable device so small and inexpensive a teenager could buy one to carry in a shirt pocket or purse and have broadcast company in any public or private space. Print too proliferated and, in conjunction with greater affluence, facilitated an army of fans with allegiance to iconic figures such James Dean, Marlon Brando, Elvis Presley, and Marilyn Monroe, stars whose personae defied rather than affirmed traditional social norms.

The corruption of youth had been a longstanding concern. In the first decades of the century, movie theaters, like pool halls, were thought to provide unsavory meeting places for unruly youths; many felt the movie theater itself was potentially as corrupting as the screen narratives presented there. Here too we see echoes of the epidemic paradigm, infused as it was with narratives about unhealthy venues. In regard to polio, the swimming pool substituted for the pool hall as the place from which youth needed protection.

Comic books were viewed as another corrupter of youth. In 1954 psychiatrist Frederick Wertham, in *Seduction of the Innocent*, championed a crusade against them, declaring "crime comics a contributing factor to many delinquent acts" (quoted in Gilbert, *Cycle* 103). Wertham wanted government to ban the sale of comic books to anyone under sixteen, a goal he pursued though numerous avenues, including congressional testimony, magazine articles, and copious media interviews. Insisting that "comics could affect all children: 'Normal ones; troubled ones; those from well-to-do families and from the lowest rung of the economic ladder; children from different parts of the city . . . ,' [Wertham believed] the universal infectiousness of violent culture was the best reason to ban it" (102).

Like the discourse surrounding polio, Wertham's attention to comic books was prophylactic, responding not to the disease but rather to anxiety about its threatening potential: a generation that violated generational norms, a demographic group so large that, if not regulated early, it might be impossible to regulate at all. Theorizing the causes of juvenile delinquency was an act of hope tinged by desperation. The moment of the delinquency crisis, like so many of the moments before the advent of the Salk vaccine, blended the hypothetical with the real. "Like a medieval wheel of fortune," Jacqueline Foertsch explains, "where polio stopped no one knew: how it entered the body and moved among the populations, whether it would strike this town or that, why the summer was such a dangerous season, how extensive or permanent the damage in each case would be, were guessing or waiting games played by patients, physicians and families countless times during the polio period" (13). As with other postwar fears—nuclear holocaust, homosexuality, Communism, nonsubmissive women, conformism, nonconformism, desegregation—the imagined consequences had more cogency than did the verifiable facts. As Oshinsky points out about polio, "In truth [it] was never the raging epidemic portrayed in the media. . . . Ten times as many children would be killed in accidents in these years, and three times as many would die of cancer" (5).

What was most frightening about polio, therefore, was not the epidemic's size but its randomness, which assaulted the social order as the virus did the nervous system. In this way, polio provided a paradigm for the early discourse about juvenile delinquency, a disease that, like its "carriers," threatened to disrupt social boundaries.

Before viewers entered the theater, they were confronted with ads and posters for *Rebel without a Cause* that described James Dean as playing "the bad boy from a good family" or announced, about the characters played by Dean and Natalie Wood: "and they both come from good families." The opening sequence of the film emphasized this point. The teenage principals, Jim Stark (Dean), Judy (Wood), and John "Plato" Crawford (Sal Mineo), have been assembled on Easter in the local police station of an unidentified Los Angeles area community. Judy, arrested for something like public indecency, comes from a middle- to upper-middle class family, and the Starks appear somewhat more upscale; Jim's father, Frank (Jim Backus), wearing a tuxedo, has been called away from the country club because Jim has been arrested for public drunkenness. Plato, arrested for shooting puppies, is both the wealthiest and the most disturbed of the three adolescents. His divorced mother apparently lives well on alimony. Frequently away, she relegates Plato's care and supervision primarily to the family maid (Marietta Canty), who seems to be his only source of genuine affection.

If the film's title indicates that delinquency has no identifiable cause, the film nevertheless targets the conditions that encourage it, all involving not authority—something against which rebels *with* a cause traditionally rebel—but its absence. Jim Stark craves authority, especially from his weak-willed father, who prefers to run from problems. Hence, every time Jim gets into trouble, the Starks move to a new neighborhood, something they have done once more at the outset of the film; Jim is set the next day to start classes at a new high school.

Before he is released from jail, Jim has an interaction with Ray Fremick (Edward Platt), the plainclothes policeman who plays several roles that are absent from Jim's life but necessary, the film implies, for his well-balanced socialization. At first Ray is curt and assertive. Then he physically overcomes Jim, and finally he speaks to him in a manner more typical of a psychiatrist than of a policeman, sympathizing with his dilemma, suggesting ways of venting his anger, and making himself available as Jim's friend or adviser. Asserting his masculinity verbally and physically, Ray earns Jim's trust by being the antithesis of his father, so much so that Jim can confess his need for a strong authority figure, and Ray can sympathize with him. Ray, as Biskind makes clear, "is another agent of the therapeutic state" (202).[7]

Although parental failure may cause Jim's rebellion, its actual nature remains murky. Ignorant of the school traditions, Jim is chastised for accidentally stepping on the school emblem, set in the pavement in front of the school, hardly an act of "rebellion." On a class trip to the planetarium that afternoon, the other students reject him when he makes a mooing noise in the dark of the auditorium. But those students who guard the school emblem and enforce the rules of silence are the same group of delinquents who slash Jim's tire. Torn between authoritarian and antiauthoritarian impulses, the teenagers who allegedly represent delinquency evoke as much confusion about its traits as about its cause. Hence, they do not represent teenage rebellion but adult fear of the unfathomable shape it may take. Delinquency has something to do with knife fights, and sexual promiscuity, and disregard for rules; equally it has something to do with peer pressure, social codes, and the failure of adult masculinity.

The apocalyptic imagery that ends the planetarium show (see figure 8.5)—ostensibly the big bang that began the universe but resonating with the nuclear holocaust that threatens to end it—conflates past fears and future anxieties by inflating them to cosmic magnitude.

In the moment of the planetarium's big bang, the nuclear anxiety infecting all aspects of the Cold War merges with the population explosion portended by the baby boom. The show thus provides an objective correlative for the pent-up emotions of adolescents set loose in a world devoid of adequate authority.

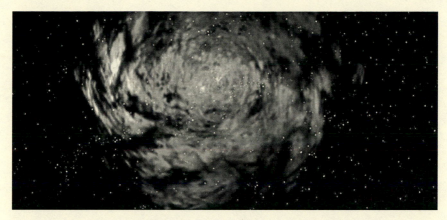

FIGURE 8-5 The apocalyptic imagery that ends the planetarium show.

In such a world, the film suggests, the knife fight with Buzz (Corey Allen), which follows his slashing Jim's tire, is inevitable. So is the game of "chicken" that evening, in which Jim and Buzz, driving in two (stolen) cars headed for a precipice, will compete to see who stays behind the wheel the longest. Before the contest, Jim bonds with Buzz over their recognition of mutual daring as way of combatting the boredom of a world without supervision (or, by inference, masculine role models). When Buzz is accidentally killed in this game, however, the nature of Jim's rebellion transforms from an embrace of delinquency to a stand against apathy. He desires to tell the police what caused Buzz's death, despite his father's urging him not to get involved and the gang of Buzz's friends warning him to keep his mouth shut.

Jim's rebellion thus turns a drama about delinquency into one about dysfunctional white, middle-class, suburban American families, in which the men are unable to fulfill the roles demanded by Luce, Kennan, and Schlesinger, so that the potentially delinquent children become symptomatic of weak or misguided mothers and fathers. As a result, the postwar parental generation brings the audience closer to the nuclear annihilation portended by the planetarium show. "It quickly becomes evident," Biskind accurately observes, "that it is not Jim, Judy, or Plato who are delinquents, but their parents" (200).

Escaping from the pressures of their peers and the failings of their parents, Jim, Judy, and Plato, hiding in an abandoned mansion near the planetarium, form an alternative family, with Plato the implicit child (see figure 8.6). This event transforms Plato's somewhat blatant homosexual interest in Jim into a childlike affection for the family that substitutes parental concern for homoerotic desire.[8] The cause of the teenagers' antisocial behavior is thus psychological rather than social.

In this regard, the film bears strong similarities to *On the Waterfront*, in which Terry also becomes a rebel by turning to authority, while Jim's parents

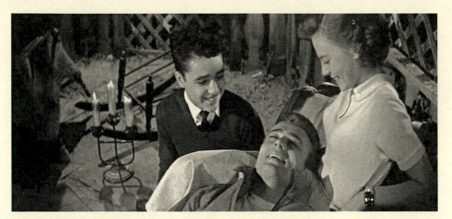

FIGURE 8-6 Jim, Judy, and Plato form an alternative family.

echo the D and D longshoremen. Like Terry, Jim wants to testify, even though the peer pressure and the code of his community preclude such acts of civic responsibility. Jim's decision to reveal the cause of the death of a young man (who was his girlfriend's boyfriend) is the same, moreover, as Terry's decision to testify about what caused the death of another young man (who was his girlfriend's brother). In "rebelling" by legitimizing authority, rather than challenging it, both men depoliticize their cause. Just as Terry in the end supports labor by discrediting unionism, Jim stands up for teenagers by demanding stronger parental control.[9]

In both films, moreover, this behavior endorses a theological rather than secular view of social benefits. We have seen how Terry, by donning Joey Doyle's jacket to suffer the stages of the cross, demonstrates his choice of Father Barry's values over "the love of a lousy buck." In the same spirit, Jim enacts an Easter story in which his red jacket identifies him with the figure whose sacrificial death helps restore social order. When Plato awakens after Jim and Judy have left him asleep so that they can run off to one of the bedrooms in the mansion, he re-experiences the parental abandonment that fomented his antisocial behavior; becoming frantic, he runs off to the planetarium, wearing Jim's red jacket. Plato's behavior and the fact that he has a gun initiate a police standoff that culminates in Plato's being killed. Because he is wearing Jim's jacket, Jim's parents, who witness the event from behind police barricades, believe that Jim is the victim, which becomes a wakeup call to his father.

The film thus achieves resolution through a number of specific economies: Plato, whose psychological scars render him unredeemable, exchanges a carnal existence for a sacrificial one. His actual name is John Crawford (J. C.), and in this story that starts on Easter Sunday he dies because of the sins of his society, that is, because of the psychological damage (including but not limited to homosexuality) caused by neglectful parents. His sacrifice enables Frank Stark to exchange roles with Ray Fremick, so that the state will no longer have to provide parental authority. Frank makes this explicit when he says, "You can depend on me. Trust me. Whatever comes, we'll . . . we'll face it together. I swear it. Come on, Jim. Stand up, and I'll stand up with you. I'll try to be as strong as . . . as you want me to be."

This reconciliation between father and son concludes with Jim's introducing Judy to his father, thereby allowing her to exchange her role as the trampy girlfriend of a delinquent for that of the kind of girl Jim can bring home to his parents. Plato's death and the possibility that Jim might have been shot enables her to gravitate toward the family, in which the father and mother resolve to assume an appropriate relationship and the wife supports rather than undermines the father's masculinity, in contradistinction to Judy's family, in which her father's hostility toward her reflects his inability to cope with the sexual desire she evokes in him.

The belief that appropriate parents, who are good role models and enforce rules, can prevent social ills differentiates *Rebel* from *Blackboard Jungle*, released the same year. *Blackboard Jungle* represents delinquency as a social, not a psychological, failure.[10] Mr. Dadier (Glenn Ford), a veteran, wants to teach English in an inner-city, all-male vocational school, populated, at least implicitly, by potential delinquents. At the outset, the boys appear behind the bars surrounding the school, dancing to rock 'n' roll, music so much associated with delinquency that its use in the film was considered scandalous.[11] In addition, an early scene in the school auditorium, in which the principal introduces the faculty to the students, echoes scenes from prison movies.

The film, however, provides an opening disclaimer identifying the school in the film as presenting a dangerous *potential* rather than *current* threat:

> We, in the United States, are fortunate to have a school system that is a tribute to our communities and to our faith in American youth.
>
> Today we are concerned with juvenile delinquency—its causes—and its effects. We are especially concerned when this delinquency boils over into our schools.
>
> The scenes and incidents depicted here are fictional.
>
> However, we believe that public awareness is a first step toward a remedy for any problem.
>
> It is in this spirit and with this faith that BLACKBOARD JUNGLE was produced.

The disclaimer appears on a black screen with a militaristic drumbeat on the sound track. The drumming segues into Bill Haley's playing "Rock Around the Clock," in effect turning the disclaimer into a warning: if not checked, unruly behavior of the sort that rock 'n' roll instigates could become dangerous. And indeed, the students at this school are dangerous. They undermine educational

activities, destroy one teacher's rare jazz record collection, commit crimes on
and off school grounds, and attempt to rape one of the teachers.

They are motivated, moreover, by malice rather than boredom or neglect.
Unlike Jim Stark, they do not crave authority; they resent it. And they do not
come from good families, if by "good" one means well off, suburban, and white.
Although there are few blacks in Dadier's class (or in the school), the ethnic
composition of the students—a smattering of blacks and Puerto Ricans (considered one group in the New York census categories of the period), as well as Italian and Irish—differs greatly from that of Jim's largely WASP suburban school.

Coming immediately after the Supreme Court's school desegregation order,
the film's urban setting, its connection to teenagers, and its focus on education reveals several problematic assumptions about the demographic disrup-
tion that *Brown* projects into the American imaginary. This school, after all, is
a "jungle," the place where uncivilized black people ("jungle bunnies") pose a
constant threat to the forces of civilization.

In 1955 Kenya was in the midst of the Mau Mau uprisings, a native rebellion
against brutal British colonial rule, news of which (well known in the West)[12]
characterized the British as protecting the colony from savages. Note, for example, these excerpts from a 1953 *Time magazine* article, "Slaughter in Kenya":

> A band of Kikuyu women, naked except for thongs of leather tied round
> their shaven heads, recently stole out from a bamboo thicket on the
> slopes of the Aberdare Mountains in Kenya. Armed with shiny pangas,
> they crept into a Kikuyu village, killed three Kikuyu men and a 14-year-old
> boy. The victims were Kikuyu guards, loyal to the white men and pledged
> to fight the Mau Mau.
>
> The women walked half a mile down a jungle track, dragging with
> them the severed head of one of the men they had slain. They showed it
> to his widow before slowly strangling her with the thongs that they wore.
> Then they hacked her four children to pieces and disappeared.
>
> Such butchery by the Mau Mau, male and female, is fast becoming
> commonplace in the rich and sorrowful land of Kenya Crown Colony.
> In the twelve months since Governor Sir Evelyn Baring declared a state
> of emergency, the Mau Mau has murdered 730 Africans. 16 whites,
> eleven Indians.* In return. British troops have killed 2,340 Africans in
> battle; have hanged 89 and jailed 27,000, have 149 of them awaiting
> execution. The fighting has busied five full battalions of British infantry
> with supporting troops (6,750 men) and 3,000 African levies; it costs
> the shuddering colony more than $820,000 a month—one-fifth of its
> revenue. One high-ranking British officer announced last week that
> "conditions are no better, and in many respects are worse, than they
> were a year ago. . . .

From Nairobi's panicky whites went a wail for regular troops to clear out the Negro locations. This meant withdrawing British infantrymen from their battle stations in the mountains, but Commander in Chief General Sir George Erskine could not resist the clamor. Six hundred young Inniskilling Fusiliers, in jungle-green uniforms and black berets, marched into Nairobi last week with orders to screen every African in the city. "Nairobi wants to rid itself of between 15,000 and 20,000 Negroes who are living in the city without permission," said Police Chief John Timmermann. The cops admitted that they could not keep any more Kukes in jail because "our prisons and detention camps are already too full."

Last week Governor Baring confessed to the boys of Prince of Wales school that "Kenya will still be in a state of stress when you are middle-aged." General Erskine had to agree. "The situation is no longer purely military," he gruffly announced. "There is no military answer to white-black tension . . . Bullets alone will not finish the Mau Mau."

. . . * Thirteen more white settlers have killed themselves by their clumsy handling of their own guns. (32)

The Mau Mau "butchers" "murder" Africans, while the British "kill" three times as many in "battle." The distinction between murdering butchers and protecting soldiers is lodged in the logic that distinguishes wild African animals from the safaris that have pushed them toward extinction. A front-page *New York Times* article, for example, referred to British general Sir George Erskine noting that "Mau Mau gangs" were reluctant "to leave the Mount Kenya *forest lairs*" (emphasis added).[13] That the "shuddering" colony must spend 20 percent of *its* revenue to support the British colonial regime suggests the same logic: that the Kenyans (even those purged from the cities or the 27,000 Kenyans in jails) benefit from British protection in a place full of wild, dangerous creatures.

The concluding paragraph of the *Time* article, extending racial logic into the Kenyan future, bases its pessimistic projection on the idea that anticolonial violence emerges from some innate trait of those with Mau Mau orientations: "Last week Governor Baring confessed to the boys of Prince of Wales school that 'Kenya will still be in a state of stress when you are middle-aged.' General Erskine had to agree. 'The situation is no longer purely military,' he gruffly announced. 'There is no military answer to white-black tension. . . . Bullets alone will not finish the Mau Mau.'" The British governor and British general anticipate a long struggle because the conflict is not military but biological. Hence resolution rests not on the swiftness of a speeding bullet but on the slow, evolutionary survival of the fittest: the law of the jungle.[14]

Because in *Blackboard Jungle* the *black*board metonymically represents the school, the film's title connects the threat posed in this "jungle" to blackness. It is a film about the "black board (of education) jungle" or simply the "black, bored jungle." There, education is threatened because the board of education has to integrate black people into a bored and alienated population. Like the movie theaters in the early decades of the twentieth century, blackboard jungles provided an alleged meeting place for lower-class teenagers who, lacking proper supervision, were ripe for delinquency.

Leerom Medovoi, reading the film through Norman Mailer's essay "The White Negro," Jerry Farber's *The Student as Nigger*, and Eldridge Cleaver's *Soul on Ice*, has pointed out that the delinquency of the sociopathic West (Vic Morrow) functions as a site of identification for teenage rebellion. Epitomizing the values of the Maileresque "hipster," West can be seen as "one of the emerging new breed of Ofays described by Cleaver, born in the fallout of *Brown vs. Board of Education*, who prefers to identify, and even to organize, with his racially oppressed cohorts rather than their colonizers, and who in exactly this way have formulated for themselves an identity independent of their elders" (155).

Medovoi also notes that this reading is close to a queer reading, in that heteronormativity was a significant component of 1950s conformity. In that regard, Medovoi points out the aspects of the film intended to disavow that queerness. The opening sequence, for example, shows boys dancing together (in this all-male school) to the rebellious rock 'n' roll music that accompanied the credits, providing a graphic link between the music of rebellion and the celebration of same-sex coupling. To counter this, in the same way that Joker's episode with Billy's mother countered the closing coupling of him and Cullen, the next shot of *Blackboard Jungle* shows the boys behind the bars of the schoolyard, leering at and reaching between the bars for an attractive young woman walking down the street (see figure 8.7). The heterosexual desire of the delinquent boys is further underscored when it manifests itself as pure lust in the attempted rape of Miss Hammond (Margaret Hayes).

But if the rebellion of the delinquents marks them as white Negroes, then it is difficult to escape the racial connotations of these two sequences. Reaching through the bars of this "jungle," the delinquents code as zoo animals, which, when they act as sexual predators, comply with the rhetoric of the segregationists who argued that blacks were animals that, in an integrated school, threatened the safety of white teenage girls.

Director Richard Brooks, according to Jon Lewis, "did as much as he could to at least introduce the problematic racial dynamics of the urban American high school" (). But as Steven Cohan makes clear, he did so by oscillating between, rather than successfully engaging, competing cultural narratives. Noting that the film attempts to embrace both the psychological and social perspectives on delinquency, Cohan correctly points out the film's confused racial perspective: "The film initially appears to be representing the problem of juvenile delinquency as as racial issue. Dadier makes [Miller] the primary target of his suspicions as well as the object of his manipulations. However, after a heated

FIGURE 8-7 The boys behind the schoolyard fence, leering at and reaching for an attractive woman.

confrontation between white teacher and black student about the former's racism, which allows the film at once to recognize and deny the place of race in its representation of both delinquency and authority, *Blackboard Jungle* then shifts gears, ignoring the ethnic and working-class composition of the student body to blame all the disturbances in Dadier's classroom on the pathology of the psychologically disturbed white teenager, West" (*Masked* 118).

Cohan has precisely identified that the difficulty of dealing with the prospect of integrated schools presented a conflict between narratives of nature and narratives of nurture. In the mid-1950s, American culture was inundated with cause-and-prevention narratives, with the scientific assertions of medical experts such as doctors Spock and Wertham, and legislative experts such as those holding congressional hearings on the causes of juvenile crime. At the same time, the southern assault on *Brown* proclaimed the prodigious danger of mixing people with different genetic proclivities.

Understandably, therefore, diversity creates a problem for Dadier, who knows there are delinquents in his class but cannot identify them. In the absence of knowledge, Dadier, relying on prejudice, decides that the ringleader must be the black student, Miller (Sidney Poitier). When events reveal West (Vic Morrow) to be the actual leader of the delinquents, Dadier learns that he shouldn't be deceived by appearances and assume that because Miller is black he must be a delinquent. Since being black does not *necessarily* make Miller a criminal, Dadier should have given him a chance to prove his innocence.

In exchange, Miller learns that not all white people are prejudiced, that Dadier does care about his potential and his future. Miller, of course, is guilty of nothing other than correctly believing that Dadier suspects him because he is black, so the economy of their educational exchange is asymmetrical: Dadier will admit that he was wrong if Miller will forget that *he* was right. This replicates exactly the racial dynamics for which James Baldwin critiqued *The Defiant Ones*, wherein the future of racial harmony burdens the black, who must forgive the white.

To the extent that Medovoi is correct that the film codes white delinquents as Negro, that coding, reinforced by Dadier's suspicion about Miller, expresses anxiety about the immanence of integrated schools, in the North as well as in the South. Throughout the decade that anxiety grew, and white flight increased *de facto* segregation at the same time that the courts acted more emphatically to end it. By the beginning of the next decade, as *West Side Story* (1961) demonstrates, the racialization of delinquency became more solidified at the same time that the expression of racial dynamics became more confused.

9

"I Want to Be in America"

Urban Integration, Pan-American Friendship, and *West Side Story*

Alfred Hitchcock, I have argued, seems to have understood that the demographic angst from which the UN was forged reflected the collision, in the postwar moment, between the demand for sovereignty and the desire for empire. The creation in the second half of the twentieth century of over one hundred nations out of former colonies certainly renounced colonialism. But for complex reasons, many of them embedded in the UN Charter, the second half of the American century also became a platform for the creation of new empires: American, Soviet, and Chinese, as well as, arguably, the Organization of the Petroleum Exporting Countries and the European market. "A 1958 NSC report praised by Eisenhower captured the dilemma for many Americans: 'The Spirit of 1776 was running wild,' it said—showing American pride in being a model for other nations—but this phenomenon was 'rather terrifying' in Africa. Other advisers to the president deplored the 'juvenile delinquencies of these new nations'" (Borstelmann 124).

West Side Story and the Exemplary, Anomalous Puerto Rican

In this regard, *West Side Story* (1961), which tries to find a place in the narrative of America for Puerto Ricans—marked as juvenile delinquents—not only consolidates conflicts between sovereignty and globalism but also underscores the gendered dynamics involved in the colonial enterprise, as reflected in the redeployment of agency after World War II and in capitalism's need for labor compliant with its own exploitation. Established as definitively (and legally) the cultural Other, the Puerto Rican raised anxiety about racial integration and attendant concerns over miscegenation, crime, and especially, juvenile delinquency, that were prevalent in 1950s American culture, especially after the *Brown v. Board of Education* desegregation decision of 1954.

Perhaps no land mass or population better epitomizes the contradictions produced by the competition for global dominance in the Cold War and thereafter than Puerto Rico. And equally, perhaps Puerto Ricans, more than any other demographic group, found their impossible condition extensively papered over by the rhetoric of self-determination and "democracy." A colony marked by the racial prejudice essential to colonial subordination, Puerto Rico at the end of the 1950s nevertheless represented America's democratic alternative to the island's Communist neighbor, Castro's Cuba. At the same time, from a Communist perspective, Puerto Rico exemplified the rationale for the Cuban Revolution: American power opposed self-determination. As Cesar J. Ayala and Rafael Bernabe point out, when Henry Luce announced the coming of the American century:

> The moment symbolically marked the rise of the United States as a global power. It has been pointed out many times that American influence as proclaimed by Luce in 1941 and as built by U. S. strategists after 1945 did not imply the construction of a new colonial empire following the British or other European models. This is undoubtedly so, but . . . there were some exceptions. For some the American Century had begun . . . when the Spanish-American War of 1898 led to the instillation of U. S. colonial governments in the Philippines, Puerto Rico and Guam. . . . Puerto Rico thus became an anomaly: a colony of a fundamentally noncolonial imperialism. (1)

"Acquired" as the spoils of war, the island and its citizens have a status markedly different from that of Cubans, for Cuba was restored to independence almost immediately after the 1898 Spanish–American War. Puerto Rico, in contrast, has for over one hundred years endured several forms of limbo. The Jones Act of 1917 gave Puerto Ricans American citizenship while constructing them as "being mostly of African descent and thus belonging to 'an inferior race,' which made incorporation into the United States impossible for some legislators. In sum, Puerto Ricans were legally constructed, by statute and constitutional opinion, as 'others' relative to the United States, and their citizenship as expressly inferior, that is, second class, at least as long as they chose to reside on the island" (Malavet 42). Upheld by a series of Supreme Court decisions, the peculiar legal duality of Puerto Ricans affected not only their right to select their own leaders but also their legal status under the leadership and the laws selected for them. In 1953 the United States declared to the UN that because "the Puerto Rican people had consented to their existing structure, no further proof was necessary to demonstrate that self-determination had been attained" (Ayala and Bernabe 172). The United States therefore no longer needed to submit the annual reports on the conditions in nonindependent territories that the UN required. In this way, the United States avoided accountability for the rights allowed or denied a specific portion of its own citizens.

Puerto Ricans attained American citizenship by being born in Puerto Rico but only attained the rights of American citizenship by leaving the island. There is no doubt, furthermore, that this strange situation arose because Puerto Ricans spoke a different language than "normal" Americans and were perceived to be of a different "race."

If the excessive normativity of the 1950s generated a panoply of anxieties, the status of Puerto Ricans, as reflected by the film *West Side Story* (1961) (based on the 1957 play of the same name), aptly focuses much of the demographic angst of the 1950s. Although not released in the 1950s, the film works as a fitting capstone to the decade I have been discussing. The Cold War started internationally with the formation of the free world and domestically with the baby boom, setting baby boomers on a collision course with the containment of Communism that would culminate at the end of the 1960s with a multi-vehicle, high-casualty pileup in Vietnam. In the interim, the size and composition of the college population altered as profoundly as the areas these college students called home and in many cases as the racial composition of those areas. By the late 1960s films would show men and women sleeping in the same bed, often with little or no clothing. Characters would speak on-screen using the same level of profanity that punctuated the vocabularies of their audience.

Most important from an international perspective, the personal habits of Americans would be much less directly connected to the international agenda of their nation. *West Side Story* marks the moment when the free world would undergo a major reformulation, with the UN membership enlarging drastically, until the white nations whose interests it privileged would be in the minority. At the same time the Cuban Revolution would further complicate attempts to reconcile the geographic globe with the geopolitical world. *West Side Story*, in other words, merges the tensions surrounding the notion of a free world troubled by the aura of colonialism with the specter of a Communist world made visible by Cuba. In the film, moreover, the shifting demographics of large American cities echo the global struggle for turf within the contemporary context of white flight and the attendant fear of urban violence.

That urban violence evoked fear of juvenile delinquency festering in the inner cities; by the end of the 1950s, the tendency to racialize delinquency, initiated in *Blackboard Jungle* (1955), had become conventional wisdom. Racial delinquency had become perceived as a social ailment rather than a psychological disorder, one that reflected symptomatically the changing demographics of the American city. The lyrics of *West Side Story*'s "Officer Krupke" make this perspective clear: "The trouble is he's crazy, the trouble is he drinks, / The trouble is he's lazy, the trouble is he stinks / The trouble is he's growing, the trouble is he's grown." Glossing the transformation of juvenile delinquency from a malady that crossed class lines to a lower-class product, Stephen Sondheim's lyrics emphatically proclaim: "No one wants a fellow with a social disease."

FIGURE 9-1 A scene showing one of the few African Americans in West Side Story at the dance, depicted as neither a Shark nor a Jet.

In *Blackboard Jungle*, Dadier *suspects* that the black student is the delinquent, but in *West Side Story* (only six years later), racialized delinquency is taken for granted. Gangs naturally divide along racial lines, so that the immanent violence over turf emanates from the changing racial composition of a neighborhood. This makes the racial composition of the film's cast particularly striking. Although in the early 1960s, in part owing to the desegregation of *de facto* segregated northern urban schools, many cities, including New York, were experiencing a demographic shift known as "white flight," *West Side Story* has almost no representation of African Americans (see figure 9.1).

The film promotes a form of Pan-American cooperation by constructing an acceptable urban space consistent with the cultural and hemispheric imperialism that has tacitly characterized US relations with Latin American countries, the problems of which the Cuban Revolution helped expose.

West Side Story, I am arguing, is deeply connected to the hemispheric politics that at the end of World War II restored a pattern of Latin American subjugation based on US-supported dictatorships committed to blocking land reform, suppressing economic self-sufficiency, and thereby maintaining a predictably and asymmetrically subordinate relationship to the economic hierarchy mandated by US postwar capitalism. While the trajectory of this economic narrative can connect the Monroe Doctrine of 1823, at one historical end, to the North American Free Trade Agreement of 1994 at the other, or can be exemplified by the history of Haiti, the moment of the film *West Side Story*'s production provides a compelling confluence of issues relating "Yankee imperialism" to both the Cold War policy of containment and northern urban white flight.

Released seven months after the failed Bay of Pigs invasion, the film version of *West Side Story* represents a Latin Caribbean island that is Cuba's mirror, that is to say, its exact reflection *in reverse*. From the moment in 1898 that the United

States acquired the adjacent islands, their trajectories have diverged radically. Cuba was never targeted for acquisition and Puerto Rico never targeted for independence. In consequence, Cuba was in a matter of years returned to self-rule—a status denied Puerto Rico to this day—through a series of maneuvers, legal actions, and legislative conditions.

Cuba's self-rule, however, was rarely independent or democratic. Instead of controlling the island nation through rules and laws, the United States used occupation, the tentacles of foreign policy, and the support of corrupt regimes. When a sovereign Cuba was formed at the turn of the twentieth century, the United States added the Platt Amendment to the Cuban Constitution, allowing "the United States to intervene into the domestic politics of Cuba whenever it believed the government lacked the ability to govern or should its independence be threatened" (Staten 42). Although the amendment was repealed in 1934, subsequent regimes continued to rule the island in coalition with the Cuban military and American corporations. In 1952 Fulgencio Batista and his supporters in the military overthrew the government to establish a very pro-US and very undemocratic Cuba, which was toppled by the 1959 revolution led by Fidel Castro. Under Castro, a Marxist government rapidly engaged in a widespread land reform program that disenfranchised several large American corporations. There were also high-profile, Nuremberg-like trials of functionaries in the Batista regime who were accused of torture, murder, and human rights violations. These trials resulted, like the Nuremberg trials, in several executions. Estimates of the number of executions in the years immediately following the revolution range from the hundreds to the thousands. While these trials may not have employed due process and in many cases the punishment may have been excessive, there seems little doubt that the bulk of those executed engaged in heinous crimes under Batista's rule. Among the high-ranking Batista officials, many had close ties to American businessmen and/or to the CIA. In addition, Cuba embarked on a program of aggressive land reform that in the US view provided inadequate compensation to the landowners. The compensation, however, was based on the low assessment that the landowners themselves had provided so as to minimize their taxes.

"The land reform was a turning point in the US relationship with Cuba," Richard Gott explains. "When the National Security Council revived its discussions of Cuba in June (1959), it decided that Castro would have to go" (180). In January 1960 the assistant secretary for inter-American affairs summarized the NSC activities, indicating that six months earlier, it had decided that "it was not possible to achieve our objectives with Castro in power" (quoted in Gott 180); throughout the summer of 1959 the NSC "had been busy drawing up a program to replace Castro" (quoted in Gott 180). Also in January 1960, the NSC decided to "accelerate the development of an opposition in Cuba which would bring about . . . a new government favorable to U.S. interests" (quoted in Gott 180).

This process was augmented by the covert support of a manufactured coun-
terrevolutionary group, formed in Miami, stationed in Nicaragua, and directed
by CIA operatives to stage an invasion at the Bay of Pigs. In addition, the United
States put in place an embargo on the import of Cuban goods, which lost much
of its effectiveness when the Soviet Union purchased the exports formerly
shipped to the United States. This growing connection between Cuba and the
USSR was a public acknowledgment of Cuba's allegiance in flagrant defiance of
the Monroe Doctrine, which claimed the Western Hemisphere as a US sphere
of influence.

This defiance was made explicit in Castro's September 1960 speech, "The
First Declaration of Havana," which announced: "The People of Cuba strongly
condemn the imperialism of North America for its criminal domination, lasting
more than a century, of all the peoples of Latin America" (quoted in Gott 184).
In the lexicon of the Cold War, Cuba threatened an informing tactic of the policy
of containment: that the United States had to make itself a visibly more attractive partner to the nations of the world than the Soviet Union. Given that the
name given US Latin American policy was "Alliance for Progress," the defection
of a member of that alliance, on the basis that it was in actuality a compact for
"criminal domination," affected not just Cuban-American relations but more
fundamentally the US public relations crusade that characterized a prolific
array of overt and covert policies on political, economic, social, and cultural
fronts. According to the United States, Castro's Cuba rejected both capitalism
and democracy, while Puerto Rico epitomized freedom and demonstrated the
opportunities that US capitalism provides.

Under the rubric of "protectorate," however, Puerto Rico was and remains
one of the last Western colonies.[1] In 1961, in other words, it instantiated most
radically the form of governance that the Cuban Revolution had rejected. But
at least from the perspective of the United States, it did so invisibly. And the
very invisibility of its colonial status forms the basis for Puerto Rico's representation in *West Side Story*. The film treats it as an independent nation, in
sharp distinction from Cuba, which the US government and media regarded as
a Soviet puppet state. Consider, for example, this excerpt from *Time magazine*
in February 1960:

> Anastas Mikoyan went to Havana last week and in effect told Fidel Castro
> that Moscow, mother of revolutions, thought well of Castro's little revolu-
> tion and was willing to help it out.
>
> Mikoyan climbed out of his plane from Moscow in the manner of a
> proconsul come to view his latest province. Waiting and happily savor-
> ing the event were Fidel Castro and Major Ernesto ("Che") Guevara, presi-
> dent of Cuba's national bank and the government's leading Red. ("The
> Proconsul Arrives" 52)

Similarly, this *Time* article, published four months later, titled "The Marxist Neighbor," surveys Castro's US baiting, fears of a planned US "intervention," and Cuban "brainwashing":

> In a third-grade Havana classroom last week, when the teacher asked what happened on Feb. 15, 1898, a tiny girl shot back the answer: "The United States blew up the Maine so they could intervene in Cuba." The rest of the "correct" answer: "most of the crew members were Negroes."
> . . . in the predictable future, the U.S. apparently will just have to get along with, without giving in to, the truculent neighbor who now presides over a people the U.S. one thought its good friends. (30–31)

In this context, Puerto Rico became the redeemable alternative to Cuba, the latter a space marked by its refusal to embrace the "American" community or "American" values; Puerto Ricans, as aspiring Americans in *West Side Story*, thus contrast sharply with the Cuban Communists, who were by definition "un-American."

Constructing Puerto Ricans in this way crucially revises *Romeo and Juliet*, on which *West Side Story* is based. By making one of the feuding groups, the Jets, original, and the other, the Sharks, the interloper, *West Side Story* changes *Romeo and Juliet*'s feud from arbitrary to historical. In so doing, it radically reinterprets Shakespeare's play, which intentionally fails to provide a substantive argument on behalf of either the Montagues or the Capulets. The absence of a potentially "right" side in *Romeo and Juliet* thematically validates Mercutio's dying words: "A curse on both your houses." Not allowing either the Montagues or the Capulets to claim the virtuous position makes *Romeo and Juliet*'s rivalry crucially different from the globally bifurcated politics of the Cold War. *West Side Story* thus rewrites Shakespeare according to the world of diametrically opposed arguments that defined Cold War sensibilities, in which both sides vie for the right to control "American" turf.

Turf Wars, Un-Americans, and (Un)Americans

West Side Story is also informed by challenges to *de facto* northern school desegregation. Castro himself chose to underscore the connection between the two. When he attended the 1960 UN September session, he moved his multiracial delegation to the Hotel Theresa in Harlem, thereby throwing an international spotlight specifically on the discriminatory treatment they had received at a downtown hotel and more generally on American racism, which remained palpable, even in the North, even six years after *Brown*.[2]

In 1960 desegregation was still moving very slowly, not only in the South, where resistant actions—legal and extralegal—were prolific, but also in the North, where demographic migrations exacerbated racial divisions faster than social policy could remedy them. It would take another four years before "the Court finally determined that the time for mere 'deliberate speed' had run out'" (Green 13).

In northern cities, the migration of white families to suburbia or to white neighborhoods within the city limits increased rather than alleviated segregation, especially when combined with the systematic gerrymandering of school districts. New York City, where *West Side Story* is set, had in 1954 forty-two *de facto* segregated elementary schools and nine segregated junior highs; five years later, the numbers had increased to seventy-two and twelve (Taylor 80). In the early 1960s, moreover, middle-class apartment developments such as Co-op City, in the Bronx, and Trump Houses, in Coney Island, along with a square mile of one-family and two-family homes built on landfill in Canarsie, facilitated a white exodus from previously integrated neighborhoods such as East New York, Brownsville, and the South Bronx.

The racial polarization of the North reflected in the postwar period a systemic coalition of racial stereotyping and public policy, wherein the stereotypes that motivated a policy decision seemed justified by the results of that decision. Writing about Detroit as paradigmatic of this problem, Thomas J. Sugrue explains,

> In the postwar city, blackness and whiteness assumed a spatial definition. . . . The completeness of racial segregation made ghettoization seem an inevitable, natural consequence of profound racial differences. . . . To the majority of untutored white observers, visible poverty, overcrowding, and deteriorating houses were signs of moral deficiencies, not manifestations of structural inequalities. White perceptions of black neighborhoods provided seemingly irrefutable confirmation of African American inferiority and set the terms of debates over the inclusion of African Americans in the city's housing and labor markets. (9)

As Sugrue makes clear, the issues of social engineering and racial demographics required both the presence of African Americans as a mythological mass and their invisibility as discrete citizens. Set in a moment of desegregation, busing, and "white flight," with which the anxieties of the 1950s transitioned into the demographic rearrangements of the 1960s, *West Side Story* reconciles racial conflicts by removing black people from the visual field and converting questions of *integration* into those of *immigration*, itself a displacement in which American citizens (Puerto Ricans) must occupy the subject position of aliens (who argue about what it is like "to be in America"). In this way, the Puerto Rican/Nyorican is used to facilitate a notion of integration that makes invisible both the imported slave labor used to build the American empire and the subjugated spaces and people used to expand that empire.

Space constraints do not permit elaboration of another sustained narrative asserting a threat to the US *de facto* postwar empire. For convenience, we can call that narrative "Only 90 Miles from Florida" (or alternatively, "Exporting Revolution . . . to an Assisted Living Community in Miami Beach"), which for half a century constructed Cuba as having designs on US turf. Suffice it to say that the Jets shared the same paranoid concern as did the CIA and the Republican Party of that era (as well as many subsequent US presidents and presidential candidates, from Barry Goldwater to Al Gore), transposed onto Puerto Rico, which becomes in the film the site of un-American activities, as affirmed by the Puerto Ricans themselves, who express both pro- and anti-American sentiments when they sing the words "I want to be in America" in a song that unites the economic and political connotations of the free world. Although the practices of the United States may fall short of its promise, the song asserts that, whether provocative or sanguine, these immigrants are looking for freedom:

> Everything *free* in America . . . for a slight fee in America.
> Here you are *free* and you have pride . . . Long as you stay on your own side.
> Free to be anything you choose . . . *Free* to wait tables and shine shoes.

Thus the problem for the Sharks, especially in light of the anti-American sentiments they express, is to prove that their designs on the West (side), on Western turf, are not perverse, that they are not an invasive force but an emigrant population, eager to adopt American values rather than to overthrow them. To do this, they must liberate Puerto Rico—that is, turn it into an independent country—so that they may turn themselves into immigrants, the huddled masses seeking freedom. This form of liberation once again makes Puerto Rico the mirror opposite of Cuba, the place that must be liberated to *protect* American freedom, just as, simultaneously, Cuba must be regarded as the colonized space, the Soviet puppet state, to occlude the colonial status of Puerto Rico. The Sharks and their Latina girlfriends must thus evoke Puerto Rico in order to erase it: "Isle of my devotion: sink back into the middle of the Ocean." Puerto Rico, of course, never was in the middle of the Atlantic Ocean, exemplifying the impossible cultural work *West Side Story* demands, which is to *return* the island to a place where it has never been.

The displacement of Puerto Rico, furthermore, is effected at the expense of displacing African Americans from the center of the issues surrounding the demographic concerns of rust-belt cities such as Philadelphia, Cleveland, Chicago, Detroit, and New York, where the national enforcement of *Brown* was impacting the composition of urban schools. Policies that included rezoning and forced busing were changing the color of school districts traditionally characterized by *de facto* segregation and with them the racial composition of urban neighborhoods.

What is striking about the opening credits of *West Side Story*, in this regard, is that it makes clear the film is about "color": the widescreen starts out completely yellow, marked by an array of thin vertical lines; then, while we hear the

FIGURE 9-2 A widescreen shot of Manhattan, taken from above Ellis Island.

musical overture, the screen morphs to red, then to orange, pink, purple, blue, green, back to orange, and then to a deeper green. At the same time the vertical lines start to thicken, ever so slightly, suggesting perhaps an abstract urban sky-line. When the screen turns blue again, the camera seems to pan back, revealing the words "WEST SIDE STORY" in block letters across the bottom of the screen, with the thick clusters of vertical lines above the title now starting to resemble Lower Manhattan. As the overture reaches its climax, the abstraction becomes a reality: a widescreen color shot of Manhattan, taken from a helicopter—we can hear the rotors—hovering roughly above Ellis Island (see figure 9.2). Next we see a God's-view shots of various parts of the city, starting with two of bridge traffic and then one of ocean liners.

This film, in other words, vividly announces itself as being about the chang-ing color of New York City, about people coming to the city and, given the Ellis Island perspective and the ocean liner, by extension coming to America. That journey, in a series of pans, always looking down from above, moves us in up from Ellis Island over the business district to the apartments and tenements of the West Side until it cuts to a playground, eventually seen at ground level: the place where we meet the Jets and the Sharks, constantly harassing one another on the basketball courts, down the streets, and through the alleys. The multi-color coding, indicated by the opening titles, becomes a constant motif in the film, maintained by the costumes, the lighting, and the set decoration. The French doors in Maria's family's apartment, for example, contain small panes of random colors that mirror the palate of the opening shots. Reds and blues, particularly, fill portions of the screen, covering walls or sides of trucks, lest we forget that against this palate of red and blue, there will be enacted issues of whiteness. Many of the Jets, who are supposed to stand for the earlier immigrant ethnicities (the Sharks call them "mick" and "wop"), have a startlingly midwest-ern appearance. Richard Beymer (who plays Tony) was born in Iowa, and his conspicuously dark makeup fails to disguise his WASP profile. The gang that actually looks "Italian" is the Sharks, all of whom have straight hair and almost all of whom have thin lips and sharp features.

And all the Latina women work in a dress-making shop, one that alludes to the garment district work that employed earlier generations of immigrants. At the same time, the work conditions indicate that this is no sweatshop. The women sewing formal gowns and wedding dresses have found good work and good working conditions in America, and have done so, moreover, without the aid of a union. While in 1961, in fact, many of the trade unions in New York City had few minority members, this nonunion shop not only has more freedom from onerous work regulations than a union shop but also allows the freedom of imagination that permits Maria to project herself into the roles valorized by American culture—the prom date and the bride—which combine to constitute, as her donning the tiara suggests, her idea of Miss America (see figure 9.3).

As the "I Feel Pretty" number is staged, in other words, Maria feels most "pretty" when she imagines herself as assimilating; that is, when she imagines herself as Natalie Wood, if she only could, which of course she can, because destiny has paired her with another Anglo, as required by the Hollywood Production Code, still in effect—although barely so—in the early 1960s.

This arrangement is a purely Anglo representation: two WASPs, made up and dubbed to look Hispanic and Italian, agree on the impossibility of a place for Puerto Ricans. This is also consistent with American judicial precedent. In a series of Supreme Court decisions, the term "non-incorporated territory" has been sustained as a way of making Puerto Rico American, in that Puerto Ricans were American citizens, and making Puerto Rico non-American, in that they were not entitled to the constitutional rights guaranteed to American citizens; while Puerto Ricans could aspire to come to America, Puerto Rico could not aspire to American statehood. As Joel Colon-Rios and Martin Hevia succinctly

FIGURE 9-3 Maria donning a tiara.

put it, "With the creation of the category of the 'unincorporated territory', the U.S. Supreme Court sanctioned the colonial condition of Puerto Rico" (7). In the Cold War period, moreover, this double identity rendered Puerto Rico an imaginary space—not independent but symbolic of American independence, it was a tourist mecca (see figure 9.4), such that US tourists, as Dennis Merrill explains, "unavoidably became participants in a Cold War cultural experience. . . . The image [of Puerto Rico] juxtaposed the island's tropical allure and its material progress, its rural simplicity and its advanced consumer offerings, its yearnings

FIGURE 9-4 Puerto Rico as Cold War paradise: travel poster.

for change and its stability. Puerto Rico shone as a Cold War paradise, an out-post for liberal capitalism in a world seemingly tempted by the promises of com-munism" (213).

At the same time, the song "Somewhere (There Is a Place for Us)" under-scores the impossibility of a place for a couple that is both foreign and Ameri-can, both white and nonwhite, both homogeneous and miscegenating. As the film proves, there is no place for them. Maria's attempt to reprise the duet, asserting that the place, "somewhere," is cut short by Tony's death, and the final sequence in which Maria is ordained by both gangs leaves her belonging to nei-ther, just as Natalie Wood, with slightly darkened makeup, which she had told us, using Marni Nixon's voice, made her feel "pretty," is equally displaced and impossible to identify. It is not that she has lost her identity, but rather that her circumstances have proliferated her identities. She is both Latina and Anglo, in her makeup violating ethnic taboos, while beneath it affirming them (see fig-ure 9.5), allowed by the casting only to make out with and, ultimately, lose her virginity to a corn-fed American actor, using makeup as dark as hers to perform Italian ethnicity in the same way that she performs Puerto Rican ethnicity, that is, with a dubbed voice, as patently nonethnic as her own.

FIGURE 9-5 Wood and Beymer, in their makeup violating ethnic taboos, while beneath it affirming them.

She thus becomes like Puerto Rico itself: in contrast to anti-American Cuba, it is pro-American, but in contrast to New York, it is un-American; in contrast to Latin America, it is America. Its citizens are in America and also aspire to go there. As a Puerto Rican American, Maria is anti-Puerto Rico, as it is the place she must reject in order to be where she wants to be, "in America," even though Puerto Rico is part of America, an invisible colony in an unacknowledged empire, forever the place that must be erased to validate the real America, as Sarah Palin called it, although Palin (in the great tradition of the film's contemporary Republican, Barry Goldwater) was locating Manhattan Island as the ersatz place, the one that should fall back into the ocean, in the same way that *West Side Story* excised Puerto Rico to establish New York City as the real America.

Urban Renewal, Slum Clearance, and the Cold War Utopia

This attitude, when juxtaposed with the actual history of the Puerto Ricans and African Americans in New York City, suggests the profound flaw at the heart of what were called the "urban renewal projects" of the period, which invoked a narrative of progress to remove African Americans from their historical neighborhoods. As Andrew Dunar explains,

> The Eisenhower administration supported a new . . . approach that became known as "urban renewal," a program that allowed for the expenditure of federal funds on much more than just slum clearance, extending its interests to education, police and fire protection, and recreational facilities. Urban renewal projects took various form, but usually included the extension of the Interstate Highway System into downtown areas, the razing of "blighted" neighborhoods, and the construction of new housing. Often, however, these efforts only served to accelerate the decline of cities they were supposed to regenerate. Blocks of residences were razed to make way for complicated interstate interchanges, and civil rights activists complained that "urban renewal" was just another name for "negro removal." When new development took place, it seldom served to provide housing for those who had been displaced, often replacing residential housing with civic centers or government buildings. Developers still hesitated to start new projects in areas where the population had been declining, and where signs of urban renaissance seemed to be the airy talk of politicians. Blocks were left undeveloped and soon became overgrown with weeds, standing signs of decay rather than renewal. (180)[3]

The neighborhood where *West Side Story* was filmed was one such urban renewal project, an area that was condemned and evacuated through the use of

FIGURE 9-6 The construction of Lincoln Center.

eminent domain to permit the construction of Lincoln Center, an important and intentional move in attempting to solidify US cultural hegemony (see figure 9.6).

The *real* America, during the Cold War, according to David Rockefeller, who in the 1950s spearheaded the public-private coalition that produced Lincoln Center for the Performing Arts, was one in which "freedom and democracy can exist . . . only [when society has] vitality in its roots" (Zipp 168–169). By this he meant the vitality of the performing arts, not of upwardly mobile immigrant populations or their ethnic neighborhoods. In the brief interim between the uprooting of a black and Hispanic community (to make room for vitality in the roots of freedom and democracy) and the razing of the buildings that housed that vital community, *West Side Story* was shot. If the goal of Lincoln Center was to bring dance to the urban masses, therefore, *West Side Story* anticipates the New York City Ballet, by dancing where the State Theater would be, but instead of bringing dance to the masses, it brings the masses to dance, as the musical *West Side Story* lured millions of people to the site that Robert Moses, head of the city Commission on Slum Clearance, officially condemned.

As if to elevate the Cold War symbolism that establishes Lincoln Center as the capitalist utopia that refutes the Marxist utopian assertions represented by Castro's Cuba, the man selected as the first president of Lincoln Center was General Maxwell D. Taylor, NATO veteran and retired US Army chief of staff. Only four months after assuming the post, Taylor had to leave and redirect his energies from a figurative refutation of Castro to the literal problem of toppling him: President Kennedy needed Taylor immediately to assist in dealing with the aftermath of the Bay of Pigs fiasco.[4]

Thus the film both anticipates and replicates the work of Lincoln Center by replacing slums with performing arts and by removing from the scene, both figuratively and literally, people of color. In fact, the mandate for the construction of Lincoln Center followed Moses's argument that "[n]o plasters, nostrums and palliatives will save this part of town" (quoted in Zipp 226). Performing what he called "bold and aseptic surgery" (226), Moses parted the West Side and oversaw the Exodus of blacks and Puerto Ricans, in order to make way for the vitality the Rockefellers deemed vital to Cold War survival. In the same way, the film's failed utopia, imagined "somewhere," prophetically evacuates the West (Side) to make way for the real cultural utopia where, replacing the Jets and Sharks, the New York City Ballet would dance on the site of Tony's white-in-black-face, imaginary grave.[5]

The End of 1950s Angst

The first baby boomers saw *West Side Story* while they were in high school, the place where they were when John Kennedy was assassinated, the place where many of them were when Lyndon Johnson escalated the number of troops in Vietnam from 25,000 to 250,000. Most of the baby boomers were still in school, kindergarten through grade 12, the following year, when Vietnam deployments increased to half a million, but a small percentage of them were in Vietnam. Over the next nine years, most of the male boomers would be old enough to serve in Vietnam; many would, and some—no doubt a significant portion of the war's 58,000 casualties—would not return.

Boomer veterans, treated very differently than their veteran fathers had been, would create a new demographic group consolidating much American angst and sorrow. College students, the counterculture, yuppies, Black Panthers, illegal Mexican immigrants, urban pioneers and gentrifiers, divorced parents, and makeshift families with complex entanglements and individualized custody agreements would, from the mid-1960s to the 1980s, contribute to a demographic map unimaginable in 1950. The range and pace of demographic reorganization that this new map illustrates makes perfect sense. However surprising the impact of a specific group, the groupings themselves and the regroupings, like the ocean's undulations, continuously break into unique waves. They attest to the normalcy of change.

My target, therefore, has not been an arbitrary set of population groups, but rather the naïve belief in their enduring normality and, for a brief period—the late 1940s to the early 1960s—an inadequate repertoire of avenues for questioning that belief or expressing the pain that it caused.

The greater 1950s was a time when foreign policy was more bipartisan than coherent, more duplicitous than transparent, a time when women's paths to happiness were treated as biologically determined, in the same way that satisfactory sexual behaviors and orientations were for men and women alike. It was a time when people worried about the changing racial composition of their schools or neighborhoods or the prospect of rampant juvenile delinquency as much, perhaps, as they feared nuclear annihilation. The 1950s saw, for the first time, a large majority of Americans afraid to identify themselves as anything but "middle class," despite vast differences in the size of their income and the ways that they earned it. In part, this was because more than half of the new families the decade produced moved into narrowly homogeneous developments with architecturally cookie-cutter units; "little boxes" one popular folk song called them. In the 1950s, the word "nonconformist" was a commonly used pejorative.

In that moment, popular films spoke the lingua franca of the American population, simultaneously asserting the normative and worrying it. The canonical films I have discussed thus reveal how popular narrative media do cultural work. They encourage stability by reconciling the contradictions that reside in what passes for natural at the same time that they focus the opposition that forges change out of its own relentless, often belligerent, delays.

NOTES

CHAPTER 1. THE CHARACTER OF POST-WORLD WAR II AMERICA

1. See Altschuler and Blumin; Humes. As Leman extensively details, the creation of the Educational Testing Service and its multifarious products—SATs (developed after World War I, but achieving preeminence after World War II), GREs, and LSATs—was an ancillary effect of the G.I. Bill, working simultaneously to promote higher education as an egalitarian meritocracy and to stratify the level of opportunity available to individuals, especially first-generation college applicants.
2. See Boyer ch. 18 (211–229).
3. See Horsman.
4. Cuordileone shows how *The Vital Center* contains the roots of Schlesinger's argument in his 1958 *Esquire* essay, "The Crisis of American Masculinity."
5. See Leibman; Spigel.
6. The singularity of the message and uniformity of the codes were in part the function of the fact that in the 1950s and 1960s, the medium had great breadth of distribution and little diversity of programming. If by 1960 more than 90 percent of American households had television sets, the majority of them received between two and five channels (seven was the maximum number possible on the UHF bandwidth), and the content in all markets was dominated first by two and later by three major networks. See Barnouw, Boddy, and Nadel (*Television*).
7. See Medovoi 91–134.
8. See Barranger.

CHAPTER 2. *SINGIN' IN THE* (HUAC) *RAIN*

1. The extent of the Hollywood blacklist has been extensively documented. Among the leading works are Englund and Ceplair, *The Inquisition in Hollywood*; and Victor Navasky, *Naming Names*. In addition, countless memoirs, biographies, and autobiographies have described the experiences of the blacklisted or nearly blacklisted.
2. See Englehardt.
3. See Wollen 12.
4. Part of the "beautiful girl" number, for example, evokes Busby Berkley's style.
5. See Boyer.
6. This figurative role, conferred on Kelly by Astaire, was more of a myth that through its iteration has retrospectively achieved the status of "fact." See Cohan 196–199.
7. Mast 249.

8. The size of college enrollment increased exponentially, and the demographic of the student body changed radically. According to Altschuler and Blumin, "by the 1950s . . . large lecture classes and the employment of graduate students to teach discussion sections had become the norm. In 1948, only 10 universities enrolled more than 20,000 students. Two decades later, 55 universities did so, and more than 60 increased the number of degree matriculates past 10,000 for the first time" (110). The bill also "demolished the contention that the core constituency was young men and women from affluent families" (111).

9. Most notable was Lucille Ball, at the time the most popular television star in America, who put on her ditzy Lucy routine in exchange for the committee's believing that she had signed certain left-wing documents without understanding them, only to please her grandfather.

10. Even late in life his testimony haunted him. In 1999, when Kazan, then eighty-nine years old, was given a lifetime achievement award at the Oscars ceremony, about 500 protesters assembled outside, and many in the hall refused to stand or applaud.

11. See Cohan 196–199.

12. Although this accurately describes what we see of *The Dancing Cavalier*, the song dubbing and the voice dubbing occur in different scenes, and the effects of both are shown in a third scene at the premiere of *The Dancing Cavalier*.

13. The voice is modeled on the one Judy Holiday created for the play *Born Yesterday*; Hagen was Holiday's understudy and also played the role in the road company.

CHAPTER 3. IT'S *ALL* ABOUT EVE

1. See also Haskell 244–247; Sayre 141.

2. Kashner and MacNair 336.

3. Among the most popular sitcoms of the mid-1950s were: *I Love Lucy*, *Make Room for Daddy* (*The Danny Thomas Show*), *Father Knows Best*, *The Donna Reed Show*, *Leave It to Beaver*, *I Married Joan*, and *The Life of Riley*.

4. In this regard, it is erroneous to regard *Modern Times* (1936) as a silent film, because it has a sound track. That sound track, like all film sound tracks, makes continuous choices among its sound options (speech, music, noise, and silence). The sound track of *Modern Times* heavily privileges music, but includes some noises and a small amount of speech.

5. The original (discarded) opening sequence begins with Joe in the morgue talking to the other corpses (Sikov 109).

6. Because *My Fair Lady*'s immense Broadway success portended a very long run, the rights were not attainable. Instead the show's composers, Lerner and Lowe, were commissioned to write a score for a musical version of the Broadway play *Gigi* that was meant to echo the plot and style of *My Fair Lady*.

7. Vanessa Schwartz explains how *Gigi*'s visually elaborate production affected critics (and underscored the film's "Frenchness"): "As one critic put it, "*Gigi* is a film made solely for the pleasure of the eyes, a purely retinal film" (50).

8. See McLean 214.

9. The disagreement over the presence and nature of evil and the formation of an "American" identity has roots in the spilt between American renaissance authors such as Nathaniel Hawthorne and Herman Melville and transcendentalists such as Ralph Waldo Emerson; see R.W.B. Lewis.

CHAPTER 4. "WHAT STARTS LIKE A SCARY TALE . . ."

1. Blackmon has traced in extensive detail the link between corrupt law enforcement, abduction, and the sale of illegally incarcerated black people to commercial interests, which since Emancipation has replicated the practice of slavery.
2. See Sayre; Neve; Girgus 165–169;, Schickel; Navasky.
3. Biskind succinctly lists the large number of details that contribute to the reading of the film as Christian allegory (178–179); Fisher examines at length the impact Father Corridan has on Schulberg's conception of the story; and Braudy notes the religious themes and allusions.
4. See Braudy 41.
5. See Nadel, *Containment Culture* 80–84.
6. See Fisher 97–100.
7. The equivalent in the twenty-first century is $1,500–$2,000.

CHAPTER 5. "LIFE COULD NOT BETTER BE"

1. As I pointed out in *Television in Black-and-White America*, television provided the common national space of these discrete, economically and racially segregated communities (43–85).
2. This is why William H. Whyte, in *The Organization Man*, published the same year that *The Court Jester* was released, regarded suburban communities as the "ideal way station" (311) for the organization man: "It is he who sets the tone, and if he is uncertain as any in keeping up with the Joneses, it is because he *is* the Joneses" (311; emphasis in original). For this reason, Whyte saw the suburbs as "communities made in his image" (296).
3. This is a Foucauldian interpretation of Mills, as reflected in Foucault's insight about the way power functions relationally, as in when, for example, the student in using the ruler replicates at the minuscule level the deployment of the Ruler, or when, via the asylum or the panopticon, the person of unreason or the prisoner's guilt is organized as an internalized mode of self-surveillance.
4. See Koenig 173–179.

CHAPTER 6. CITIZENS OF THE FREE WORLD UNITE

1. Filippelli 5.
2. Filippelli 112.
3. His coauthor accepted the award as sole author. In 1992 Trumbo's coauthorship was acknowledged by the Motion Picture Academy.
4. Dina Smith notes the importance of Hepburn's Cinderella quality; see also William A. Brown and Rachel Mosley.
5. Eisenberg subsequently critiques the causes and effects of the traditional Berlin Airlift narrative, but her description here captures well the public perception of it at the time (and, for the most part, thereafter).
6. Shandley 62.
7. See Ma; Houston; McConachie.
8. Among the prolific citations of this saying, see, for example, Bailey (97) or Maloney: "Anyone who's ever been in the army has heard the saying—'There's *the right way, the*

wrong way, and the army way.' As far as the army goes, it's true" (63). The huge number of references indicates that assumptions about incompetent US military procedures were so widely accepted as to have become a cliché. Retrospective over-praising of the US military in contemporary American political discourse tends to obscure the fact that proclamations about military efficiency would have been laughable in the 1950s.

9. Nadel, *Containment Culture.*

10. *Containment Culture* 13–37.

11. See Corber (*In the Name of National Security, Homosexuality in Cold War America*); Johnson; Epstein.

12. Although today the US census data distinguishes "white" from "Hispanic," throughout the history of American cinema, many light-skinned leading men of Hispanic background (in addition to Montalban, Fernando Lamas, and Cesar Romero, as well as fictional characters such as Zorro and the Cisco Kid), in terms of romantic pairing with white women, were considered "white," but not until the mid-1960s were any black men paired with white women. Thus the extremely chaste *Guess Who's Coming to Dinner* (1967) still seemed groundbreaking.

CHAPTER 7. EXPEDIENT EXAGGERATION AND THE SCALE OF COLD WAR FARCE IN *NORTH BY NORTHWEST*

1. See Keane; Shumway 107; Cavell 762–763;Wood 141; Allen 59–60; Meola 123.

2. Cavell spends much time describing himself observing the film's extensive references to *Hamlet*, only to conclude that (1) Hitchcock wishes to compete with Shakespeare's most famous play and (2) the play has a famous Oedipal interpretation. The first point requires not only that Hitchcock was egomaniacal, but that he was a stupid egomaniac, and the second point, focused on Ernest Jones's interpretation of *Hamlet*, requires that Hitchcock was competing with Shakespeare by subordinating himself to Jones. Cavell fails to consider that *Hamlet* is a famous play *about something*; it is about a student pulled out of his studies and thrust into a world of murder and intrigue for which he has had no preparation and of which he has no understanding. His ability to navigate his circumstances is relentlessly complicated by his inability to distinguish illusion from reality and by the necessity to assume a false identity with real consequences.

3. Nadel, *Containment Culture* 13–37.

4. Schlesinger, *Act of Creation*, contains a copy of the *United Nations Charter*. All *charter* material is quoted from that copy, pages 295–321.

5. As Pomerance points out, a central irony of the film is "our protagonist is a man who can learn to survive only from those who fail to acknowledge him as Roger O. Thornhill (the person *he* supposes himself naturally, automatically, simply, merely, and wholeheartedly to be), persistently recognizing him as a person they believe him naturally, automatically, simply, merely, and wholeheartedly to be, George Kaplan. Even though he insists he is *not* Kaplan (and one of the lovely ironies of the film is that we tend to agree with him), his denials must be directed toward a small and powerful audience convinced that he *is*" (16).

6. See Kunz. See also Meisler 94–114; LaFeber 187–192; Walker 99–101; Dunar 159–165.

7. For an extended examination of the role that American Cold War television, and especially adult westerns, played in promoting the notion of the United States as exemplar of the Western bloc, see Nadel, *Television in Black-and-White America.*

8. About the casting of Grant, Hitchcock said: "You are actually playing a character, but you are also playing the personality of Cary Grant. The value of having Cary Grant, the

film star, is that the audience gets a little more emotion out of Cary Grant than they would from an unknown, because there is identification" (Gottlieb 92).

9. See Wood 140; Allen 199; Millington 150.

10. See Camp; Dynia; Wood; Cavell 767–768; Spoto 342–344.

11. See Trento; Weiner. This is also the general impression conveyed by Allen Dulles's *The Craft of Intelligence*.

12. Wilford extensively details the vast range of organizations and public figures who were knowingly funded by and/or cooperated with the CIA in its covert propaganda agenda, including, for example, William Paley and Gloria Steinem.

13. Kinzer has documented the extensive impact of the Dulles brothers in formulating and disguising US interventionism.

14. As Hitchcock demonstrated in *Blackmail*, the first talkie in British film, he understood the dimensions of film sound years before they would be adequately theorized.

15. For an elaboration of star theory, see Dyer (*Stars* and *Heavenly Bodies*); Fisher and Landy.

16. Like the comment in the scene about laughing, this remark, paraphrasing comedian Jimmy Durante (whose trademark sign-off was "Good Night, Mrs. Calabash, wherever you are"), serves as a piece of metacommentary signaling the film's farcical mode.

CHAPTER 8. DEFIANT DESEGREGATION WITH NO (LIBERAL) WAY OUT

1. Bartley, *Massive Resistance* 120.

2. See Nadel, *Television in Black-and-White America: Race and National Identity*.

3. Boddy 201; Barnouw, *Television Writer* 28.

4. It is noteworthy that although Gladys is a significant character in the film, who appears in more than one scene and has more lines than other white characters, her performance is uncredited.

5. We now know that, in light of Kaufman's corrupt collusion with the FBI and the Justice Department, Ethel Rosenberg's sentence was predetermined, as an attempt to exert coercive leverage on Julius. Because the Rosenbergs were not convicted of giving atomic secrets to the Soviets but with *conspiring* to do so, the sentence, even if it were the result of a fair trial, would have been unconscionably excessive. Given that exculpatory evidence was suppressed to allow Kaufman to give the sentence decided upon before the trial, it does not seem inappropriate to call Ethel's execution state-sanctioned murder. See Clune.

6. See Kennedy 63.

7. See also Medovoi 182.

8. In a period when the Production Code prohibited acknowledging the existence of homosexuality, the closest to an explicit indication of Plato's orientation is the pinup picture of Alan Ladd in his locker; when Jim drops Plato off at his house after Buzz's death, Plato's invitation to sleep over is acted and shot so as to suggest romantic chemistry between the two boys.

9. If Terry served as a surrogate for Kazan, moreover, it is worth noting that *Rebel* director Nicholas Ray, having come under HUAC scrutiny and barely avoided the blacklist (Medovoi 178), chose a central plot mechanism that affirms cooperating with the state. This seems particularly significant since James Dean was Ray's surrogate, in that Dean modeled his performance after Ray, who was his mentor in the months preceding the production (Kashner and MacNair 99–122).

10. Biskind sees *Rebel* and *Waterfront* as being basically "the same film" as *Blackboard Jungle*, in that "they all set out to solve the same problem: social control" (163). Sayre

sees the film as more generally reflecting "adults' feeling of being endangered by the young" (116).

11. See Medovoi 91–135; Doherty 54–82; Jones *Great Expectations*, 61–62.

12. Poitier two years later would star with Rock Hudson in *Something of Value*, based on Robert Ruark's novel about the rebellion.

13. "Mau Mau Block Kenya Surrender," *New York Times*, April 12, 1954, p. 1.

14. See also, for example, Sanderson; "Native Terrorists Raid a Kenya Mission," *New York Times*, September 13, 1952, p. 2; "Chiefs in Kenya Discuss Terror," *New York Times*, October 28, 1952, p. 5; "Mau Mau Massacres 150 Natives in Night Raid Near Kenya Capital," *New York Times*, March 28, 1953, pp. 1+.

CHAPTER 9. "I WANT TO BE IN AMERICA"

1. Hence the title of Malavet's book on the political and cultural conflict between the United States and Puerto Rico: *America's Colony*.

2. Borstelmann 132–133.

3. See also Sugrue; Jones, *The Slaughter of Cities*. Regarding the interstate highway system, see Mowbray.

4. Olmstead 179

5. Zipp sees *West Side Story* as an ironic allegory for the policy of urban renewal: "The play's narrative arc parallels the historical progress of urban renewal's aspirations. If the conflict between the gangs provides some rationalization for the negative impetus for urban renewal, the play's central love story illuminates its utopian hopes and tragic fall. The promise of love in the story acts like the promise of renewal in postwar New York: it offers to deliver people from worry, want and danger and to usher in possibility. But, of course, *West Side Story* is a tragedy, and the collapse of the lovers' hopes mirrors the corruption and decline of urban renewal's city-remaking visions" (248).

FILMOGRAPHY

Abbot and Costello Meet Dr. Jekyll and Mr. Hyde. Directed by Charles Lamont. Universal International Pictures, 1953.

All about Eve. Directed by Joseph L. Mankiewicz. Performances by Bette Davis and Anne Baxter. Twentieth Century Fox, 1950.

The Big Lift. Directed by George Seaton. Performances by Montgomery Clift and O. E. Hasse. Twentieth Century Fox, 1950.

Blackboard Jungle. Directed by Richard Brooks. Performances by Glenn Ford and Sidney Poitier. MGM, 1955.

Blackmail. Directed by Alfred Hitchcock. British International Pictures, 1929.

Casablanca. Directed by Michael Curtiz. Performances by Humphrey Bogart and Lauren Bacall. Warner Brothers, 1942.

The Court Jester. Directed by Melvin Frank and Norman Panama. Performance by Danny Kaye. Dena Enterprises and Paramount Pictures, 1955.

Daddy Long-Legs. Directed by Jean Negulesco. Performances by Fred Astaire and Leslie Caron. Twentieth Century Fox, 1955.

The Defiant Ones. Directed by Stanley Kramer. Performances by Tony Curtis and Sidney Poitier. United Artists, 1958.

Far from Heaven. Directed by Todd Haynes. Performances by Julianne Moore and Dennis Quaid. Focus Features, 2002.

Follow the Fleet. Directed by Mark Sandrich. Performances by Fred Astaire and Ginger Rogers. RKO, 1936.

Gigi. Directed by Vincent Minnelli. Performances by Leslie Caron. MGM, 1958.

The Group. Directed by Sidney Lumet. Performance by Candice Bergen. United Artists, 1966.

Guess Who's Coming to Dinner. Directed by Stanley Kramer. Performances by Katherine Hepburn, Sidney Poitier, and Spencer Tracy. Columbia Pictures, 1967.

The Inspector General. Directed by Henry Koster. Performance by Danny Kaye. Warner Brothers, 1949.

Invasion of the Body Snatchers. Directed by Don Siegel. Performance by Kevin McCarthy. Allied Artists, 1956.

It Happened One Night. Directed by Frank Capra. Performances by Clark Gable and Claudette Colbert. Columbia Pictures, 1934.

The Jazz Singer. Directed by Alan Crosland. Performance by Al Jolson. Warner Brothers, 1927.

A Kid from Brooklyn. Directed by Norman Z. McLeod. Performance by Danny Kaye. Produced by The Samuel Goldwyn Company. Distributed by RKO Radio Pictures, 1946.

The King and I. Directed by Walter Lang. Performances by Yul Brenner and Deborah Kerr. Twentieth Century Fox, 1956.

Knock on Wood. Directed by Melvin Frank and Norman Panama. Performances by Danny Kaye and Mai Zetterling. Paramount Pictures, 1954.

The Lady Vanishes. Directed by Alfred Hitchcock. Performances by Margaret Lockwood and Michael Redgrave. MGM, 1938.

Lili. Directed by Charles Walters. Performances by Leslie Caron and Mel Ferrer. MGM, 1953.

Love in the Afternoon. Directed by Billy Wilder. Performances by Gary Cooper, Audrey Hepburn, and Maurice Chevalier. Allied Artists, 1957.

The Manchurian Candidate. Directed by John Frankenheimer. Performances by Frank Sinatra, Laurence Harvey, and Angela Landsbury. United Artists, 1962.

Merry Andrew. Directed by Michael Kidd. Performance by Danny Kaye. MGM, 1958.

Modern Times. Directed by Charlie Chaplin. Performance by Charlie Chaplin. United Artists, 1936.

My Fair Lady. Directed by George Cukor. Performances by Audrey Hepburn and Rex Harrison. Warner Brothers, 1964.

Niagara. Directed by Henry Hathaway. Performances by Joseph Cotton and Marilyn Monroe. Twentieth Century Fox, 1953.

Ninotchka. Directed by Ernst Lubitsch. Performance by Greta Garbo. MGM, 1939.

No Way Out. Directed by Joseph L. Mankiewicz. Performances by Sidney Poitier and Richard Widmark. Twentieth Century Fox, 1950.

North by Northwest. Directed by Alfred Hitchcock. Performances by Cary Grant and Eva Marie Saint. MGM, 1959.

Notorious. Directed by Alfred Hitchcock. Performances by Cary Grant and Ingrid Bergman. RKO, 1945.

On the Riviera. Directed by Walter Lang. Performances by Danny Kaye and Gene Tierney. 20th Century Fox, 1951.

On the Waterfront. Directed by Elia Kazan. Performances by Marlon Brando and Karl Malden. Columbia, 1954.

Peyton Place. Directed by Mark Robson. Performances by Lana Turner and Lee Phillips. Twentieth Century Fox, 1957.

Quo Vadis. Directed by Mervyn LeRoy. Performances by Robert Taylor and Deborah Kerr. MGM, 1951.

Rebel Without a Cause. Directed by Nicholas Ray. Performances by James Dean, Natalie Wood, and Sal Mineo. Warner Brothers, 1955.

Roman Holiday. Directed by William Wyler. Performances by Gregory Peck and Audrey Hepburn. Paramount, 1953.

Romeo and Juliet. Directed by Franco Zeffirelli. Performances by Leonard Whiting and Olivia Hussey. Paramount, 1968.

Royal Wedding. Directed by Stanley Donen. Performances by Fred Astaire and Jane Powell. MGM, 1951.

Sayonara. Directed by Joshua Logan. Performances by Marlon Brando and Red Buttons. Warner Brothers, 1957.

The Secret Life of Walter Mitty. Directed by Norman Z. McLeod. Performances by Danny Kaye and Virginia Mayo. The Samuel Goldwyn Company, 1947.

Singin' in the Rain. Directed by Stanley Donen and Gene Kelly. Performances by Gene Kelly, Donald O'Connor, and Debbie Reynolds. MGM, 1952.

Some Came Running. Directed by Vincent Minnelli. Performances by Dean Martin and Frank Sinatra. MGM, 1958.

Something of Value. Directed by Richard Brooks. Performances by Rock Hudson and Sidney Poitier. MGM, 1957.

Sunset Boulevard. Directed by Billy Wilder. Performances by William Holden and Gloria Swanson. Paramount, 1950.

Susan Slept Here. Directed by Frank Tashlin. Performances by Debbie Reynolds and Dick Powell. RKO, 1954.

The Teahouse of the August Moon. Directed by Daniel Mann. Performances by Marlon Brando and Glenn Ford. MGM, 1956.

The Ten Commandments. Directed by Cecil B. DeMille. Performances by Charlton Heston, Yul Brenner, and Anne Baxter. Paramount, 1956.

That's Entertainment. Directed by Jack Haley. Documentary with numerous performances. MGM, 1974.

The 39 Steps. Directed by Alfred Hitchcock. Performance by Robert Donat. Gaumont British Picture Corporation, 1935.

Topper. Directed by Norman Z. McLeod. Performances by Cary Grant and Constance Bennett. MGM, 1937.

West Side Story. Directed by Jerome Robbins and Robert Wise. Performances by Natalie Wood and Richard Beymer. United Artists, 1961.

Wonder Man. Directed by Bruce Humberstone. Performance by Danny Kay. The Samuel Goldwyn Company, 1945.

You Gotta Stay Happy. Directed by H. C. Potter. Performances by Joan Fontaine and James Stewart. Universal Pictures, 1948.

WORKS CITED

Allen, Richard. *Hitchcock's Romantic Irony*. Columbia University Press, 1989.

Altschuler, Glenn C., and Stuart M. Blumin. *The G.I. Bill: A New Deal for Veterans*. Oxford University Press, 2009.

"The Atlantic Report on the World Today: Japan." *Atlantic*, August 1956, pp. 19–20.

Auerbach, Jonathan, and Lisa Gitelman. "Microfilm, Containment, and the Cold War." *American Literary History*, vol. 19, no. 3, 2007, pp. 745–768.

Ayala, Cesar J., and Rafael Bernabe. *Puerto Rico in the American Century: A History since 1898*. University of North Carolina Press, 2007.

Bailey, Beth. *America's Army: Making the All-Volunteer Force*. Harvard University Press, 2009.

Balasz, Bela. *Bela Balasz: Early Film Theory*. Translated by Erica Carter and Rodney Livingston. Berghahn Books, 2010.

Baldwin, Kate A. *The Racial Imaginary of the Cold War Kitchen: From Sokol'niki Park to Chicago's South Side*. Dartmouth College Press, 2016.

Barnouw, Erik. *The Television Writer*. Hill & Wang, 1962.

———. *A Tube of Plenty: The Evolution of American Television*. 2nd rev. ed., Oxford University Press, 1990.

Barranger, Milly S. *Unfriendly Witnesses: Gender, Theater, and Film in the McCarthy Era*. Southern Illinois University Press, 2008.

Bartley, Numan V. *The Rise of Massive Resistance: Race and Politics in the Deep South During the 1960s*. Louisiana State University Press, 1999.

Barthes, Roland. *Mythologies*. Translated by Annette Lavers. Hill & Wang, 1978.

Bell-Metereau, Rebecca. "Movies and Our Secret Lives." *American Cinema of the 1950s: Themes and Variations*, edited by Murray Pommerance, Rutgers University Press, 2003, pp. 89–110.

Bently, Eric. "Farce." *Comedy: Meaning and Form*, edited by Robert Corrigan, Harper & Row, 1981, pp. 193–211.

Bermel, Albert. *Farce: The Comprehensive and Definitive Account of One of the World's Funniest Art Forms*. Simon and Schuster, 1982.

Billingsley, Kenneth Lloyd. *Hollywood Party: How Communism Seduced the American Film Industry in the 1930s and 1940s*. Prima Publishing, 1998.

Biskind, Peter. *Seeing Is Believing: How Hollywood Taught Us to Stop Worrying and Love the Fifties*. Henry Holt, 1983.

Blackmon, Douglas A. *Slavery by Another Name: The Re-Enslavement of Black Americans from the Civil War to World War II*. Anchor, 2009.

Boddy, William. *Fifties Television: The Industry and Its Critics*. University of Illinois Press, 1990.

Bordwell, David, Janet Staiger, and Kristin Thompson. *The Classical Hollywood Cinema: Film Style and Mode of Production to 1960*. Columbia University Press, 1985.

Borstelmann, Thomas. *The Cold War and the Color Line: American Race Relations in the Global Arena*. Harvard University Press, 2001.

Boyer, Paul. *By the Bomb's Early Light: American Thought and Culture at the Dawn of the Atomic Age*. Pantheon, 1985.

Braudy, Leo. *On the Waterfront*. BFI Publishing, 2005.

Brockman, Stephen. *A Critical History of German Film*. Camden House, 2010.

Brown, Daniel. "Wilde and Wilder." *PMLA*, vol. 119, no. 5, October 2004, pp. 1216–1230.

Brown, William A. "Audrey Hepburn: The Film Star as Event." *Larger Than Life: Movies Stars of the 1950s*, edited by R. Barton Palmer, Rutgers University Press, 2010, pp. 130–146.

Buruma, Ian. *Inventing Japan, 1953–1964*. Modern Library, 2004.

Byars, Jackie. *All that Hollywood Allows: Reading Gender in 1950s Melodrama*. University of North Carolina Press, 1991.

Camp, Jocelyn. "John Buchan and Alfred Hitchcock." *Literature and Film Quarterly*, vol. 6, no. 3, 1978, pp. 230–240.

Cavell, Stanley. "North by Northwest." *Critical Inquiry*, vol. 7, no. 4, 1981, pp. 761–776.

Ceplair, Larry, and Steven Englund. *The Inquisition in Hollywood: Politics in the Film Community, 1930–1960*. Anchor/Doubleday, 1980.

Champlin, Charles. *The Movies Grow Up: 1940–1980*. Ohio University Press, 1981.

Charney, Maurice. *Comedy High and Low: An Introduction to the Experience of Comedy*. Oxford University Press, 1978.

"Chiefs in Kenya Discuss Terror." *New York Times*, 28 October 1952, p. 5.

Chown, Jeffrey. "Visual Coding and Social Class in *On the Waterfront*." *On the Waterfront*, edited by Joanna E. Rapf, Cambridge University Press, 2003, pp. 106–123.

Chums, Peter, II. "Dance, Flexibility, and the Renewal of Genre in *Singin' in the Rain*." *Cinema Journal*, vol. 36, no. 1, Fall 1996, pp. 39–54.

Clapp, James A. "The Romantic Travel Movie Italian-Style." *Visual Anthropology*, vol. 22, no.1, 2009, pp. 52–63.

Clover, Carol. "Dancin' in the Rain." *Critical Inquiry*, vol. 21, Summer 1995, pp. 722–747.

Clune, Lori. *Executing the Rosenbergs: Death and Diplomacy in a Cold War World*. Oxford University Press, 2016.

Cohan, Steven. *Incongruous Entertainment: Camp, Cultural Value, and the MGM Musical*. Duke University Press, 2005.

———. *Masked Men: Masculinity and the Movies in the Fifties*. Indiana University Press, 1997.

Colón-Ríos, Joel L., and Martin Hevia. "The Legal Status of Puerto Rico and the Institutional Requirements of Republicanism." *Texas Hispanic Journal of Law and Policy*, vol. 17, no. 1, Spring 2011, pp. 1–25.

Corber, Robert. *Homosexuality in Cold War America: Resistance and the Crisis of Masculinity*. Duke University Press, 1997.

———. *In the Name of National Security: Hitchcock, Homophobia, and the Political Construction of Gender in Postwar America*. Duke University Press, 1993.

Crossman, Richard. *The God That Failed*. Edited by Richard Crossman. Bantam Books, 1951.

Cuordileone, K. A. *Manhood and American Political Culture in the Cold War*. Routledge, 2005.

Damerell, Reginald G. *Triumph in a White Suburb*. William Morrow, 1968.

Derrida, Jacques. "Plato's Pharmacy." *Dissemination*, translated by Barbara Johnson, University of Chicago Press, 1981, pp. 65–171.

Doane, Mary Ann. *Femmes Fatale: Feminism, Film Theory, Psychoanalysis*. Routledge, 1991.

Doherty, Tom. *Teenagers and Teenpics: The Juvenilization of American Movies in the 1950s*. Temple University Press, 2002.

Dower, John W. *Embracing Defeat: Japan in the Wake of World War II*. Norton, 1999.

———. "Preface." In Eiji Takemae, *The Allied Occupation of Japan*, translated by Robert Rickets and Sebastian Swann, Continuum, 2002, xix–xxiv.

Dudziak, Mary L. *Cold War Civil Rights: Race and the Image of American Democracy*. Princeton University Press, 2000.

Dulles, Allen. *The Craft of Intelligence: America's Legendary Spy Master on the Fundamentals of Intelligence Gathering for a Free World*. The Lyons Press, 2006.

Dunar, Andrew J. *America in the 1950s*. Syracuse University Press, 2006.

Dyer, Richard. *Heavenly Bodies: Film Stars and Society*. 2nd ed., Routledge, 2003.

———. *Stars*. 2nd ed., BFI Publications, 1998.

Dynia, Philp. "Alfred Hitchcock and the Ghost of Thomas Hobbes." *Cinema Journal*, vol. 15, no. 2, 1976, pp. 27–41.

Eisenberg, Carolyn. "The Myth of the Berlin Blockade and the Early Cold War." *Cold War Triumphalism: The Misuse of History After the Fall of Communism*, edited by Ellen Schrecker, New Press, 2004, pp. 174–200.

Empson, William. *Some Versions of Pastoral*. New Directions, 1974.

Endy, Christopher. *Cold War Holidays: American Tourism in France*. University of North Carolina Press, 2004.

Englehardt, Tom. *The End of Victory Culture*. Basic Books, 1995.

Epstein, Barbara. "Anti-Communism, Homophobia, and the Construction of Masculinity in the Post War U.S." *The Cold War, edited by Lori Lyn Bogle*, Routledge, 2001, pp. 73–96.

Falk, Andrew. *Upstaging the Cold War: American Dissent and Cultural Diplomacy, 1940–1960*. University of Massachusetts Press, 2010.

Feuer, Jane. *The Hollywood Musical*. 2nd ed., Indiana University Press, 1993.

Filippelli, Ronald L. *American Labor and the Postwar Italy, 1943–1953: A Study of Cold War Politics*. Stanford University Press, 1989.

Fisher, James T. *On the Irish Waterfront: The Crusader, the Movie, and the Soul of the Port of New York*. Cornell University Press, 2009.

Fisher, Lucy, and Marcia Landy. *Stars: The Film Reader*. Routledge, 2004.

Foertsch, Jacqueline. *Bracing Accounts: The Literature and Culture of Polio in Postwar America*. Fairleigh Dickenson University Press, 2008.

Frommer, Arthur. *Europe on 5 Dollars a Day*. Wiley Publishers, 1957.

Gaddis, John Lewis. *Strategies of Containment: A Critical Appraisal of American National Security Policy During the Cold War*. Oxford University Press, 2005. Originally published in 1982.

Georgakas, Dan. "Schulberg on the Waterfront." *"On the Waterfront"*, edited by Joanna Rapf, Cambridge University Press, 2003, pp. 40–60.

Gerteis, Christopher. "Subjectivity Lost: Labor and the Cold War in Occupied Japan." *Labor's Cold War: Local Politics in a Global Context*, edited by Shelton Stromquist, University of Illinois Press, 2008, pp. 258–290.

Gibney, Frank. "The Birth of a New Japan." *Life Magazine*, 10 September 1951, pp. 134–153.

Gilbert, James. *A Cycle of Outrage: America's Reaction to the Juvenile Delinquent in the 1950s*. Oxford University Press, 1986.

———. *Men in the Middle: Searching for Masculinity in the 1950s*. University of Chicago Press, 2005.

Girgus, Sam. *Hollywood Renaissance: The Cinema of Democracy in the Era of Ford, Capra, and Kazan*. Cambridge University Press, 1998.

Goldfield, Michael. *The Decline of Organized Labor in the United States*. University of Chicago Press, 1987.

Goodman, Paul. *Growing Up Absurd*. Random House, 1960.

Gott, Richard. *Cuba: A New History*. Yale University Press, 2004.

Gottfried, Martin. *Nobody's Fool: The Lives of Danny Kaye*. Simon & Schuster, 1994.

Gottlieb, Sidney. *Alfred Hitchcock: Interviews*. University Press of Mississippi, 2003.

Green, Robert L. "Desegregation." *Metropolitan Desegregation*, edited by Robert Green, Plenum Press, 1985, pp. 1–36.

Gundle, Stephen. *Between Hollywood and Moscow: The Italian Communists and the Challenge of Mass Culture, 1943–1991*. Duke University Press, 2000.

Halberstram, David. *The Coldest Winter: America and the Korean War*. Hyperion, 2007.

———. *The Fifties*. Villard Books, 1993.

Haralovich, Mary Beth. "Movies and Landscapes." *American Cinema of the 1950s: Themes and Variations*, edited by Murray Pommerance, Rutgers University Press, 2003, pp. 21–42.

Harvey, James. *Movie Love in the Fifties*. DaCapo Press, 2001.

Haskell, Molly. *From Reverence to Rape: The Treatment of Women in the Movies*. 2nd ed., University of Chicago Press, 1987.

Head, Earl J., and Pratibha A. Dabholkar. *Singin' in the Rain: The Making of a Masterpiece*. University Press of Kansas, 2009.

Hofstadter, Richard. *The Paranoid Style in American Politics*. Vintage Books, 2002. Originally published in 1952.

Horsman, Reginald. *Race and Manifest Destiny: The Origins of American Racial Anglo-Saxonism*. Harvard University Press, 1981.

Houston, Kerr. "'Siam Not So Small!': Maps, History, and Gender in *The King and I* (1956)." *Camera Obscura*, vol. 20, no. 59, August 2000, pp. 73–117.

Humes, Edward. *Over Here: How the G.I. Bill Transformed the American Dream*. Harcourt, 2006.

Hunter, Edward. *Brainwashing: The Story of the Men Who Defied It*. Pyramid Books, 1964. Originally published in 1956.

Hurrell, John Dennis. "A Note on Farce." *Comedy: Meaning and Form*, edited by Robert Corrigan, Harper & Row, 1981, pp. 212–216.

Johnson, David K. *The Lavender Scare: The Cold War Persecution of Gays and Lesbians in the Federal Government*. University of Chicago Press, 2004.

Johnston, Ruth. "Technologically Produced Forms of Drag in *Singin' in the Rain* and *Radio Days*." *Quarterly Review of Film and Video*, vol. 21, 2004, 119–129.

Jolly, Richard, Louis Emmerij, and Thomas G. Weiss. *UN Ideas That Changed the World*. Indiana University Press, 2009.

Jones, E. Michael. *The Slaughter of Cities: Urban Renewal as Ethnic Cleansing*. St. Augustine's Press, 2004.

Jones, Landon Y. *Great Expectations: America and the Baby Boom Generation*. Coward, McCann & Geoghegan, 1980.

Kashner, Sam, and Jennifer MacNair. *The Bad and the Beautiful: Hollywood in the Fifties*. Norton, 2002.

Keane, Marian. "The Designs of Authorship: An Essay on *North by Northwest*." *Wide Angle*, vol. 4, no. 1, 1980, pp. 44–54.

Kennan, George F. "The Sources of Soviet Conduct." *The Cold War: A History through Documents*, edited by Edward H. Judge and John W. Langdon, Prentice Hall, 1999, pp. 28–37.

Kennedy, Randall. *Race, Crime, and the Law*. Pantheon, 1997.

Kinzer, Stephen. *The Brothers: John Foster Dulles, Allen Dulles, and Their Secret World War*. Times Books, 2013.

Koenig, David. *Danny Kaye: King of Jesters*. Bonaventure Press, 2012.

Kristeva, Julia. *Powers of Horror: An Essay on Abjection*. Columbia University Press, 1982.

Kunz, Diane. *The Economic Diplomacy of the Suez Crisis*. University of North Carolina Press, 1991.

LaFeber, Walter. *America, Russia, and the Cold War, 1945–1975*. John Wiley & Sons, 1976.

Lee, Lance. *"On the Waterfront:* Script Analysis Conventional and Unconventional." *"On the Waterfront"*, edited by Joanna Rapf, Cambridge University Press, 2003, pp. 61–84.

Leibman, Nina. *Living Room Lectures: The Fifties Family in Film and Television*. University of Texas Press, 1995.

Leman, Nicholas. *The Big Test: The Secret History of American Meritocracy*. Farrar, Straus and Giroux, 1999.

Lev, Peter. *The Fifties: Transforming the Screen 1950–1959*. University of California Press, 2003.

Lewis, R.W.B. *The American Adam: Innocence, Tragedy, and Tradition in the Nineteenth Century*. University of Chicago Press, 1959.

"Life with a Key," *Time*, 10 November 1958, p. 42.

Luce, Henry. "The American Century." *Life Magazine*, 17 February 1941, pp. 61–65.

Lundberg, Ferdinand, and Marynia Farnham. *Modern Woman: The Lost Sex*. Harper & Brothers, 1947.

Ma, Sheng-mei. "Rogers and Hammerstein's 'Chopsticks' Musicals," *Literature/Film Quarterly*, vol. 31, no. 1, 2003, pp. 17–26.

Malavet, Pedro A. *America's Colony: The Political and Cultural Conflict between the United States and Puerto Rico*. New York University Press, 2004.

Maloney, H. Newton. *When Getting Along Seems Impossible*. Fleming H. Revell Co., 1989.

Marx, Karl. "The Eighteenth Brumaire of Louis Bonaparte." *Surveys from Exile*, edited by David Fernbach, Penguin, 1973.

"The Marxist Neighbor." *Time*, 20 June 1960, pp. 30–31.

Mast, Gerald. *Can't Help Singin': The American Musical on Stage and Screen*. Overlook, 1987.

"Mau Mau Block Kenya Surrender." *New York Times*, 12 April 1954, p. 1.

"Mau Mau Massacres 150 Natives in Night Raid Near Kenya Capital." *New York Times*, 28 March 1953, pp. 1+.

May, Elaine Tyler. *Homeward Bound: American Families in the Cold War Era*. Rev. and updated ed., Basic Books, 1999.

Mazower, Mark. *No Enchanted Palace: The End of Empire and the Ideological Origins of the United Nations*. Princeton University Press, 2009.

McConachie, Bruce. "The 'Oriental' Musicals of Rogers and Hammerstein and the U.S. War in Southeast Asia." *Theater Journal*, vol. 46, no. 3, 1994, pp. 385–398.

McIlroy, Brian. "White Nagasaki/White Japan and a Post-Atomic Butterfly: Joshua Logan's *Sayonara* (1957)." *A Vision of the Orient: Texts, Intertexts and Contexts of Madame Butterfly*, edited by Jonathan Wisenthal et al., University of Toronto Press, 2006.

McLean, Adrienne. "1958: Movies of Allegories and Ambivalence." *American Cinema of the 1950s: Themes and Variations*, edited by Murray Pommerance, Rutgers University Press, 2005, pp. 201–221.

Medovoi, Leerom. *Rebels: Youth and the Cold War Origins of Identity*. Duke University Press, 2005.

Meisler, Stanley. *United Nations: The First Fifty Years*. Atlantic Monthly Press, 1995.

Meola, Frank M. "Hitchcock's Emersonian Edges." *Framing Hitchcock*, edited by Sidney Gottlieb and Christopher Brookhouse, Wayne State University Press, 2002.

Merrill, Dennis. *Negotiating Paradise: U.S. Tourism and Empire in Twentieth-Century Latin America*. University of North Carolina Press, 2009.

Millington, Richard. "Hitchcock and the American Character: The Comedy of Self-Construction in *North by Northwest*." In *Hitchcock's America*, edited by Jonathan Freedman and Richard Millington, Oxford University Press, 1999, pp. 135–154.

Mills, C. Wright. *The Power Elite*. Oxford University Press, 1959. Originally published in 1956.

——. *White Collar: The American Middle Class*. 50th anniv. ed., Oxford University Press, 2002. Originally published in 1951.

Mills, Harry A., and Emily Clark Brown. *From the Wagner Act to Taft-Hartley: A Study of National Labor Policy and Labor Relations*. University of Chicago Press, 1950.

Monge, Jose Trias. *Puerto Rico: The Trials of the Oldest Colony in the World*. Yale University Press, 1997.

Mosley, Rachel. *Growing Up with Audrey Hepburn: Text, Audience, Resonance*. Manchester University Press, 2003.

Mowbray, A. Q. *The Road to Ruin*. J. B. Lippincott, 1969.

Myrdal, Gunnar. *An American Dilemma: The Negro Problem and Modern Democracy*. Harper & Bros., 1944.

Nabokov, Vladimir. *Lolita*. Vintage, 1989. Originally published in 1955.

Nadel, Alan. *Containment Culture: American Narratives, Postmodernism, and the Atomic Age*. Duke University Press, 1995.

——. *Television in Black-and-White America: Race and National Identity*. University Press of Kansas, 2006.

"Native Terrorists Raid a Kenya Mission." *New York Times*, 13 September 1952, p. 2.

Navasky, Victor S. *Naming Names*. Hill & Wang, 1980.

Neve, Brian. "The Personal and the Political: Elia Kazan and *On the Waterfront*." *"On the Waterfront"*, edited by Joanna E. Rapf, Cambridge University Press, 2003, pp. 20–39.

Olmstead, Andrea. *Julliard: A History*. University of Illinois Press, 1999.

Oshinsky, David M. *A Conspiracy So Immense: The World of Joseph McCarthy*. Oxford University Press, 2005.

——. *Polio: An American Story*. Oxford University Press, 2006.

Packard, Vance. *The Hidden Persuaders*. IG Publishing, 2007. Originally published in 1957.

——. *The Status Seekers*. Pocket Books, 1964. Originally published in 1959.

Patterson, James T. *Brown v. Board of Education: A Civil Rights Milestone and Its Troubled Legacy*. Oxford University Press, 2001.

——. *Grand Expectations: The United States, 1945–74*. Oxford University Press, 1996.

Peucker, Brigitte. "The Cult of Representation: Painting and Sculpture in Hitchcock." *Alfred Hitchcock Centenary Essays*, edited by Richard Allen and S. Ishii Gonzales, British Film Institute, 1999, pp. 141–158.

Phillips, Louis. "Wherein the Truth Lies: Honesty and Deception in Hitchcock's *North by Northwest*." *Armchair Detective*, vol. 20, no. 3, 1987, pp. 254–259.

Pomerance, Murray. *American Cinema of the 1950s: Themes and Variations*. New Brunswick, NJ: Rutgers University Press, 2005.

——. *An Eye for Hitchcock*. Rutgers University Press, 2004.

Prock, Stephan. "Music, Gender and the Politics of Performance in *Singin' in the Rain*." *Colby Quarterly*, vol. 36, no. 4, 2000, pp. 295–318.

"The Proconsul Arrives." *Time*, 15 February 1960, p. 52.

Radosh, Ronald, and Allis Radosh. *Red Star Over Hollywood: The Film Colony's Long Romance with the Left*. Encounter Books, 2005.

Rapf, Joanna E., ed. *"On the Waterfront"*. Cambridge University Press, 2003.

Riesman, David. *The Lonely Crowd*. Yale University Press, 1961. Originally published in 1950.

Rogin, Michael. *Blackface, White Noise: Jewish Immigrants in the Hollywood Melting Pot*. University of California Press, 1996.

Rossell, Christine H., and Willis D. Hawley. "Understanding White Flight and Doing Something about It." *Effective School Desegregation: Equity, Quality, and Feasibility*, edited by Willis D. Hawley, Sage Publications, 1981, pp. 157–184.

Rothman, William. *The "I" of the Camera: Essays in Film Criticism, History, and Aesthetics*. Cambridge University Press, 2004.

Sanderson, Sandy. *Matthew and the Mau Mau. Harper's Magazine*, 1 August 1953, pp. 83–89.

Sayre, Nora. *Running Time: Films of the Cold War*. Dial Press, 1980.

Schickel, Richard. *Elia Kazan: A Biography*. HarperCollins, 2005.

Schlesinger, Arthur M. "The Crisis of American Masculinity." *Esquire*, November 1958, pp. 63–65.

———. *The Vital Center: The Politics of Freedom*. Transaction Publications, 1998. Originally published in 1949.

Schlesinger, Stephen C. *Act of Creation: The Founding of the United Nations*. Westview Press, 2003.

Schrecker, Ellen. *The Age of McCarthyism: A Brief History with Documents*. 2nd ed., Bedford/St. Martin's, 2002.

———. *Cold War Triumphalism: The Misuses of History After the Fall of Communism*. New Press, 2004.

———. *Many Are the Crimes: McCarthyism in America*. Little, Brown, 1998.

Schwartz, Vanessa. *It's So French: Hollywood, Paris, and the Making of Cosmopolitan Film Culture*. University of Chicago Press, 2007.

Seavy, Nina Gilden, Jane S. Smith, and Paul Wagner. *A Paralyzing Fear: The Triumph Over Polio in America*. TV Books, 1998.

Shakespeare, William. *Hamlet*. Simon & Schuster, 1992.

Shandley, Robert T. *Rubble Films: German Cinema in the Shadows of the Third Reich*. Rutgers University Press, 2001.

Shaw, Tony. *Hollywood's Cold War*. University of Massachusetts Press, 2007.

Shumway, David. *Modern Love: Romance, Intimacy, and the Marriage Crisis*. New York University Press, 2003.

Sikov, Ed. *Laughing Hysterically: American Screen Comedy of the 1950s*. Columbia University Press, 1994.

Silverman, Kaja. *The Acoustic Mirror: The Female Voice in Psychoanalysis and Cinema*. Indiana University Press, 1988.

Silverman, Stephen M. *Dancing on the Ceiling: Stanley Donen and His Movies*. Alfred A. Knopf, 1996.

Slater, Leon. *Not in Vain: A Rifleman Remembers World War II*. Louisiana State University Press, 1992.

"Slaughter in Kenya." *Time*, 2 November 1953, p. 32.

Smith, Dina. "Global Cinderella: *Sabrina* (1954), Hollywood, and Postwar Internationalism." *Cinema Journal*, vol. 41, no. 4, Summer 2002, pp. 29–51.

Spigel, Lynn. *Make Room for TV: Television and the Family Ideal in Postwar America*. University of Chicago Press, 1992.

Spock, Benjamin. *Baby and Child Care*. Pocket Books, 1952. Originally published in 1946.

Spoto, Donald. *The Art of Alfred Hitchcock: Fifty Years of His Motion Pictures*. Anchor, 1991.

Stam, Robert. "Hitchcock and Bunuel: Desire and the Law." *Studies in the Literary Imagination*, vol. 16, no. 1, 1983, pp. 7–27.

Standley, Fred H., and Louis H. Pratt. *Conversations with James Baldwin.* University of Mississippi Press, 1989.

Staten, Clifford. *The History of Cuba.* Palgrave/Macmillan, 2003.

Stromquist, Shelton. *Labor's Cold War: Local Politics in a Global Context.* University of Illinois Press, 2008.

Sugrue, Thomas J. *The Origins of the Urban Crisis: Race and Inequality in Postwar Detroit.* Princeton University Press, 1996.

Taylor, Clarence. *Knocking at Our Own Door: Milton Galamison and the Struggle to Integrate New York City Schools.* Columbia University Press, 1997.

Trento, Joseph J. *The Secret History of the CIA.* Basic Books, 2001.

Walker, Martin. *The Cold War: A History.* Henry Holt, 1993.

Wang, Jessica. "The United States, the United Nations, and the Other Post-Cold War World Order: Internationalism and Unilateralism in the American Century." *Cold War Triumphalism: The Misuses of History After the Fall of Communism,* edited by Ellen Schrecker, New Press, 2004, pp. 201–234.

Weiner, Tim. *Legacy of Ashes: The History of the CIA.* Doubleday, 2007.

Westad, Odd Arne. *The Global Cold War.* Cambridge University Press, 2007.

White, E. B. *The Wild Flag: Editorials from "The New Yorker" on Federal World Government and Other Matters.* Houghton Mifflin, 1946.

Whyte, William H., Jr. *The Organization Man.* Doubleday, 1956.

Wilford, Hugh. *The Mighty Wurlitzer: How the CIA Played America.* Harvard University Press, 2008.

Wilson, George M. "The Maddest McGuffin: Some Notes on *North by Northwest.*" *Modern Language Notes,* vol. 95, no. 5, 1979, pp. 1159–1172.

Wollen, Peter. *"Singin' in the Rain".* BFI, 1992.

Wood, Robin. *Hitchcock's Films Revisited.* Columbia University Press, 1989.

Wylie, Philip. *The Generation of Vipers.* Dalkey Archive, 1996. Reprint of 1955 20th ed., originally published in 1942.

Yamamoto, Traise. *Masking Selves, Making Subjects: Japanese American Women, Identity, and the Body.* University of California Press, 1999.

Yudkoff, Alvin. *A Life of Dance and Dreams: Gene Kelly.* Backstage Books, 1999.

Zipp, Samuel. *Manhattan Projects: The Rise and Fall of Urban Renewal in Cold War New York.* Oxford University Press, 2010.

INDEX

ABOUT THE AUTHOR

ALAN NADEL, William T. Bryan Chair in American Literature and Culture at the University of Kentucky, has most recently published *Television in Black-and-White America: Race and National Identity* and coedited *Henry James and Alfred Hitchcock: The Men Who Knew Too Much.* His other books include *Containment Culture: American Narratives, Postmodernism, and the Atomic Age; Flatlining on the Field of Dreams: Cultural Narratives in the Films of President Reagan's America;* and *Invisible Criticism: Ralph Ellison and the American Canon.* He has also edited two collections of essays on playwright August Wilson. He has won prizes for the best essay in *Modern Fiction Studies* and the best essay in *PMLA,* and his poetry has appeared in several journals, including *Georgia Review, New England Review, Partisan Review, Paris Review,* and *Shenandoah.*